Korea and Manchuria
Between Russia and Japan
1895-1904

The Observations of
SIR ERNEST SATOW
British Minister Plenipotentiary to
Japan (1895-1900) and China (1900-1906)

SELECTED AND EDITED
WITH A HISTORICAL INTRODUCTION BY
GEORGE ALEXANDER LENSEN

The Diplomatic Press
TALLAHASSEE, FLORIDA

Other Books by George Alexander Lensen

REPORT FROM HOKKAIDO

RUSSIA'S JAPAN EXPEDITION OF 1852 TO 1855

THE MEANING OF YALTA
(with John L. Snell, Charles F. Delzell, and Forrest C. Pogue)

THE RUSSIAN PUSH TOWARD JAPAN

THE WORLD BEYOND EUROPE

RUSSIA'S EASTWARD EXPANSION

REVELATIONS OF A RUSSIAN DIPLOMAT

SOVIET UNION AND EASTERN EUROPE

The Diplomatic Press
2305 Amelia Circle
Tallahassee, Florida

Spy

To T'ing-yi

Contents

Introduction

THE DECADE FROM 1895 to 1905 forms a historical divide in modern Far Eastern international relations. Until 1895 initiative and pressure had come from the West—from England, France, Russia, Germany, and the United States. After 1905 initiative and pressure emanated from the East—from Japan and, more recently, from China. The Sino-Japanese War of 1894-95 and the Russo-Japanese War of 1904-1905 mark off the historical divide.

The victory of Japan over China reversed the power status of the two countries. Japan emerged as the leading Asian nation, and Western statesmen shifted their attention from Peking to Tokyo. Whatever restraint they had exercised in their demands on China, lest the "sleeping giant" be awakened, was removed by the exposure of Chinese weakness, and the partition of China seemed at hand. Different countries had different interests. Some favored partition, others not. But whether they deemed it to their advantage to seek to preserve the territorial integrity of China or whether they schemed to secure a choice slice of the country for themselves, they now had to consider Japan, be it as aid or as obstacle to their plans.

The victory of Japan over Russia had even more serious consequences. It shook the Russian monarchy to its foundations. It raised Japan from an Asian power to a world power, and exploded the myth of white superiority. It strengthened Japanese ambitions at the same time that it aroused belated Chinese interest in modernization. Only thirty-seven years separate the surprise attacks on Port Arthur and on Pearl Harbor, and but half a century has passed between the Chinese

1

empire's utter prostration and its dynamic resurgence as a nuclear power.

The decade between Japan's defeat of China and Japan's defeat of Russia is more than a historical divide. It is a transition period of great importance. In it we see the development of attitudes and trends that were to shape international relations in later years. We find the seeds of conflict, of war and revolution in our own day.

Aside from China proper, which was, as noted, on the verge of partition after the Sino-Japanese War, Korea and Manchuria played an important part in the rivalries of the Powers. Korea was the "Sick Man" of the Far East. A tributary state of the Chinese empire, it had been "opened" to the world by Japanese warships in 1876. China gradually tried to reassert her suzerain authority and a triangular struggle developed between China, Japan and Russia. The first phase ended with the victory of Japan over China in 1895 and the proclamation of Korean independence; the second phase ended with the Japanese victory over Russia in 1905 and the eventual annexation of Korea by Japan (1910). But Chinese, Japanese, Russian, and Korean intrigues smouldered beyond these dates, to flare up anew in later years.

International rivalry over Korea has been due in part to the strategic importance of the peninsula. It is a bridge between the continent and Japan; it borders unto China and Russia by land and unto Japan by sea; it possesses ice-free ports and by this and its location can facilitate or hinder Russian outlet to the Pacific. To a large extent international rivalry in Korea was encouraged, if not invited, by the weakness, corruption and division of the Korean government. Korean disunity provided an opportunity for foreign interference, and the various Powers deemed it necessary to forestall each other's control of the region. Moreover, the Chinese and the Koreans sought to strengthen their own hands by playing the foreigners against each other. Japanese meddling in the internal affairs of Korea during the transition decade was climaxed in 1895 with the

2

assassination of the Queen. The height of Russian influence was reached the following year directly as a result of this outrage, when the Korean King sought refuge from the Japanese in the Russian legation. Russian attempts to establish a settlement at the Korean port of Masanpho (Masampo) aroused international concern.

Manchuria, like Korea, was a major object of Chinese, Japanese and Russian contention. It was of special territorial interest to China's Manchu rulers, who hailed from there; to the Russians, to whom it offered a shortcut for their trans-continental railway; and to the Japanese, who wanted a grain basket for their empire. But Manchuria, with its abundant natural resources, also attracted the interest of the United States and Great Britain as a place for investment. Its separation from China by either Russia or Japan would have closed the door to Western enterprise. The rivalry over Manchuria, like the rivalry over Korea, was highlighted but not ended during the transition period. It was to be an important factor in the outbreak of the Second Sino-Japanese War in the 1930's and the Pacific War thereafter.

In the wake of the Sino-Japanese War of 1894-95, contention focussed at first on only a portion of southern Manchuria—the Liaotung Peninsula. By the Treaty of Shimonoseki, which ended the war, the Liaotung Peninsula, containing Port Arthur and Dalny (Dairen), as well as the island of Formosa and the Pescadores Islands were ceded by China to Japan. Russia, Germany, and France intervened, however, to prevent Japan from obtaining a foothold on the continent. Japan was to give up her claims to the Liaotung Peninsula in return for an increased war indemnity on the part of China, on the ground that control of this region by a foreign power would threaten the Chinese capital of Peking. Yet within three years, by 1898, Russia, which had spearheaded the Tripartite Intervention, had herself moved into the Liaotung Peninsula and had obtained leases at Port Arthur and Dalny.

Manchuria as a whole became the object of international

3

rivalry with the outbreak of the Boxer uprising in 1899-1900. Popular antagonism toward Christianity and the West had been building up in China for more than half a century. Goaded on by the Boxers (the Society of Harmonious Fists) and by other revolutionary groups and ultimately by the Manchu government itself, the Chinese tried to expel the foreign intruders from the land. They murdered many Christians and besieged the foreign legations at Peking. An international expeditionary force had to be sent to the rescue, and the Empress Dowager and the Manchu court fled from the capital, to return later in great humiliation. While the Boxer uprising originated in China proper, it spread to Manchuria. Thither the Russians, whose railway building crews and families were endangered, sent large relief forces. The conflict that ensued between Russian and Chinese armies in 1900 is still called the "Russo-Chinese War" in the Soviet Union.

The pacification of Manchuria did not entail an immediate withdrawal of Russian troops. A convention was laboriously negotiated between Russia and China and only some Russian units were withdrawn. Russian reluctance to pull out completely, aroused Japanese and Western alarm. Direct negotiations between Japan and Russia followed in a vain attempt to reach an agreement over Manchuria and Korea. The negotiations failed partly because Russia did not take Japan seriously enough, partly because Japan, after concluding an alliance with England in 1902, felt confident that she could impose her will by force. The Japanese attack on Russia in 1904 (which terminates our account) was motivated in part by a desire to avenge the humiliation of Japan by Russia and her allies in 1895 (the beginning of our account).

There are a number of scholarly studies on the international rivalry over Korea and Manchuria and on the diplomacy of the Russo-Japanese War. Of necessity, they paint the picture in broad strokes, dealing with the general sweep of events. There are also some detailed accounts of the negotiations between Russia and Japan, based on official sources. Generally

4

they concentrate on what was said rather than on what was thought and on actions rather than on motivations.ᵃ A more intimate, behind-the-scenes glimpse of international relations can be gleaned from the memoirs of diplomats and statesmen, but these, if written for publication, are often slanted to portray the author and his policies in a favorable light. It is in the unpublished diaries of major personalities that we must seek the unadorned record of the ideas and aspirations, the hopes and fears, the frame of mind and temper of statesmen and diplomats, which as much as specific events affect the course of history. In this connection the diaries of Sir Ernest Mason Satow, British Minister to Japan from 1895 to 1900 and British Minister to China from 1900 to 1906, are of particular interest.

The son of a Swedish merchant who had migrated to England from Riga in 1825 and of an English mother, Satow was born at Clapton, in Northeast London, on June 30, 1843.[1] Raised in a strict Lutheran, Orthodox Nonconformist way, Satow received a broader outlook at University College, London. Bright and studious, Satow was admitted to the college at the age of 16, receiving his B. A. degree two years later, in the fall of 1861. The *Narrative of the Earl of Elgin's Mission to China and Japan,* which one of his brothers chanced to bring home, aroused Satow's interest in Japan; an account of Commodore Matthew C. Perry's expedition deepened it. When he ran across a notice in the college, announcing competitions for three student interpreterships in China and Japan, he entered, placing first on the list. Given his choice of country, Satow selected Japan, and shortly after graduation, at the age of 18, departed for the Far East. He arrived in Japan in September of 1862 and there stayed, except for two seasons of home leave, continuously for twenty years.

ᵃ "I did not say what I thought," Sir Ernest Satow noted in his diary after a conversation with the French Minister to China, and added: "It would be interesting to see *his* journal of our conversation, and amusing to see what he gets out of it."

Those were years of turmoil in Japan. Foreigners were not safe. Laurence Oliphant, author of the book that had lured Satow to Japan, had just been seriously wounded by an assassin; others were yet to feel the cold steel of the samurai swords, Satow himself escaping by inches. The contradictions of Japan's dual government, with the military dictatorship, the Tokugawa Shogunate, in Edo and the legitimate but powerless Imperial Court in Kyoto, were coming to a head and civil war loomed on the horizon. Satow took great interest in the momentous events, but he remained true to his primary purpose—the study of Japanese language and culture—and thanks to his talent and will power made rapid progress in the mastery of the written and spoken tongue.

Satow's family, like any family, was not happy with their son living so far away from home. In March of 1864, Satow received a letter from his father offering him 100 pounds per year if he went back and studied law. He recorded in his diary:

It is not easy to put down on paper any expression of what I thought and felt on receiving this letter, but I was put in a great state of perplexity. On the one hand a free and easy life with something of adventure, and means of gratifying my desire of studying Japanese; on the other, fortune, probable if not certain, the prospect of marriage and of being able to live a decent life instead of the immoral one I have led lately, the pleasures of travel in Europe and the enjoyment of good music. For some time I was under the impression that I should be compelled by these latter considerations to go back to Europe, and wrote almost confidently about it to my people at home. I remained thus up to the date of March 14, when I had an interview with [Sir Rutherford] Alcock [the British Minister], and asked him what chance I had of promotion and what my prospects were; he replied very kindly, listened to my arguments very patiently, and promised to write home for my promotion. But although I decided to stay, I am not quite sure whether this was the whole reason, for after all it was small comfort. It is more probable that I felt that to leave Japan and return to that dull old England, would be to destroy the real happiness of my life and to cut off all the ties I have formed during the last two and a half years. Not only ties of friendship, for they are weak compared with what I have at home, but attachment to the country, to the language, and to the people. Having now decided which course to take, I must stick to it, and try to win the position of a great Japanese scholar; for to know this language well is my intention, and to this end are all my efforts directed. . . . [3/26/1864]

The opposition of various clans to the opening of Japan and attacks on foreign individuals and vessels triggered Western reprisals in the form of punitive naval expeditions. Satow participated in these as interpreter. It was on one of these missions in 1864 that the important friendship between Satow and Ito Hirobumi began. Young Ito, who had stolen to England with several comrades and had been studying at Satow's alma mater in London, had hastened back to Japan with his friend Inouye Kaoru to warn his Choshu clansmen of the folly of their policy in the face of the military might that he had seen abroad. Offering to act as mediators, Ito and Inouye had been taken aboard the warship on which Satow was traveling. Meeting as young men—Satow was then 19, Ito 23, and Inouye 29—they matured together during the next two decades and in personal talks and letters, especially between Satow and Ito, taught each other a great deal. Their bond was cemented by their efforts on behalf of the restoration of the Imperial government to power.

The difficulty of dealing with Japan's dual government prompted the British to help turn the Emperor's "phantom sceptre" into real sovereignty. While the British Ministers, in view of their position, had to shun any public involvement in Japan's internal affairs, Satow, as Student Interpreter, Interpreter, Japanese Secretary and ultimately Second Secretary, felt no such inhibitions and in articles in the *Japan Times*, later translated into Japanese and circulated in pamphlet form as "The English Policy of the Englishman Satow," openly advocated a confederation of the feudal chiefs under the supremacy of the Emperor. So highly respected were Satow's views, that in 1867, as the dual government came to an end, he was invited by the Prince of Tosa to enter Japanese service and help in the formation of parliament. Though Satow chose to remain in his position, he continued to cultivate his intimate contacts with the country's foremost statesmen, and did much to acquaint the leaders of Japan and England with each other's thoughts.

In the closing days of 1882, Satow left Japan. He had been interested in law for many years. In the summer of 1876, while on home leave, he had attended lectures on the history of Roman law at the University of Marburg in Germany. Now he resumed his studies in England and in 1883 passed the legal examination "a long way first of all the men in." While in London, Satow was asked whether he would like to have an independent post in Siam. When it was pointed out to him that the Foreign Office was resolved not again to appoint a local man Minister to Japan and that his going to Siam might open the way for his eventually becoming Minister to Japan, Satow agreed. In 1884, Satow became Consul-General at Bangkok and the following year was promoted to Minister Resident, moving from the Consular to the Diplomatic Service. He maintained an active interest in Japan, seeking refuge there from the climate of Siam for months on end. Returning to England in 1887, he finished the legal studies he had commenced during earlier leaves and qualified as a barrister-at-law. In his other readings, Satow was greatly affected by Thomas à Kempis's *Imitation of Christ* and turned to religion, his childhood faith having been corroded by the materialistic influence of Herbert Spencer.

In 1888, Satow proceeded with his faithful Japanese servant Saburo as Minister to Uruguay, and in 1893 became Minister to Morocco. Catapulted from the quiet paradise of Montevideo into the maelstrom of English-French-German-Spanish-Italian rivalry, Satow displayed admirable diplomatic tact and skill, and in 1895 was rewarded with the cherished appointment of

Her Majesty's Minister Plenipotentiary in Tokyo, the Edo of yesteryears. Thus, at the age of 51, Satow returned as an important and experienced diplomat to the country which had shaped him as much as he had shaped her during his previous twenty years of service there. No other European was so qualified or able as he to observe and evaluate conditions in Japan.

In Satow's absence much had happened. When he returned in 1895, he found a Constitutional Monarchy, dominated by a clan oligarchy, consisting of his old Choshu friends. Satow's position was unique. Western diplomats and Japanese statesmen alike conferred with him constantly, for no one knew better than he the intentions and detailed provisions of the early treaties and agreements, that now formed the basis and "tradition" of international relations. These talks with leading Japanese and Western actors on the Far Eastern scene, Satow recorded in his diaries.

On March 29, 1900, Satow received a telegram from Lord Robert Arthur Salisbury. "Peking is likely to be vacant soon, as Sir Claude MacDonald's health cannot be relied on," the Foreign Secretary wired. "I should be very glad to appoint you there, as I am sure I could not leave [it] possibly in better hands. In that case MacDonald would not unprobly [sic] take your place." Satow accepted, and the switch in positions was arranged, MacDonald becoming Minister to Japan and Satow Minister to China.

In the summer of 1900, Satow returned to England before assuming his new duties. But the Boxer uprising and the siege of the Western legations in Peking made his home leave uncertain and restless, as Satow went to the Foreign Office to read telegrams from China and to discuss the crisis with many individuals. Told that Sir Claude MacDonald, with whom he was trading places, was delighted to go to Tokyo and that it was hoped that he would not mind Peking, Satow retorted that "it would be interesting in many ways."

On May 31, on the very day of his return from Japan,

9

Satow had hastened to the Foreign Office and had talked to key officials. "[Francis Leveson] Bertie [Assistant Under-secretary of State for Foreign Affairs] seemed to think the news from Peking about the 'Boxers' serious, and that the Powers will have to use such strong measures against the Empress Dowager as will bring China to the ground and hasten on partition," Satow noted in his diary. On June 21, William St. John Brodrick, the Secretary of War, asked Satow whether he thought Japan would accept a mandate from the Powers to intervene in China. "I said that if they did, probably they would not be contented to take a backseat when affairs were finally arranged," Satow replied.

Baron Redesdale Mitford, British Attaché in Japan in the 1860's, had proposed the removal of the capital of China from Peking. Satow discussed this with Mitford and afterwards with Bertie on June 25. Bertie said that the Russians would never agree.

But Bertie's idea is that if the Chinese have really massacred the Legations, the integrity of China is at an end [Satow recorded in his diary]; if the Russians occupy Peking we must give up the North, and establish a scion of the Mings [the Chinese dynasty dethroned by the Manchus] in the South. . . . I expressed a strong opinion that if the Legations have been massacred, women, children and all, not one stone should be left standing on another.

Satow discussed the same topic with Sir Thomas Sanderson. "He thinks that if the Legations have been destroyed, we ought to raze the Imperial city to the ground, and I agreed with him. I suggested that we had gone on the wrong track during the last forty years, and that the old gunboat policy was the right one." (7/3)

When Satow had returned from Japan, it had been agreed that he should set out for his new post in mid-September. But as the situation in China became more critical and hope for the survival of the foreigners in Peking dwindled, Sanderson instructed Satow in mid-August to go out at once. "Rather a sudden blow," Satow confided to his diary, "and when the sun sat I felt quite downhearted at so soon leaving this beautiful land."

Before departing, Satow had some final conferences with Foreign Office officials. In his diary he summed up the views of Bertie, with whom he had a long talk on August 20:

His main idea is that we should hold aloof if possible from interference in the internal affairs of China, and if there is civil war, to let them fight it out among themselves till a strong man comes out on top. We can assure the Yangtze viceroys of our protection and support, and say we confide in them to maintain order and protect foreigners. [Customs Commissioner Alfred E.] Hippisley's idea was recently that Yüan Shih-k'ai [the Acting Governor of Shantung] would offer the Empress Dowager [T'zu Hsi] and Emperor [Kuang Hsü] an asylum at Tsinan-fu. He thinks no Power would want to take advantage of a civil war to appropriate territory except Russia and perhaps Germany: Lord Salisbury suspects the Emperor William of big designs in China. Russia would have enough to do to absorb Manchuria. . . .

On August 25, Satow sailed from England by way of America and Japan. When he stopped at Kobe in the latter part of September, he confided to his dairy: "Kobe Chronicle expresses doubt as to my being 'strong' enough for Peking post, but adds that I am somewhat of a heretic to popular ideas, since I believe that Orientals have rights as well as Occidentals, and that imperial necessities sometimes override local interests," and commented: ". . . I was pleased with this appreciation of my character." (9/23)

In Shanghai, where Satow proceeded from Japan, he talked with Sir Robert E. Bredon, the Deputy Inspector-General of the Chinese Customs Service, on October 1. Satow learned that the Manchu Court had fled from the capital city. Bredon expressed the thought that demand for return of the Court to Peking should precede demand for extradition of the ringleaders, and observed that it would have been disastrous if the palace had been destroyed. "I said at the time of the relief if

Palace had been destroyed I should have liked it, but now it was too late," Satow noted. "What was required was that the Court should be made to understand the heinousness of the attempt to destroy the Legations, and even the foreign residents needed to see this too." The matter of extradition came up also in a conversation which Satow had with Odagiri Masunosuke, the Japanese Consul General. "He said Japan would probably object to the German demand for extradition of the ringleaders, but would have to give way if she found herself alone," Satow recorded in his diary. "I said I knew nothing, but my personal preference would be in favour of letting China whip her naughty children herself, rather than undertake that duty for her." (10/1)

Sir Claude MacDonald was still in China, awaiting Satow's arrival. He was to brief him on the state of the negotiations with the Chinese and to present him to the Chinese authorities and the Western colleagues before leaving for his post in Japan. Satow reached Peking on October 20, after a long and dusty ride from T'ung-chou. Weary from cold and fatigue, Satow dismounted and moved his numb legs along the devastated legation street. "A feeling of profound melancholy took possession of me, such as I have never experienced," he recalled in his diary. "It was like entering a huge city of the dead where the tombs had been thrown down and enveloped in dust."

Many were the problems that faced Satow as he took over as the British plenipotentiary, for its was not merely a matter of coming to terms with Manchu China, but with his own colleagues. The unity that had prevailed among the Powers at the time of crisis, had dissolved with victory, and they vied with each other in despoiling China, directly through looting and indirectly through padded demands for reparations and concessions. For eleven months the Representatives of Germany, Austria-Hungary, Belgium, Spain, the United States, France, Great Britain, Italy, Japan, the Netherlands, and Russia haggled over the "price" of the Boxer Rebellion. Satow's relationship with Chinese officials was not as close, of course, as his relationship with Japanese statesmen whom he had known for many years, but Chinese and Westerners respected his advice and conferred with him constantly.

The partition of China was a definite possibility. It was averted for no moral or political principle, but because some of the Powers were not yet ready for the task and could not allow the others to get a head start. If in the jealousy and mutual distrust of the allies there lay the salvation of China, so in the peace that seemed to descend over the land there were imbedded the seeds of later war. Lord Salisbury had talked of Russian absorption of Manchuria, and Manchuria was to demand the attention of Satow throughout his stay in China.

The Russo-Japanese War, which broke out in 1904, did not settle the Manchurian question to China's advantage. When Satow told a Japanese newspaperman in April of 1906, that the Chinese spoke strongly against Japan and said the Russians were preferable, the Japanese merely smiled and replied, "*nigeta sakana itsudemo ōki* [a fish that got away is always large]." If China did not get back control over Manchuria, neither did Japan fully displace Russia. The two countries in effect divided Manchuria between them. But Satow foresaw the trend of events. "I think the ambitions of Japan will rather grow than be restricted in the hands of the younger generation, and that these men will be very go-ahead." (1/13/ 1906)

In a conversation with the American Commissioner Plenipotentiary William W. Rockhill in November of 1905 he had reviewed the Far Eastern situation.

As to Japan, she would have to repair her losses in men and material, and would lie low for the next ten years, when there would be another outburst of energy.[b] She, like every other nation, would expand where she could; there was no finality

[b] In 1915 Japan presented to China the Twenty-one Demands in an attempt to make her into a Japanese satellite.

13

about the present arrangement. The next time anything happened, it would be Vladivostok or perhaps the Amur province. Then subsequently the position of Germany at Kiaochou would become precarious, as everybody in the province had been saying during the war. Then as a third stage, the French in Indo-China. These would be stages in a long evolution of Japan, the only Asiatic Power that had backbone enough to maintain her independence and expand.

Satow left China in May, 1906. On May 3, he had a farewell audience at the Imperial Court. "The Emperor as usual spoke not a word. Empress-Dowager very good humour, and said she was giving me a water colour drawing by herself," he recorded in his diary. In the latter part of May and in early June, as he was passing through Japan, Satow was received by Emperor Meiji and by leading Japanese statesmen. He learned from Viscount Hayashi, the Foreign Minister, that he had been recommended for the Order of the Rising Sun. Hayashi, incidentally, urged Satow to write the history of the Restoration in Japan. "I confess I do not feel very much inclined to take up the subject, but we shall see," Satow noted in his diary.

In June, 1906 Satow set sail for the United States and from there, in July, returned back to England. He had been treated badly by the Foreign Office. He had not been elevated to the rank of Ambassador, and was conscious that Lord Lansdowne wanted to get rid of men like himself, "and replace the 'outsiders' by members of the diplomatic service pure and simple." "Satow had bad luck," the late Sir George Sansom wrote in a personal letter to me (August 6, 1963), "for when he was transferred to Peking, he remained a Minister, whereas his successor in Japan (Sir Claude MacDonald) became an Ambassador because of the friendly relations of U. K. with Japan." Though Satow would have liked to stay in the active Foreign Service till the age of 65, he had felt that he was no longer wanted when his appointment to Peking had been renewed "at least another year" rather than for five years, and had declared that for reasons of health he did not wish to return to the Chinese capital.

On July 25, Satow was received in audience by King Edward VII. "He spoke of my not returning to China, but that at present there was no post which could be given me," Satow recorded. "My services must not be lost. I replied that I had no desire to retire if I could be of use, and he said I must consider myself on disponibilité [on the reserve list]." Later in the day Satow got official notice that he was to be sworn in as a member of the Privy Council, "which was what His Majesty meant." On October 13, Satow received a letter from F. A. Campbell announcing the Foreign Office's intention of applying for a pension for him. It was a most complimentary letter, full of nice things about his services. Satow replied that he was grateful to Campbell for the consideration he had always shown him since taking charge of Chinese affairs, and confided that his retirement did not come as a surprise to him: "I had expected to go on the shelf sometime in the autumn. . . ."

Following retirement from the Diplomatic Service, Satow was appointed British Member of the Court of Arbitration at the Hague and one of four Plenipotentiaries at the Second Peace Conference there. In the fall of 1907, Satow retired to Ottery St. Mary in Devonshire and there lived until his death on August 26, 1929. No longer in the forefront of government, he continued to be consulted by friends in the Foreign Office.

Over the years Satow had contributed scholarly articles on Japanese, Korean and Siamese subjects to the *Transactions of the Asiatic Society of Japan*. Now he wrote a chapter on the Far East for the *Cambridge Modern History* (1909) and notable historico-legal articles for the journals *Nineteenth Century and After* (1913) and the *Cambridge Historical Journal*. In 1917, Satow published a *Guide to Diplomatic Practice*, which is still widely used by students and practitioners of diplomacy in its up-dated fourth edition, edited by Sir Nevile

Bland in 1957, and commonly known as *Satow's Guide to Diplomatic Practice*. In 1920, he brought out a work on *International Congresses*. The following year Satow published *A Diplomat in Japan*, a book which he had begun writing in 1885-87, while serving as British Minister in Siam. In appreciation of his achievements he was awarded the honorary degree of D.C.L. from the University of Oxford and that of LL.D. from the University of Cambridge. As the *Dictionary of National Biography* stated: "Satow is one of the few British Ministers abroad who have shown themselves as accomplished in the theory as in the practice of diplomacy, and of the still fewer who have written history."[2]

A Diplomat in Japan is well known to students of Japanese history. It is an important eyewitness account. But it deals with only a fraction of Satow's early stay in Japan. It goes up to 1869 and is confined to the series of events that led to the restoration of imperial rule in Japan. Furthermore, as H. W. V. Temperley has noted in the *Dictionary of National Biography*, "Satow's comments on history and politics are difficult to find in his published works, as he remained invariably discreet."[3] It is to Satow's diaries, not intended for publication, that we must turn for Satow's personal views.

Satow kept a series of diaries throughout most of his long life. They became more detailed with time, as Satow's responsibilities increased and as his conversations gained in importance. Thus Satow's personal record of his stay in Japan and China in 1895-1906 is about twice as long as his account of the two decades that he had spent in Japan earlier. It consists of over 3,000 manuscript pages. Although handwritten, the entries, particularly during the stay in Japan, are greatly abbreviated by a form of "speedwriting," so that they would total, if published in full, about the same number of printed pages. To have published the Satow diaries, even those dealing only with the period from 1895 to 1906, in their entirety would have been prohibitive. Nor would it have been worthwhile. The Satow diaries, like any diaries, are cluttered with personal reminders of passing interest and with the humdrum of office routine. Instead, it seemed best to delete trivia and to paraphrase the less significant entries. Even then the material remained too bulky and disconnected for publication. After several editing drafts, it became apparent that the Korean and Manchurian questions ran like a theme throughout the diaries during the crucial period from 1895 to 1904. Just as Satow in the writing of *A Diplomat in Japan* focussed on "one of the most interesting episodes" in which he had been concerned, so this edition of his diaries focusses on the major topic which absorbed his interest during his return to the Far East.

To add clarity to the succession of events, the book has been divided into two parts. The first part covers Satow's stay in Japan, the second most of his stay in China. Although the chronological arrangement of the diary entries has been retained in most of the book, the Korean and Manchurian questions were separated in the first part to achieve continuity of thought and presentation. It was found advisable also to supplement the diary entries with excerpts from Satow's diplomatic dispatches. Although published by the Foreign Office in the *Confidential Correspondence and Papers, China* (popularly called the *Confidential Prints*), they were distributed in very limited quantity for official use only, and have but recently been opened to the public. While the weighty prose of diplomatic correspondence does not have the charm of such diary comments as "Churchill rather rubbed the Japanese up the wrong way, by going to the War Department in dittoes and a straw hat when other military attachés went in frock-coat and tall hat," the dispatches fill in gaps in the diaries and round out the story of international rivalry in the Far East.

The Satow who emerges from the diaries (including the early diaries) is a man of learning, discrimination, diplomatic skill and influence. He fits the thumbnail sketch drawn by the Baroness Albert d'Anethan, wife of the Belgian Minister, upon his arrival in Japan in 1895: "He is a tall, slight, rather careworn-looking man, with an intellectual face and the stoop of the student. He seems most agreeable and interesting."[4]

Satow had a very good hand, a virtue which entailed some disadvantages when Satow first came to Japan and wanted as much "free" time as possible for the study of Japanese. "My handwriting was, unfortunately for me, considered to be rather better than the average, and I began to foresee that a larger share of the clerical work would be given to me than I liked," Satow recalled. Satow had a fine understanding of music. He enjoyed going to concerts and commented on the various compositions and their performances with insight. Satow had a deep interest and knowledge of art and frequented galleries and museums in Asia and in Europe. He appreciated nature and knew the names of the flowers and shrubs and trees about him. In short, he was a cultured gentleman.

In addition to his legal studies, mentioned above, Satow delved deeply into linguistics. At one time or another, he studied Latin, Greek, German, French, Chinese, Japanese, Spanish, Korean, Italian, Portuguese, Manchu, and Siamese. For his diversion and language practice, he liked to memorize such pieces as the "Commedia di Dante" and Italian sonnets. His diaries are sprinkled with foreign expressions, sometimes because they were effective (for example, that Japan had "Groszmachtkitzel"—the itch to become a great power), other times because they would veil the meaning from Japanese eyes, should his servant or someone else get at the diaries (Greek, for example, was like a secret code in Japan). Sir George Sansom wrote me that "Satow was a good linguist and spoke Japanese very fluently." As he put it in an assessment of the great pioneers in the study of China, Japan, and Korea:

Satow was perhaps a rather dry scholar, but he was a prodigious worker. Besides being a most valuable member of the British Legation in Japan at a crucial period, he added to his

18

understanding of Japanese politics a remarkable command of the Japanese language and a scholar's interest in Japanese history and literature. Much of his work is still not superseded. He is one of the Founding Fathers of modern Japanology.[5]

If Satow's scholarship and some of his dispatches ring "dry," his diary entries and a number of his experiences sparkle with wit and vitality. During a home leave in England, for example, he recorded that "a good way of changing the conversation is to remark to the lady of the house that a cobweb is hanging from the ceiling." Although Satow is very discreet about his personal life in his diaries, he speaks of his love for a schoolfriend—"dear devil of a fellow"—correspondence with whom his parents forbade and, after his move to Japan, of *musume* (girls) and *onna gochisō* (women feasts), though usually when he did not get them—when he was "badly screwed," as he puts it. He was less discreet about other people. Writing of the Bavarian naturalist Philipp Franz von Siebold, who had two children, one of them "secret," Satow observed: "Old Siebold it appears had the misfortune to get another child on the body of a female domestic when he was last in Japan."

Satow's diaries for the years of his stay in Japan, both in 1862-82 and 1895-1900 are silent about the Japanese woman by whom he himself had, it appears, two children. So are his biography by Bernard M. Allen and the biographical sketch in the *Dictionary of National Biography*, as well as Japanese reference works. In fact, the biographies state that Satow "never married." Yet old British diplomats and elderly Japanese intellectuals alike remember that Satow had a Japanese wife and at least one son. Sir George Sansom, in response to a query from me, replied: "As to Sir Ernest Satow's progeny, I have never heard of any but one son, who ca. 1930 was practicing as a doctor in or near Tokyo. He had a Japanese surname and I presume that Satow was not married to the Japanese mother by English law."

While Satow does not refer to his wife and children directly, the diaries for the period from 1895 to 1900 state now and again that he dined at Gembei "con los muchachos." "With the boys" could refer to colleagues; it could mean his sons. The solitary entry in Japanese, on November 26, 1899, that he dined with "oyako" ("Mother and child" or "mother and children") points to his family, as may statements on April 17 and 21, 1900, that he ate "con tutti e tre" ("with all three"), especially because he added: "Said nothing about possibility of not returning. . . ." The most direct references appear in his China diaries, when on his way home from Peking in 1906, he stopped in Japan. On May 22, he visited O. K. and Hisayoshi. "O.K." may have been a nickname or an abbreviated spelling of the name Okei, popular for girls in those days; it may have been his wife's initials. Hisayoshi seems to have been his younger son. "The idea of the latter is to go as an assistant to Sapporo Agricultural College, whence he could always get back in vacation and at any time in these days, if he is wanted," Satow recorded. The next day Satow went to O.K.'s house on Fujimi Street again. "O.K. brought out a treasure of gold coins, eighty-seven yen of the old currency, which she divided between the two boys, and gave me half to carry to Eitaro." Eitaro seems to have been Satow's other son. The "Ei" of Eitaro probably is the character for "English" and the "taro" suggests elder son. Eitaro lived in Colorado by this time, which would explain why old residents like Sir George Sansom had not heard of him. On May 26, Satow gave O.K. "some checks up to September of next year." On May 28, he went to bid farewell. "O.K. says that she has given up the idea of adopting a little girl, and will think of getting Hisayoshi married, as soon as he is able to earn a livelihood."

On June 8, Satow said goodbye to O.K. and Hisayoshi again, and the next day departed from Tokyo. On June 27, on his way back to England, Satow stopped in Colorado to visit Eitaro. "Looking bronzed and well," Eitaro met Satow at the station in Denver. The following day they went to

Eitaro's ranch near Berthoud. "Very rough kind of life, but healthy," Satow jotted down in his diary. On June 30, Satow saw Dr. Sewall about Eitaro. "He says his health is excellent, but it is better for him to live here and carry on farming, but must take care of his health. No harm in his paying short visits to Japan and England during the autumn dry season."

It is probable, as Sir George Sansom presumed, that O.K. was Satow's common law wife. A formal marriage to a Japanese would have been quite impossible for a British diplomat in those days. When Queen Victoria had asked Satow in 1897 if Japanese were not a very difficult language, he had replied that it was, "because one could not learn it by living in a Japanese family as one would do in Europe."

Another intriguing relationship of Satow may be gleaned from his diaries for the period of 1895 to 1900—the relationship with Asaina Kansui (Asahina Masahiro) whom he paid for miscellaneous information. Asaina, who appears in the official dispatches merely as "a confidential source," not only expounded his views of men and politics, but supplied Satow with such materials as the shorthand notes of the financial committee of the Lower House. On March 2, 1896, Asaina told Satow that Japan "does not want to move again for another eight or nine years, till she is ready" (i.e. until 1904-1905, when she attacked Russia). On April 21, Asaina informed Satow that "Japan is arming with greater rapidity and secrecy than she did for her war with China." In October of 1899 Asaina communicated to Satow that the Japanese fleet was "in full fighting order" and that "the naval people would like to go in at the Russians." Asaina also gave Satow the name of a secret agent, the Japanese Foreign Minister had sent to Seoul to "buy" some Korean officials.

Occasionally Satow asked Asaina for specific information: "I told him to try and find out whether the Russians have informed his government of their desire to lease Port Arthur and Talienwan Bay and whether the Cabinet have made any observations to Russia on the subject," Satow recorded in his diary on March 12, 1898. Asaina could not always procure the desired information. One day he told Satow that a communication had been received in the Foreign Office from Russia, but that he had not been able to find out the content, since Foreign Minister Nishi Tokujiro, who had recently been Japanese Minister to Russia, kept his mouth closed and did all the translations from Russian himself, without sending them out of his office. Asaina received fairly regular compensation for his information and occasionally bonuses—"50 extra for papers procured," as one entry states. As in the case of Satow's relations with O.K., the diary references are often camouflaged in foreign words, in this instance primarily in Greek and Latin.

Mr. Tani Moriki, Chief of the Archives Section of the Secretariat to the Minister for Foreign Affairs of the Japanese Foreign Office, was so kind as to furnish a biographical sketch of Asaina, prepared by the Historical Materials Compilation Institute of the University of Tokyo. Asaina came from a "hatamoto" family (hereditary vassals of the Shogun before the Imperial Restoration), receiving an allowance of 500 *koku* of rice. His father, Asaina Masatoshi, served as "konando-todori" (an official title of the period) and "karo" (principal retainer) of the Tayasu family, as well as Governor of Nagasaki, etc. In 1859, Asaina was employed as a page, assigned to the "Chuoku" (Living Room of the Shogun). In 1861 he succeeded to the headship of his family. The following year he was appointed the head of an infantry unit. From 1864 to 1866 he was Governor of Nagasaki, though he did not actually serve there. In 1865 he was named concurrently Commissioner for Foreign Affairs, in 1866 Commissioner of Financial Affairs. In March of 1867 Asaina was appointed Commissioner for Foreign Affairs, in June Acting Minister for Foreign Affairs, in July concurrently Governor of Edo. As the Imperial government was being restored to power, Asaina at first seemed to remain in public office. Thus in January of 1868 he was reappointed Commissioner for Financial Affairs, but he was relieved of the position within a fortnight. No information is available as to his moves after the downfall of the Shogunate till his death in August, 1905. In the words of the Historical Materials Compilation Institute: "Probably, he did not enter into government service, but lived free from worldly cares."

As Commissioner for Foreign Affairs, Asaina had had contact with many foreign envoys, including Satow. The existence of some official documents exchanged between Satow and Asaina testifies to their acquaintance. But while the Historical Materials Compilation Institute agreed, in response to my query, that Asaina "might have supplied Satow with a great deal of information," it objected that, "it would be too much, without any specific evidence, to think that 'Satow paid Asahina for this information.'" The evidence is overwhelming.

In his diary Satow recorded that he paid Asaina on September 10 and November 20, 1896, 100 each; on January 12 and March 3, 1897, 20 each. No payment is mentioned on seventeen other recorded meetings with Asaina during this period, but on April 27, Satow notes that Asaina "has received 500 last year 200 this." When money was first given is not clear. On December 2, 1895, when Satow and Asaina first met after the former's return to Japan, Satow jotted down in his diary: "He said he would make inquiries among his friends and tell me all he could." On February 19, 1896, Asaina informed Satow of a secret Japanese troop movement to Korea, but it is not clear whether any money changed hands. On May 3, 1897, Satow gave Asaina $300, on November 26, 100; on January 12, 1898, and on March 12, May 10, July 5, October 4, November 22, 100 each, with 50 extra for papers added on July 5. On December 4, Satow noted that Asaina "cannot get any Bills yet"; two weeks later he gave him 30, whether for the Bills or not. On January 10, 1889, he resumed the almost regular bimonthly payments of 100, shelling out again on March 11, May 11, July 17, September 11, November 7,

January 19, 1900, and on March 1. On April 28 there was a final payment of 300. Calculating from the April 27, 1897 entry that Asaina had received 500 the year before and 200 that year, it is clear that Asaina was paid by Satow at least 2,880 yen (the currency is not certain, being indicated only once with a $ sign).

On the other hand, Asaina in turn received information from Satow. For example, on February 19, 1897, Satow recorded the feeling that Asaina was trying to "pump" him "to find out whether there was an understanding between England and Japan," and three days later he wrote that Asaina "took away with him copies of papers relating to accession of colonies, including translation of my two notes-verbals." Nor was payment by a foreign diplomat unusual. Ito asserted that "Hitrovo [the Russian Minister] spends a good deal of money on Japanese, some high official persons," and that "former Chinese Minister used to employ uneducated Japanese as spies, but was sometimes misled, because they did not know what they saw." The Japanese did the same. Foreign Minister Okuma Shigenobu, according to Asaina, "sent Toda, a merchant, over to Corea to act as a secret agent, and buy some Corean officials."

What were some of the impressions that Satow gathered from his talks with Asaina, with leading Japanese and Chinese statesmen, and with his Western collegaues? What were some of his own feelings? Satow was, first of all, sympathetic toward Japan. He congratulated Prime Minister Ito on the success of Japanese arms in the Sino-Japanese War. (8/1/1895) Satow told Count Inouye Kaoru that his idea had always been "that Japan was more fitted to lead Corea in the path of progress, as there was much more similarity between them than between the Coreans and Chinese." (10/4/95) Satow concurred with Ito that obtaining independence for Korea would have its disadvantages, as Russia would then be able to deal with Korea directly. "We agreed that 'neutralization' was rather the term to employ than independence." (8/1/95)

24

Ito stated another time that the idea of Korean independence was "quite impractical." "She must be either annexed, or be placed under the protection of some other Power." When Satow inquired what Power that would be, Ito replied laconically, "the strongest." (9/26/95) Edwin Dun, the American Minister in Tokyo, held that the best arrangement for Korea would be for it to be governed by an union of the Powers, with Denmark or Switzerland as their mandatory in the name of the king. But when Satow asked whether the United States, as "a Power known to be disinterested" would "put her finger into such a fire," Dun replied, "certainly not." (10/17/95)

Satow objected to Ito's position that Russia was more directly concerned with Korea than other Western Powers. "If Russia was Corea's neighbour by land," he protested, "Great Britain was her neighbour by sea, and it would never be admitted by Great Britain that Russia had more vital interests at stake in Corea than herself." He warned Ito that "by treating Russia as if that Power was alone to be dealt with, he would be making her the sole arbiter of Corea's future." (10/23/95) To a Korean who came to him to ask for British protection of Korea from Russia, however, Satow replied that British political and other interests in Korea "were less than those of Japan and Russia, which were her immediate neighbours" and that it was difficult to help from such a great distance. (2/13/1896)

Satow believed that, if prudence were observed, Russo-Japanese rivalry over Korea—"Russia wanted to keep Japan out, and Japan wished to keep out Russia"—could be balanced so as to insure the independence of the country. When a Japanese newspaperman observed that the Russians would intrigue, Satow countered that he was "quite sure the Japanese could beat them at that." (1/17/96) Satow expressed displeasure with Japanese involvement in the Korean coup d'état and the murder of the Queen, and when the Japanese who had participated in the conspiracy were acquitted at a trial that seem-

25

ingly had proven their guilt, Satow conveyed to Acting Foreign Minister Saionji Kinmochi his personal dissatisfaction and noted that it would make an unfavourable impression on the world in general. (1/23/96) Satow advised Ito that Korean affairs be left to quiet down; "they should be treated as ordinary incidents, and no heroic remedies applied." (12/20/95)

When the Korean King fled to the Russian legation, Satow observed that apparently "the Russians had lulled the Japanese into a false security about Russia," (2/14/96) but he told a group of Koreans that he "did not think Russia wished to destroy the independence of Corea, only to prevent the Japanese taking possession." (2/19/96) Satow discerned in Japan at that time "an earnest desire to arrive at an understanding with Russia as regards the future of Corea," but noted that "it is difficult. . . to see what form of compromise is feasible which would insure to Japan a joint influence in the affairs of the Peninsula." (2/24/96) When Satow heard that several Japanese had privately suggested to the Russian Minister that Korea be partitioned between Japan and Russia, Satow told Foreign Minister Mutsu Munemitsu that he did not think "a partition satisfactory to both Powers was feasible." (4/16/96)

In May 1896, Satow informed the Japanese that England's interest in Korea was secondary to that of China, Japan, or Russia, and that one of the latter should take the initiative in concerting with the other interested Powers to find a remedy for Korea's anarchy. Although Mutsu, in May of 1896, was concerned about Russian naval pressure on Korea, he thought that Russia had no idea of annexing Korea. Satow expressed his concurrence with Mutsu's view, "as her objects could be attained without attempting to govern such an unruly race as the Coreans had proved themselves to be." (5/21/96) Satow felt that the substitution of Russia for China in Korea in 1896 was "so far satisfactory that Russia was more easy to negotiate with." (8/10/96) When Japan and Russia concluded an agreement about Korea, Satow reflected that the necessity of coming to an understanding with Russia must have been "a bitter humiliation" for Count Okuma Shigenobu, who during the Sino-Japanese War had "expressed himself somewhat too boastfully respecting the ability of his countrymen to carry through their policy in Corea in despite of European Powers and. . . advocated a 'strong' attitude towards foreign Governments." (3/1/1897)

Satow reported in a confidential dispatch in February 1897 that Marshal Yamagata Aritomo had proposed the partition of Korea in 1896 during his talks in Russia, but that the Russian Foreign Minister had declined "on the ground that Russia did not desire any Corean territory." (3/1/97) Russian attempts, in April 1897, to increase their military influence in Korea and to strengthen their hold over the country aroused Satow's concern. He foresaw "great risk of complications arising . . . should Russia endeavor . . . to play in that country the part which China had assumed prior to the war of 1894." He noted that the Japanese "already hold themselves to be more than able to cope on land with the army of Eastern Siberia" and that the arrival of two English-built battleships in Japan "will no doubt strengthen the confidence of the Japanese Government in their belief that time alone is necessary to render this country a match for Russia at sea." (4/29/97)

It was the view of Lord Salisbury in October of 1897 that Great Britain should not interfere with Russian commercial ambitions in Korea, only with possible military movements. Meanwhile she should counsel the Japanese "to get on happily with the Russians." (10/7/97) But in December Satow reported that he doubted that the Japanese believed that the Korean people would get tired of the Russians and turn again to Japan for assistance. He felt that "they must have some other hopes of recovering their lost influence by means which it is thought prudent to make no allusion to at present." (12/16/97)

Satow told Vice Minister of Foreign Affairs Komura Jutaro in May 1898 that his government "had always recognized that the interests of Japan and Russia [in Korea] came first." (5/9/1898) When Foreign Minister Aoki Shuzo informed Satow in January 1899 that Japan would arrange about Korea "direct with Russia without English intervention," Satow rejoined that "we should observe a disinterested attitude, but that Japan had our sympathy." (1/25/1899) Before Satow left Japan in May of 1900, he had a final conversation with Ito. He stated that it was not to the advantage of Japan to fight Russia, though many people talked about it. "Japan and Russia as to Corea like . . . a pretty woman with two suitors; no need however to come to blows." Ito replied that there was strong sentiment in Japan for fighting. Upon his return to England Satow told the Secretary of War that Japan "would not act in any case before 1903 when her fleet and army will have obtained their full expansion, and even then only if England backs her up." (5/2/1900)

The Japanese reaction to the Tripartite Intervention was not exclusively one of anger and frustration. Satow felt (and the German Minister Freiherr von Gutschmid agreed) "that Japanese are rather flattered than otherwise that in the Liaotung question, though forced to retrocede, they have been treated as if they belonged to the European concert." (8/21/1900) Yet the Japanese people were for war against the three Powers, which blocked their acquisition of the Liaotung Peninsula. Asaina told Satow, that "if the Japanese people were polled, their voice would be for war unprepared as they were." Satow cautioned that it would be disastrous for Japan to go to war: "I knew the courage of the people and that the 40,000,000 of them would fight to the last breath rather than give in, but their navy was not strong enough." (2/19/96) Satow also warned that Japan should not expect England to come to her rescue in her dispute with Russia, Germany and France, since she had disregarded British advice. But he assured Asaina that if any attack were made on the independence of Japan, England would come to her rescue. (2/19/96)

Satow advised Ito to agree to the retrocession of the Liaotung Peninsula and the acceptance of a reasonable indemnity (smaller than the one demanded by Japan). Satow discussed the matter with his European colleagues and tried to bring about agreement on this issue. Satow urged Ito to settle the Liaotung issue as soon as possible to put an end to the constant intervention by Russia, Germany, and France, so humiliating to both China and Japan. Satow decried the fact that as a result of the Tripartite Intervention the prestige of Russia, Germany, and France had increased at the expense of Japan. This seemed to him "of serious import for the future of Eastern Asia." The reason why Japan did not negotiate with China directly, as Satow suggested, but through the three Powers was that Ito, as he told Satow, "had no confidence in the good faith of any Chinese statesman with the exception of Li Hungchang, and he had yet to learn that the latter possessed any real power." (10/7/1895) The Japanese simply did not know how to cope with the seizure of Port Arthur by the Russians in 1898. As Satow described the frame of mind of the Japanese government: "They have the appearance of being thoroughly disheartened, and they do not seem to appreciate the value of diplomacy, except as a preliminary to the use of force." (3/26/98)

Satow regarded Russia as "an absorbing Power." "She aimed at universal domination, being the youngest of the nations, full of sap; Eastern Europe and the whole of Asia was what she aimed at." (12/24/1903) He likened the Russians to "a tree that was always putting out branches over the neighbour's wall" and to "the bamboo, that sends its roots along under ground, and then suddenly comes up where you least expect it." (10/12/1899) Satow, therefore, bolstered Japanese and Chinese resistance to Russian demands. He advised the Japanese to take an active role in the defense of their interests. When Okuma complained to him about Russian occupation of Port Arthur, Satow "rubbed it into him about the 'mere spectator' policy of the Japanese." (3/25/98) When Li Hung-chang told him that he had refused Russia's offer to take over a portion of the railroad line outside the Great Wall in part payment for damages to the Manchurian line, Satow told him "he should stick to that," adding that he knew "he was strong enough to refuse sometimes what Russians asked." (1/25/1901) To Prince Ch'ing's query in February 1902, what would happen if Russia refused to sign the Russo-Chinese agreement providing for evacuation of Manchuria (and continued pressing China for concessions), Satow replied: "I told him that the Anglo-Japanese agreement was not a mere *brutum fulmen* [insensible thunderbolt, i.e. futile threat of force] but meant business." (2/20/1902) Another time Satow scolded the Chinese for weakly giving in on every occasion to Russian demands uttered in a loud voice and remarked that Li Hung-chang's idea to obtain good treatment by making concessions was a false one. "It only increased appetite." (3/18/1902)

While in London on home leave, Satow suggested to Lord Lansdowne that someday England might have to fight Russia, and that "she was not so strong as she looked." (4/29/1903) He told the editor of the *Spectator* that England ought to oppose Russia in Manchuria "tooth and nail." He said that "tooth and nail meant war," and expressed the opinion that "a challenge would not be accepted by Russia." He did not think that either England or Japan would resort to force, "but it would not do to say so." (5/13 and 5/15, 1903) In his diary he recorded a remark by Sir Thomas Sanderson, which appears timeless: "Of course we should be glad to come to an understanding with Russia, but it seems impossible, though there are indications that they desire it; but they want us to take them on trust, which will not do." (5/16/03)

Satow told Foreign Minister Aoki in April 1899 that "privately" he had "long been of opinion that China would not hold together." (4/20/99) But Satow tried to prevent the partition of China for practical reasons. As he told the French Minister at Peking: "How could we possibly find the men to carry it out, and then just think of the difficulties among ourselves." As Russia sought to conclude a secret convention with China before withdrawing from Manchuria, the position of China was ticklish. While Great Britain and the European Powers wanted to be informed of the demands that Russia made on China, the communication of these demands to the other Powers could be regarded as an insult and thus a cause for war by Russia. China feared to reveal the text unless first assured of British mediation, while Britain first wished to see the text before deciding on mediation. Satow advised Li to reject Russian demands on China "if it is desired to prevent her disruption," (2/27/1901) and told Prince Ch' ing "that China need not fear Russia breaking off negotiations, and that if he remained firm the articles imparing Chinese sovereignty would be taken out." (3/15/1901) He also wired to the British Consul at Nanking to urge Viceroy Chang Chihtung "to memorialize the Emperor against it," lest Li Hungchang sign in spite of Satow's remonstrances. (12/14/1903) In a conversation with Sir Robert Hart, Inspector General of the Chinese Customs Service, Satow summed up the British position regarding a Russo-Chinese convention. "I said all we really cared for was freedom of commerce, but if the Chinese gave away what would conflict with the most favoured nation clause, we should ask for compensation." (1/14/1902)

Russian designs on Manchuria were partly "preventive." As Charles Hardinge wrote in a confidential dispatch from St. Petersburg in November 1902, Finance Minister Sergei Witte realized that "the existence of Dalny as a free port at the terminus of the Manchurian railway will offer great facilities for the development of British, Japanese, and American trade and industry in Manchuria" and that if Manchuria were allowed to become a manufacturing country (rather than a market for Russian products), it "would be able to flood Russian territory with manufactures produced at so cheap a cost that no Russian industry would be able to compete." (11/3/1902)

While Satow evaluated the prevailing Chinese feeling as "one of despair at the impotence of which they are conscious," he warned in a dispatch to the Foreign Office that the Boxer events had shown that "the Chinese are people capable of suddenly taking fire, and in that condition of performing acts of the rashest desperation." (12/31/1903) But for the moment he did not trust Chinese ability to resist Russian pressure, backed by French "advice." "They would I believe rather sacrifice Manchuria even, provided it were not done openly, rather than let the Japanese have a chance of taking the place of the Russians, for Dubail [the French Minister] would demonstrate that it is more easy in every way and more profitable to their pockets to be friends with Russia than with Japan." (2/5/1904)

In November of 1895, Satow felt that the Tripartite Intervention had forced Japan to moderate her policy, "putting water into the wine." Foreign Minister Mutsu Munemitsu told Satow in April 1896 that "it was absolutely necessary for Japan to have peace for the next five years." (4/16/1896) Satow agreed that "peace was necessary to enable Japan to develop her resources." But on May 9, 1896, Satow recorded a fascinating conversation with Hayashi Kenzo, an old friend, now a retired Vice-Admiral:

He says that two years ago the question was whether they should go for the Russian squadron first and smash them up, and then go for the Chinese, or vice versa. Ultimately they decided on the latter course, because they concluded that their ships would be less damaged. By the time they had polished off the Chinese, the Russians had increased their navy too much. They always anticipated that Russia would interfere on the side of China. For years past they have felt that sooner or later they must fight Russia, and they will have to do it yet. If last spring they had already possessed the *Fuji* and *Yashima* they would not have given way about Liaotung.

Satow gave thought to British naval support of Japan. He told Vice-Admiral Sir Alexander Bullock in May 1896, that if England undertook to keep Tsushima Strait for the Japanese, the latter could pour enough soldiers into Korea to prevent the Russians from coming in. "We could account for the Russian fleet, and the Japanese would undertake the French." (5/16/96) Goto Shojiro, a prominent Japanese statesman, expressed to Satow fear that Russia would assert herself in Korea. "The only thing is for England and Japan to make common cause against the enemy," he told Satow. (10/14/95) In November of 1897 Satow discussed the question of an Anglo-Japanese alliance with Asaina. "Told him we thought the moment had not come for joint action, and till then a formal alliance undesirable, but in meanwhile to cultivate the closest possible understanding." (11/26/97) Satow told Foreign Minister Aoki in December of 1898 that England could do nothing in the Far East until her disagreements with France about Newfoundland and Siam had been settled (Fashoda had been "arranged for"). "However Japan would not be ready till 1903," Satow added, "and by that time our hands also might be free." (12/7/98) When Aoki in March 1899 told Satow that "if Russia has Corea Japan cannot sleep in peace," Satow observed that "Japan would not be ready until 1903." Aoki replied, "she might be obliged to act before." (3/30/99)

In 1898 Ito told Satow that the Chinese government had asked Japan to give assurance that Japan intended no agression. "He answered they had given no reply, or rather had said they could give none, as *they could not undertake* anything of the kind!" Satow recorded in his diary, and added: "I laughed and said they could not possibly contemplate anything of the kind." (3/31/98) When Aoki came to Satow to get his reaction to Japanese acquisition of a Chinese port, Satow warned him that "the British Government would not approve of any aggressive measures against China." (10/15/99) Reports of a Russo-Chinese agreement led a Japanese politician to state that "it was no longer merely a Corean question, but a Chinese question, and . . . that the very independence of Japan was at stake." (3/14/96)

When Okuma told Satow in 1896 about the extent of Japanese military preparations, Satow said to him that "the half-million men might excite suspicion as to Japanese intentions in certain quarters, as it was too large for mere self-defence." (11/5/96) On February 22, Asaina had told Satow that "the real motive of war with China was to obtain justification for increasing army and navy." (2/22/96) Reviewing the Far Eastern situation in a "very confidential" dispatch to Lord Salisbury in March of 1898 Satow added another factor: "Whatever the ostensible reason for going to war with China may have been, there can be little doubt that the main object was to anticipate the completion of the Siberian Railway and to prevent Russia gaining free access to the Pacific Ocean." (3/26/98) On April 5, 1898, after a talk with Inouye, Satow summed up what the latter had said: "Japanese naval preparations not ready yet; though the scale had been enlarged, the body has not been filled up. Five years hence when the Siberian Railway is finished, a great struggle will take place." On March 4, 1900 Satow reiterated that he did not think the Japanese would take the initiative in war, "at any rate not before 1903."

When Russia in 1903 began to exploit a timber concession in Korea (which it had negotiated in 1896), Russo-Japanese relations reached a crisis stage. The likelihood of war was mentioned in dispatches from everywhere in 1903. As the British Minister reported from St. Petersburg, "Russia's mistrust of the intentions of Japan probably at present equals, or even surpasses, Japan's mistrust of Russia." (8/5/1903) On August 29, 1903, after talking to the Japanese Minister at Peking, who told him of the presentation of Japanese proposals at St. Petersburg, Satow noted in his diary: "From his tone I drew the conclusion that he expects war." On September 7, Uchida openly told Satow he thought "it would be difficult to avoid war." When Tang Shao-yi, whom Viceroy Yüan Shih-k'ai sent to Satow, expressed the fear that "if Japan were victorious [in a war with Russia], she would become very domineering," Satow replied that he deemed it "unlikely . . . that she would feel inclined to herself domineer over China, but rather to afford her assistance." (10/29/1903) In November 1903 as talk of war persisted, Satow noted in his diary: "My conjecture is that if war breaks out, it will take first the form of an endeavour to destroy or neutralize the Russian fleet, and be followed by an attack on Vladivostok. . . . (11/1/03)

In Japan the international situation created political pressures which in turn affected the international situation. Satow noted in his diary on November 12, 1903, that Uchida Yasuya, the Japanese Minister at Peking, had confided to him that "his government must conclude something before 5 December, for which date the Diet is summoned, for if they don't the Cabinet must fall under impeachment, and if they try to quiet things by dissolving the Diet and so preventing the impeachment, [Premier] Katsura or [Foreign Minister] Komura will certainly be assassinated!"

In November 1903, Satow jotted down the prescient remarks of the American Minister Edwin H. Conger about the unrest in Central China and along the Yangtze. "The people attribute the heavy burdens imposed on them in consequences of the events of 1900 to the Tartar dynasty, and feel that the only hope for China is in getting rid of them." (12/7/1903) As Russia and Japan negotiated in 1903, Satow counselled the Chinese to keep quiet until the negotiations were decided, lest they invite the hostility of Russia, "which was looking for an opportunity to seize Peking." (11/21/03) At the same time it was Satow's view that "the whole [Japanese] nation and the Diet were for war." (12/13/03)

In December 1903, General Yamane asked Satow for his "private" view, whether Japan ought to fight now or delay. "I pondered, and then said yes," Satow recorded in his diary, "for if Russia is left undisturbed in Manchuria out of which she will never retire willingly, she will end by taking Corea, and the position of Japan would then be imperilled." (12/14/03) Satow told the French Minister that the Russians misunderstood the temper of the Japanese people when they thought their military preparations would frighten them. The Japanese were willing to fight. People had told the Japanese after their victory over China that their campaign had been "a mere military promenade" and that "they would never get their position as a nation recognized until they crossed swords with an European power. That was a strong motive with them." (12/24/03)

The American Minister told Satow in January 1904 that the Russian Minister and all the others thought that war between Russia and Japan would be "an easy business" and that "these dwarfs were quite out of their reckoning in thinking they would stand up against European troops." "I said to him," Satow recorded, "I did not think England could stand by and see Japan crushed, or allow Corea to pass into the possession of Russia, as Masampho directly threatens the Yangtze, and seeing the interests United States have in Japan, which she brought into the world and educated, I did not think they would either." (1/17/04)

Fearing that a war between Russia and Japan would be at their expense, the Chinese asked Satow whether Great Britain would be willing to mediate between Japan and Russia to avert war. Satow replied that "all experience was against the success of attempted mediation, when it was desired by neither of the hostile Governments or by only one of them." He added: "Generally speaking, it was only after war had resulted in the defeat of one party, or both had begun to feel exhausted, that the interposition of other Powers was asked for, or could be usefully rendered." (1/19/04) When Chinese asked him why England, America and France could not talk to Japan to get her to moderate, so as to avoid war, Satow replied "as befitted such nonsense that His Majesty's Government would not think of making a suggestion of this kind to Japan, because they considered her to be entirely in the right." (1/23/04)

In February 1904, after talking to the German Minister at Peking about the probability of war between Japan and Russia, Satow noted in his diary: "I conceive that the Germans will not be at all sorry to see Russia engaged out here, as that will weaken them at Constantinople." (2/3/04) Upon the outbreak of war, Satow and the German Minister speculated about the future. "As to the results of a Japanese victory, I did not think they would be so extensive as he feared," Satow recorded. "The Japanese had not a light hand, and their endeavours to exercise predominant influence in Corea in 1894-95 had been altogether unsuccessful. Like most people of a determining character, they failed in tact, because they could not bring themselves to humour other people's susceptibilities. . . . The Chinese were a proud people and would resent the feeling that they lay under an obligation to Japan. . . . I did not anticipate that Japan would be any more successful with China than she had been with Corea." He added in his diary parenthetically: "I certainly think that a little disturbance of the balance of power in the Far East in favour of Japan is better than Russia having her own way. The rise of Japan as a military and naval Power and the construction of the Siberian railway have completely altered the situation out here for us as for all other European Powers, and we cannot expect to have things entirely our own way, as in 1842. But Japan will not be able to rule China. The latter will rely on European Powers to prevent Japan having her own way entirely." (2/14/04)

As can be seen from these excerpts, Satow had a remarkable grasp of attitudes and events. Though naturally he modified his views somewhat over the years, his basic evaluations remained the same and his predictions have stood the test of time surprisingly well. He was ever mindful of Russian designs on Korea, Manchuria, and China. He was alert also to the danger of Japanese militarism, but feared it less because he understood its inherent weaknesses. He appreciated the potential resurgence of China and realized that the days of the white man's undisputed domination of the world were past.

To preserve the flow of events and a certain narrative force, footnotes have been kept to a minimum, explanations and additions being added, where possible, in the paraphrased passages or bracketed in the text proper. The notes that were deemed unavoidable have been divided into two categories: footnotes, indicated by a small letter, provide information which is necessary for understanding the text; notes at the back of the book, marked by numbers, cite source data that only researchers may want to consult occasionally. No page or volume documentation was practical for the diary entries, the dates, provided in the text directly or in parentheses forming the most useful means of locating passages in the original manuscript.

As stated already, Satow was blessed with a good hand, and question-mark-warnings of an educated guess due to illegibility of the manuscript are rare. Satow had his own system of speedwriting. To have printed his abbreviations would have been quaint but burdensome for the reader. To have moored the text with footnote references to abbreviations would have prevented the flight of Satow's impressions from getting off the ground. Thus Satow's speedwriting has been transcribed in full words without annotation, except for occasional question marks where the rendering of a word was likely but not certain. Satow's spelling of names, with occasional variations, has been retained. Foreign words with which Satow sprinkled his diaries have been rendered faithfully, with English translations in brackets, except that the Japanese and Chinese characters and Greek letters have been romanized for convenience of publication.

The present book would not have seen the light of day without the generous aid of the Florida State University Research Council, which supported my work in London and

Introduction

enabled me to locate, photoduplicate and edit all the necessary sources. I am most grateful to the Secretary of the Public Record Office for permission to publish excerpts from the Satow diaries and the *Confidential Prints*. The friendly, courteous and ever-willing assistance of everyone else connected with the Public Record Office and the Ashridge Repository is likewise acknowledged. The frontispiece portrait of Sir Ernest Satow has been taken from *Vanity Fair* (23 April 1903). Last but not least I am indebted to my colleagues at the Florida State University, particularly to Professor Victor S. Mamatey, Chairman of the History Department, for their understanding and encouragement of my research.

GEORGE ALEXANDER LENSEN

Tallahassee, Florida
January, 1966

PART ONE
1895-1900

Japanese-Russian Rivalry in Korea

ON AUGUST 1, 1895, Sir Ernest Satow, who had recently arrived in Tokyo as the new British Minister Plenipotentiary, called on Prime Minister Ito Hirobumi, a friend of long standing. Satow congratulated Ito upon the success of Japanese arms in the Sino-Japanese War and on the course of the peace negotiations "which had turned out so well for Japan." They then spoke of Korea.

He asked me whether England had any interest there [Satow recorded in his diary]. Commercially I replied it was not of great importance, but we were anxious that what Japan was trying to prevent should not come about. I asked whether it was the desire of Russia to bring their railway through Manchuria or to a port in Corea. He answered that what they aim at is something much greater than a port, and then went on to tell me confidentially that Hitrovo [Mikhail Khitrovo, the Russian Minister to Japan] had visited Saionji [Kimmochi, the Acting Minister of Foreign Affairs] the day before, and after repeating as far as he could the language used by him went upstairs and fetched down a memorandum which he read to me, and afterwards I read it over so as to fix it in my memory. . . . The gist was that Russia expected Japan to conform her acts to her declarations as to the independence of Corea, and asserting that the King is anxious to make reforms, but fears authority will be weakened by Japanese interference. I remarked that the communication was couched in very polite terms, to which he responded that that was the Russian method, of beginning very mildly, and then gradually increasing in peremptoriness. I inquired whether Kato [Takaaki, the Japanese Minister in London] had reported a conversation he had with Lord K[imberley, the British Foreign Secretary] about recurring to a proposal made by Great Britain at an earlier

43

period of the war for the guarantee of Corean independence.
He said yes. Then I remarked that it seemed to me advisable
to join other Powers besides Russia and Great Britain. Explained
the relations between Great Britain, Spain and Italy regarding
status quo in Mediterranean, and suggested that Italy would
be very willing to join, also perhaps Austria. He observed that
it would be best to invite all the Great Powers, but it was not
yet opportune. That 'independence' of Corea would leave the
question open, and he hinted that Russia would then be able
to deal directly with Corea, and obtain her aims more easily
and securely. We agreed that 'neutralization' was rather the term
to employ than independence.

On August 25 Satow informed the new Foreign Secretary,
Lord Robert Arthur Salisbury, that Lieutenant-General Viscount Miura Goro had left for Korea as Envoy Extraordi-
nary and Minister Plenipotentiary. Describing his background
and character, Satow reported: "He is credited with moderate views respecting the introduction of reforms into Corea,
being opposed to heroic measures, and holding that the work
must be carried out slowly and steadily."[6]
On September 26, Satow discussed Korea with Ito.

His Excellency said that recently, troubles having broken out
at Sang Wön, in the Province of Phyöng-an-do, the Corean
Government had requested the aid of Japanese troops in suppressing them, but that General Miura, the present Minister at
Seoul, had refused, considering it preferable that such assistance
should not be afforded until the Corean Government had exhausted all the means at their disposal. The present force stationed in Corea amounted to six battalions, or about 4,800 men,
and this it was shortly intended to reduce to a material extent.
Corea, it had been shown, was quite incapable of reform from
within, and those which Japan had endeavoured to introduce
seemed a long way off of being realized.
I observed that, at any rate, Japan had gained two things by
the [Sino-Japanese] war, namely, the annexation of Formosa;
and secondly, that Corea was now independent of Chinese tutelage. Marquess Ito replied that the idea of Corean independence
was quite impracticable. She must be either annexed, or be
placed under the protection of some other Power.

In reply to the question what Power that would be, his Excellency replied laconically, "the strongest."

I took the opportunity of saying that somewhat indiscreet observations had been made by responsible Japanese officials that the object of the [Sino-Japanese] war had been to forestall the completion of the Siberian Railway, but his Excellency repudiated the notion with great energy, and declared emphatically that in that case the war with China would have been altogether unjust. The sole object with which Japan had dispatched troops to Corea had been the suppression of the Tong Hak insurrection and the subsequent reform of the Administration, and she had made every exertion to come to an agreement with China for equal participation in the establishment of a sound system of government. Unfortunately her endeavours had not met with success, and the war had been the consequence of China's refusal to co-operate. It was true, of course, that Japan had dispatched a larger force to Corea than China, but the reason for that was the disadvantage in which she had been placed on a former occasion by her forces being numerically inferior to the Chinese. However, had the Chinese Cabinet agreed to the proposals made by Japan, the latter would have withdrawn, and there would have been no war.

From the manner in which Marquess Ito spoke, I am disposed to infer that he will not be disposed to resist Russian demands in order to maintain the Japanese position in Corea, nor even the annexation of Corea by Russia, although, as he remarked, the latter event would entirely change the face of Eastern Asia. But having been compelled to give way with respect to the Liao-tung Peninsula, owing to the inferiority of the Japanese fleet, he naturally feels that Japan by herself is powerless to oppose Russian advance towards the open sea.[7]

On October 4, Count Inouye Kaoru, one-time Premier and Home Minister and a leading figure on the political scene, called on Satow. "We talked about Corea and I said my idea had always been that Japan was more fitted to lead Corea in the path of progress, as there was much more similarity between them than between the Coreans and Chinese," Satow jotted down in his diary. "In 1869 Kido [Takayoshi (Koin)] had advocated war with Corea as a means of quieting Japa-

45

nese internal dissensions, but Saigo Kichinosuke opposed; several years later the two had changed roles."

That afternoon Satow went to Count Okuma Shigenobu, one-time Foreign Minister who had lost one leg to a bomb hurdling would-be-assassin. Okuma was very friendly and spoke very highly of Sir Harry Parkes, the British Minister to Japan from 1865 to 1883.

When Sir Harry left in 1883 he had called to say good-bye, and remarked that sooner or later they would have trouble with China on account of Corea. For a long time past Japan had been greatly provoked by China on more than one occasion, especially when Admiral Ting [Ju-ch'ang] came to Nagasaki with the Chinese squadron and there were rows between the crews and the townspeople, provoked by the Chinese. Then the decoying of Kim Ok-kiun [a pro-Japanese Korean leader] to Shanghai, his murder there, the interference of the Chinese to prevent his body being brought to Japan by a steamer of the N.Y.S.K. and sending it with the murderer to Corea in a Chinese man of war, where the body was cut in pieces and exposed as members of a traitor and the assassin rewarded. But the Government had behaved with the greatest self-restraint. It was not true that Japan had sought to make war with China, though she was fully prepared, and the War Department was anxious to prove the weapon they had perfected. Luckily for them they had managed to get a quantity of quickfiring guns just before war was declared, and they had twice as many as were needed for their navy. Still, they were very anxious for the result of a battle, as the Chinese vessels were stronger and they had many foreign officers; but as for the army they were quite at ease in their minds, even if there had been foreign officers, as the Chinese troops were not ready to fight, and there was such an enthusiasm in Japan that they would easily have raised and equipped another 100,000 men. At present they were not ready to encounter another enemy, for their manufacturing power (i.e. of weapons) and finance were not sufficently developed. The present magazine rifle was not good and they were working to supply another better model, but it would be some time before they could furnish 300,000 men with rifles. Of ships they could easily purchase enough, and their maritime population gave them a source of supply which a couple of years would convert into efficient sailors. But officers took many years longer. However there were more entries than before to the naval college.

On October 10 Satow went to Saionji, "who talked rather freely about Corean affairs." In a dispatch to the Foreign Secretary Satow elaborated:

Your Lordship will have learnt from other sources of the *coup d'État* effected on the 8th instant by the father of the King of Corea, together with the disappearance of the Queen, and the appointment of the King's elder brother, I Je-myon to be Prime Minister.

The Japanese Acting Minister for Foreign Affairs informed me to-day, confidentially, that there were reasons for supposing that Japanese subjects were concerned in the affair, and, as it was a matter of the gravest import, he had this morning dispatched Mr. Komura [Jutaro], the Head of the Political Bureau, to Seoul, to inquire into all the circumstances. The Japanese Government would view with the greatest displeasure the participation of Japanese subjects in a treasonable conspiracy against the Sovereign of a friendly State.

His Excellency also informed me that the order to dispatch men-of-war to the Corean coast had been revoked.

As an indication of the very changed tone that has been adopted here with regard to Corea, I beg to inclose an extract from the *Nichi Nichi Shimbun*, foreshadowing an appeal to the Powers which have Treaties with Corea to join with Japan in some common arrangement with regard to the future of that country.

The language in which it is framed reads like that of a semi-official "Communiqué," and is evidently designed to conciliate Russia.[8]

On October 14, Satow called on Goto Shojiro, a prominent personality in the Restoration and most recently Minister of Agriculture and Commerce.

Seems much alarmed about the turn things may take in Corea, and that Russia will take this opportunity of asserting herself there. The only thing is for England and Japan to make common cause against the enemy. Told him Lord Salisbury very busy just now in bringing the Turks to reason about Armenia, and the Chinese about the missionary massacres, and I did not know what he would do, but for my own part I should greatly regret if England allowed Japan to be crushed.

Goto says [General Charles W.] LeGendre [one-time adviser to the Japanese Foreign Office] came here three or four years ago when Enomoto [Takeaki] was Minister for Foreign Affairs on a mission from Corean Government about Japanese fishermen poaching in the seas off Quelpart, and even landing there and building huts. But as he had no credentials, Japanese Government refused to treat with him. Since then he has been unfriendly, and acted as a go between of the Queen and Russian Minister [Karl Ivanovich] Wäber. It was in his presence that the Queen was killed, either in his room or hers. It is said her head was cut off, which looks like a Japanese performance. No doubt Japanese were mixed up in it. General Miura [the Japanese Minister at Seoul] was at the Palace five minutes later in his uniform. All this came in a long telegram from LeGendre to [Edwin] Dun [the American Minister in Japan], who went at once to the Foreign Office and saw Hara [Takashi, Vice Minister of Foreign Affairs], but the latter pretended not to know anything of what had happened. The Queen it seems had stuffed up Inouye that the Min family were the real friends of Japan, and he came back so fully embued with that idea that he made a speech at Kobe saying that the whole policy of Japan hitherto had been based on a mistake. Inouye, he says, has a head after the European pattern! He tried to introduce all sorts of reforms when he went over there last summer, and the Palace people pretended to accept them, but in reality detested the changes, to carry out which it would be necessary for Inouye to be made King of Corea. He was in fact talking of the good dispositions of the Min family at the very moment the news arrived. Goto said further that the German, French and Russian men-of-war had arrived simultaneously at Inchhön, and that they were going together about Corea as they had about Liaotung. Formosa [which Japen had acquired by the Sino-Japanese War] of course partly crippled Japanese military resources, but as far as Japan herself goes, no invasion was possible. Her fleet however was not ready, as she had only cruisers. Russia had intended to wait till the completion of the Siberian Railway but the events of last year had given her a good opportunity which she did not miss, and what had now happened in Corea would also be turned to good account by her. Some people advocated Japan allying herself with France and Russia, but what good would that do her. He quite understood German policy was not unfriendly to Japan, but circumstances were too strong for her. If she had gone on the side of Japan, what help could Japan have given her in Europe against France and Russia.

On October 16 Satow wrote, and the following day telegraphed, to London that the Japanese Government had issued a decree forbidding Japanese subjects to go to Korea and had dispatched the Director of the Political Bureau of Foreign Affairs to Seoul to make an on-the-spot investigation.

Marquess Saionji expressed to me his great concern lest it might be imagined that the Japanese Government had had a hand in what has occurred, inasmuch as the new Cabinet belongs more or less to the party of progress which is disposed to lean on Japan. The Japanese Government, he assured me, are determined to clear up the whole affair, and to punish the guilty, so far as they come under Japanese jurisdiction, so as to make it clear to the Powers that they are in no way responsible for acts of which they have the greatest detestation. Full information had been communicated to the Russian Government by the Japanese Minister at St. Petersburgh, and he was glad to learn from Mr. Nissi [Nishi Tokujiro] that his frankness had produced an excellent impression. At the same time he viewed with some apprehension the fact that about forty Russian sailors had been sent up to Seoul, and he thought there were indications of an intention to further increase their number.[9]

On October 17, Satow called on Edwin Dun, the American Minister in Tokyo.

Dun is sure that some Japanese were concerned in coup d'état at Söul. [Horace N.] Allen the United States Chargé d'Affaires (in the absence of John M. B. Sill [the American Minister]) is very much under the influence of the Russian. Dun's idea is that the best arrangement as to Corea would be for it to be governed by an union of the Powers, with Denmark or Switzerland as their mandatory in the name of the King. I said the question would be who could propose it, only a Power known to be disinterested, such as the United States, but I doubted whether she would put her finger into such a fire. Dun said certainly not. Dye is the name of the American general who was present at the affair in the Palace. He and Allen declare they recognized Japanese leaving the Palace among the assailants, but Dun thinks this is not certain, as Coreans in European dress would have the same look, and only language would identify. Watanabe Shujiro told [John Harington] Gubbins [Secretary of the British Legation in Japan] that ex-Major Okamoto who was concerned in the Guard's mutiny some years ago, and was cashiered then is supposed to have been in the coup d'état. Dun also told me this.

On October 18 Satow learned that General Miura, his secretary, the interpreter, the military attaché, the police inspector and more than forty other Japanese had been recalled from Korea and that Komura Jutaro, who was replacing Miura as Minister Resident in Korea was to make an investigation jointly with the Russian representative.[10]

On October 23, Satow called on Ito. "He was evidently anxious to have a talk about Corea, and almost immediately asked my opinion, which I gave him pretty straight, regretting the necessity of having to speak plainly," Satow noted in his diary. He elaborated in a dispatch:

I replied to his Excellency that I thought Japan could no longer look forward to having a preponderant voice at Seoul after what had occurred. The whole circumstances must naturally create a feeling of distrust in the minds of foreign Governments. Japan must therefore be prepared to share equally with other Treaty Powers the influence to be exercised at the Corean Court. Before the war she had proposed to act in concert with China for the introduction of necessary reforms. The victories achieved had placed her in a position of predominance, but that could no longer be maintained, and she must content herself with acting in combination with the Powers on a footing of equality.

His Excellency said that he believed the whole facts, which the Japanese Government had no intention of concealing, had been already made public in Europe, and he thought he saw signs of an exchange of views taking place between the Powers.

50

This he inferred from a telegram in this morning's papers stating that Prince [Aleksei] Lobanoff [-Rostovskii, the Russian Foreign Minister] had informed the German Emperor that Russia would not tolerate the Japanese establishing themselves in Corea. He was anxious that they should know everything, and had given instructions to the Japanese Representatives to give full information to the Governments, especially that of Russia.

I remarked that it would, if I might venture to say, be more politic to take all the Powers equally into his confidence as to Corean matters, which he could do by addressing a Circular despatch to the Japanese Ministers in Europe and the United States relating what had happened, and explaining what the Japanese views were of the policy necessitated by the present situation.

Marquess Ito replied that his reason for taking special pains to make things clear to Russia was that that Power had alone called upon Japan soon after the war to give effect to her previous declarations regarding the independence of Corea, and that Russia possessed greater interests in that country than any other Power.

I rejoined that it was very possibly the aim of Russia to lay claim to a special position on account of the proximity of her Eastern Asiatic dominions. But if Russia was Corea's neighbour by land, Great Britain was her neighbour by sea, and it would never be admitted by Great Britain that Russia had more vital interests at stake in Corea than herself. By treating Russia as if that Power was alone to be dealt with he would be making her the sole arbiter of Corea's future.

His Excellency inquired what, speaking not as Her Majesty's Minister, but for myself, I thought Japan should do in case Russia addressed a peremptory demand for the withdrawal of the Japanese garrisons.

That, I said, was a contingency which Japan should by all means endeavour to avoid or anticipate. If such a summons came she would be exposed to the alternative of refusal, which in the present condition of her navy would be extremely dangerous, or of submission, which would be a severe blow to her prestige. I had understood both from himself and Count Inouye that they considered the garrisons need not be maintained there much longer. (To this his Excellency assented, remarking, however, that this idea had not been as yet communicated to any

51

of the foreign representatives.) That being so, why not make a beginning by at once withdrawing the whole of the present garrison at Seoul, some of whom, both officers and men, had taken part in the attack on the Palace, replacing them not by fresh troops, but by a detachment from those already in Corea? That would probably be understood as a commencement of withdrawal.

His Excellency appeared to approve of this idea, but added that, as he had said on a previous occasion, troops were still necessary to guard the telegraphic communication with the Liao-tung Peninsula. I suggested, with reference to the latter point, that as soon as the negotiations with China for the evacuation of the peninsula were concluded, which I hoped would be soon, the Japanese Government might inform the Powers that the remaining troops were provisionally kept in Corea for that specific purpose. In this way it might be possible to avoid a summons from Russia.

The point about which his Excellency seemed to be most anxious was the possible recurrence of disturbances after the final retirement of the garrisons. Russia, he said, had brought forty sailors up to Seoul and had offered to protect the King, who had, however, declined. But if he were left without the support of any Japanese troops at all, he might later on be disposed to accept the Russian offer. There was another matter, he said, of even more pressing importance. The foreign Representatives, at least some of them, he believed the Russian and United States' Chargés d'Affaires, had asked their Governments for instructions as to whether they should recognize the present Cabinet. Some of the latter, especially the Minister of War, Cho Wi-yon, and the Prime Minister, Kim Hoing-chun, and O Yun-jung, the Minister of Finance, were partizans of the Tai-Wön-Kun [father and regent of the King], and more or less mixed up in the late affair. It was doubtful whether they could be maintained in power, and he was uncertain whether the whole Cabinet might not have to resign. He had, however, instructed Mr. Komura, the Minister Resident appointed to supersede Viscount Miura, to consult with his colleagues as to the possibility of a compromise by which the Tai-Wön-Kun should return to his retirement, leaving the present Cabinet in power. The King being more or less a nonentity, they were the only men who could possibly carry on the Government with any hope of success.

I responded that, if feasible, this seemed a good way out of the difficulty, and I expressed the hope that Mr. Komura would receive instructions to communicate freely with his colleagues, and especially with Mr. [Walter C.] Hillier [the British Consul General at Seoul] and the German Consul, Herr Krien. I also counselled his Excellency to acquaint all the foreign Representatives in Tokio with any steps the Japanese Government might decide upon in connection with their policy in Corea.[11,e]

On October 26, Goto Shojiro came to Satow.

Said Inouye must be very stupid if he did not foresee what was about to happen when he left Corea, for the murder of the Queen occurred only a week after his return here. He was responsible for presenting to the Corean Government as Military adviser Okamoto Riunoske, the man accused of taking the Queen's life. . . . I told him I feared the Queen's murder would cause much trouble to the Japanese Government and give the Russians a handle for demanding withdrawal of the Japanese garrisons. That my advice was to inform the Powers that they would withdraw (in fact what I said to Ito on the 23rd), and invite them to settle Corean affairs by a general agreement. He said that was his view also, but Ito was not the proper person to do it; there must be a new government. I replied that as a foreigner I of course could not offer an opinion on such a topic as a change of Cabinet. He assented, and proceeded to say that Ito was too undecided, always changing his mind. Thus he had promised Matsugata to insist on a large indemnity and no territory on the mainland, but the war-party afterwards induced him to break his word.

On October 28, Satow handed Ito a note in brief headings of his advice about Korea.

He read it attentively, ejaculated 'Not quite,' then produced from a large bundle of telegrams the draft of one that he despatched on the 25 to all the Powers except Holland, and embodying my suggestions [Satow recorded in his diary.][12] Then he talked about the demand [of the foreign Representatives in Korea, influenced, he believed, by the Russian Chargé d'Af-

e The policy of Count Inouye and the overbearing conduct of Japanese subjects in Korea toward the natives are described in a Japanese newspaper article, enclosed in No. 292, Oct. 25, 1895, F.O. 405-65, pp. 69-70.

faires,] that the *Kunrentai* [Korean Court guards trained by Japanese] should be dismissed, and I told him I would telegraph home.[d] He had telegraphed to Nissi about it. Also telegrams from Awoki [Aoki Shuzo, the Japanese Minister to Germany] and the Minister in Paris [Sone Arasuke], which he said I must keep entirely to myself, about friendly attitude of France and Germany. Told him Komura ought to try and win the confidence of Krien and Hillier, so that we might balance Russian intrigues.

On October 30, Satow noted in his diary that the instructions received by the German Minister were not the same as his. "Has had the telegram about Corea communicated to him, and so has Hitrovo, who expressed to the Japanese a slightly more definite fixing of the date of evacuation."

On November 7, Satow learned from Vice Minister of Foreign Affairs Hara Takashi that Japanese withdrawal of troops from Korea would not be immediate. The following day he reported home that the Japanese Government had initiated criminal proceedings against the civil and military officials recalled from Korea.[14]

On November 12 Satow had a discussion with Saionji concerning the state of affairs in Korea and the desires of the foreign powers there. Reporting the conversation to Lord Salisbury, Satow expressed the view that the best hope for reform and stability lay in the "complete retirement" of the Tai-wŏn-kun, the late Queen's rival, and in "leaving the present Cabinet to carry on the Government independently of direct foreign control.[15]

On November 13 Satow lunched with the Thomas's. "[Freiherr von] Gutschmid [the German Minister to Japan] says that according to Hitrovo the proposal to substitute Japanese guard for the Corean guard came from Inouye! That

---

[d] In the telegram Satow reported the demand of the foreign Representatives for the disbandment of the Korean drilled troops and their refusal to recognize the current Korean Cabinet. "Personally," he wired, "I consider the proposal unsafe, and I think it unwise to deny recognition to the Corean Government.[13]

Waeber [the Russian Consul at Soeul] telegraphed to Lobanof, and was told he could consent!" The following day Satow called on Saionji and asked whether it was true that Inouye had proposed the substitution.

He said he did not yet know but had telegraphed. Hitrovo's
telegram was to the effect that the Russian Government had no
objection to the temporary (*pour le temps*) occupation of Palace
by Japanese guard, but left it to Waeber to consent or not as he
thought opportune. I said that at the time Inouye went I thought
his selection was a mistake, being a person of political importance, who was likely to intervene if he was inclined: that for
the diplomatic business Komura was quite enough, and an officer of the Kunaisho [Department of the Imperial Household]
would do for the message of condolence. This I said was only
for his own ear. He agreed that it was a mistake. He had selected
Komura thinking him enough, but the Government had
thought otherwise. . . . I impressed on him the necessity of
continuing in the line they had announced to the Foreign Representatives. He said that the Japanese Government would not
agree to the proposal. If there were any bloodshed the blame
would be thrown on Inouye. Object evidently to get the Japanese Government to turn out the Cabinet, and restore the status
quo ante 8 November. . . . Despatches from Hillier of 5 November show that the proposal was discussed in a meeting of
Inouye and Komura with the Foreign Representatives, and
agreed to unanimously, and that for some time past the Foreign
Representatives have been demanding it. So Waeber's report to
St. Petersburg not quite frank.

On November 15 Saionji sent his private secretary, Nakada
Takanori, to inform Satow that he had received a reply from
Inouye, in which the latter telegraphed "that he has sent Komura and Inouye Katsunosuke [an official of the Foreign Of-
fice] to American and Russian Legations to ask whether it
was he who initiated the proposal to substitute Japanese troops
as the Palace Guard, and both had acknowledged that he did
not propose it."[16]
On November 19, Satow informed Saionji that "in the opinion of Her Majesty's Government, Japan, while in military oc-

cupation of Corea, was naturally responsible for the maintenance of order at the capital, and inclusively for the safety of
the King."[17]

On November 29, Aleksei Speyer [Shpeier], the new Russian Minister to Seoul, called on Satow.

Talked a little about Corea. I said that the Japanese seemed to
have recognized their error in going in for forcing reforms and
undertaking to establish a protectorate. Speyer said he trusted
that things would settle down. I rejoined that the Japanese having recently displayed moderation, their willingness to keep the
peace could be guaranteed. Speyer said (of course) that no disturbance would come from the side of Russia. I also observed
that since the intervention of the three Powers the Japanese had
seen the necessity of 'putting water in the wine.' Newspapers
and the ordinary man in the street out here who uttered rubbish
were ignorant of European politics through being all their life
in the East, and were not aware of the way in which the great
Powers pulled together at home and that the Extreme East hung
upon Europe.

On December 16, Satow talked with Saionji about the Russian and Japanese positions in Korea.

Says Speyer has not proposed anything. But had spoken about
Corean affairs in a moderate manner, and told Japanese Government that he had instructions to report on the dissensions in that
country between different parties, in order that Russian Government might have a full understanding of the situation.
I said that I had expressed to Speyer my conviction that Japan would act very moderately, at which Saionji thanked me for
the assurance I had given. I added that Speyer had replied that
Russia would not give cause for any disturbance of the peace
in regard to Corea.[18]

On December 20, Satow called on Ito by appointment.
"[As for] Corea, I said I thought Corean affairs should be
left to quiet down, they should be treated as ordinary diplomatic incidents, and no heroic remedies applied," he noted in
his diary.

The following day Satow called on Dun, the American Minister. "He says Inouye huffed at the nonadoption of his proposal to accept foreign Representatives' suggestion to replace palace-guard by Japanese soldiers: says 'do they think I am a child?' Has gone off therefore, and does not intend to come back for a month or so." But Ito and Saionji, Satow observed in a dispatch, were satisfied that the Japanese Government had acted rightly in refusing the proposal.[19]

On January 17, 1896 Satow discussed Korea with Kawasaki Saburo, Editor of the *Chuwo Shimbun*. "I said the position was like that of Morocco," Satow recorded. "Russia wanted to keep Japan out, and Japan wished to keep out Russia. Therefore I thought the rival interest, if prudence were observed, would insure its not being annexed. He said the Russians would intrigue: I laughed and said I was quite sure the Japanese could beat them at that, which tickled him immensely. Warned him not to quote anything I had said to him as coming from me."

On January 23, Satow conveyed Japanese fears of Russian scheming in Korea in a confidential dispatch to Lord Salisbury.[20] On the 28th he sent a lengthy report on the court-martial which had tried and acquitted the Japanese involved in the murder of the Korean Queen and entourage. He commented:

Much surprise has been produced by the apparent *non sequitur* involved in the dismissal of the charges against the defendants, who, as the Judgment plainly states, conspired to bring about a change of government and to compass the Queen's death. The Acting Foreign Minister admitted to me, on the 23rd instant, that the result had appeared strange to him; and added that it would give rise to much debate, even among the members of the Cabinet. He endeavoured, however, to explain that the Judgment amounted only to a verdict of "Not proven." It did not absolutely acquit the accused, but merely declared the evidence insufficient to convict them of a punishable offence.

I observed to his Excellency that the Judgment admitted the fact of a conspiracy against the Queen's life, narrated the preparations made by providing weapons, the issue of orders to various persons calculated to insure the end contemplated, and brought them as far as the entrance to her apartments. The next fact, which was patent to everybody, was the murder of the Queen. Putting two and two together, the Court could hardly have any doubt as to the identity of the murderers. In fact, I heard that the best possible evidence was in existence—that of a person who saw the attack on the Queen, and recognized her assailants. I felt convinced that the world in general, which is not familiar with the precise meaning of the Japanese Code of Criminal Procedure, could not but take an unfavourable view of a Judgment that practically acquitted the criminals.[21]

On February 12 Gutschmid came to Satow. "Says that Speyer received a snub from Lobanof for sending home sensational telegrams about Corean affairs. Thinks Ito certainly wishes to go to Russia." Gutschmid was followed by Kawasaki, the editor of *Chuwo*. "He says most of the Cabinet ministers object to Ito's going and Mutsu especially. That there is no doubt a Japanese killed the Queen of Corea, and the sentences published at Soul on Coreans are not genuine. The whole has come out. But he says that the statements of Miura and the others are not in accordance with the preliminary judgment delivered."

On February 13, a Korean by the name of Kwön Yong-chin called on Satow, accompanied by a Japanese-speaking Korean youth. Both wore European clothes and had their hair cut short.

Hardly had they sat down when Gubbins came in with an extra published by the *Asahi* reporting a revolution at Söul and that the King had taken refuge at the Russian Legation. I showed it to him and he pointed out his own name among those for whose decapitation and pillorying orders are said to have been issued. He has been here a week. In reply to my suggestion that the news might not be quite so bad in reality he said he knew this was coming: preparations had been made some time back, and clothes for the King and his son to escape in from the Palace had been supplied by the Russians and Americans who were acting together. He said Corea was a small and weak country, and the inhabitants had no desire to be protected by Russia. Would not England the greatest Power in the world come to their rescue.

I said that for a couple of years past the Coreans had looked to Japan as their chief protectors. That England sympathized with the Corean nation and was anxious to see progress in that country, but her political and other interests were less than those of Japan and Russia, which were her immediate neighbors.

He replied that Japan was of no help to them, and had been falling back for some time past. So he came to ask me for the help of England.

I said the distance from England was very great 10,000 or 12,000 and it was difficult to help from so great a distance.

He retorted that India at any rate was half away. England's interests made it a matter of importance that Russia should not get possession of Port Lazaref. He knew there was already drafted an agreement between Russia and the King giving the latter authority to bring the railway from Vladivostok to Port Lazaref, and only needed his seal to be affixed. If they established themselves there Great Britain's commerce would be at their mercy. Would we not help to prevent such a consummation as that.

I replied that to bring a railway from Vladivostok to Port Lazaref was no easy matter. There were high mountains to cross.

He said that is true, but it can come along the shore the whole way.

I said that Her Majesty's Government had given me no instructions about Corea, as there was a Consul-general at Soul, to whom they would send instructions direct.

He said that being the case it was no good his seeking an interview, and took his leave.

During the conversation I asked who had killed the Queen, Coreans or anyone else. To this he returned an evasive answer. When the Kunrentai entered the Palace, a few Japanese troops entered with them, and shots were fired. So she lost her life, but no one knew how.

I recommended him, as his name was on the list of the proscribed, to stay here and see how things turned out before returning back, but he said that if the independence of his country were to be destroyed, he would return and die in her defence.

I made an observation about the division of Corea into factions which he did not seem to like very much.

On February 14 Satow noted in his diary: "From all the indications it would seem that the Russians had lulled the Japanese into a false security about Corea, and that it [the flight of the Korean King to the Russian Legation] came on them as a surprise."

The following day Satow saw Ito.

Read me telegram from Komura transmitting the King's proclamation dated from Russian Legation. Nothing newer. Gutschmid who lunched with Hitrovo told him this afternoon that the latter said he had no news, but Ito doubts this. I said [Zinovii] Polianovsky [a Russian language student] had said last night that Hitrovo was delaying his departure on account of the troubles. I added that our experience in Central Asian affairs had been that Russian Government constantly assured us that nothing would be done, then some zealous officer on the spot did that very thing, and the Government then said they could not avoid a 'fait accompli.'

Ito said that his only fear was that *Soshi* [political bullies] might resent what had happened, and make a row.

From this I gather that Japanese Government accept the inevitable, and will not resist what has been done. The line to Wiju is no longer of any use since Japanese troops withdrawn. That to Fusan is interrupted, some Japanese telegraph people have been killed.

Komura, he says, had no suspicion of what was coming. He telegraphed the landing of Russian sailors, as he fancied intended to prevent Japanese troops going to aid in putting down the rebels; though Japanese Government has refused aid of that kind, and has done nothing except when their own people were attacked. . . .

I told him, though without mentioning the man's name or personality, what Kwön told me the day before yesterday in order to alarm me into promising British aid. Did not mention his disparaging remarks about Japan.

On February 16, Baron Albert d'Anethan, the Belgian Minister to Japan, visited Satow, "Says the Japanese and Russians had an arrangement to communicate to each other everything the King [of Korea] said to them! [Captain Frank] Brinkley reported to have said that the Japanese would rather fight than give way, even with the insufficient means at their disposal."

On February 17, Satow called on Saionji and thanked him for the copy of the telegram from Komura.

He said they had received another, which was in process of being decyphered, and would let me have it. He was anxious to know whether I thought the Russian Government knew beforehand what was going to be done. I said the same thing as to Ito, that they always declared in such cases that a 'fait accompli' could not be undone, so it came to the same thing. He re-echoed my words. Many of the Japanese about Chhun-chhön had been killed, also one in the streets of Sŏul, but the murderer had not been captured. Asked him whether he had noticed that the King's proclamation said he had put himself under the protection of the Powers.[e] He said that would be just what Japan would desire. But it was not clear whether he meant his personal safety under protection of the Representatives or of his Kingdom under that of their Governments.

On February 19, Asaina Kansui (Asahina Masahiro), formerly Lord of Kai, who became a "confidential source" of information for Satow, related that 400 Japanese troops had been secretly sent to Korea.

Fears there will be a collision. Some people seeing that England stands aloof think it would be better to join hands with the three Powers [Russia, Germany, and France]. I told him that Japan had disregarded the advice given at the outbreak of the [Sino-Japanese] war, and that she could not expect England now to help her against Russia. But if any attack were made upon the independence of Japan we would come to her

[e] The King's declaration read as follows: "Disorder still reigns in our country, and it is due to the increasing number of turbulent Ministers and rebellious subjects. We have, therefore, proceeded to the Russian Legation and placed ourselves under the protection of the foreign Representatives. Do you people, nevertheless, refrain from creating disturbance, and pursue your several occupations quietly. Cut off and bring for my inspection the heads of the ring leaders responsible for the present disorders, namely U-pöm-sön, Ri-tu-hwang, Ri-pom-rai, Ri-chin-no, Cho-wi-yön, and Kwön-hyöng-chin."[22]

61

rescue. I reviewed the whole from the beginning, including Miura, and said that what had now happened had been foreseen by people in Europe before I left. He agreed with my view, but said that if the Japanese people were polled, their voice would be for war unprepared as they were. They did not think much of either Russian or French navy. I said it would be disastrous for Japan to go to war. I knew the courage of the people and that the 40,000,000 of them would fight to the last breath rather than give in, but their navy was not strong enough.

Asaina told Satow that Fukuchi Genichiro [a journalist] had had a talk with Hitrovo at the beginning of the Sino-Japanese War and offered Russia Hangyöngdo, if Russia would let Japan have the rest. Hitrovo clapped his hands and said that it was a capital idea. Then Fukuchi proceeded to say that Japan would conquer China, but being too big a morsel to swallow, would divide with others. Suppose each power were to say what she would take. Nothing came of it however!

That day three Koreans called on Satow: I Sun-yong, Pak Yong-hoa [Yong-hyo] and O Yun-yök, the latter of whom also spoke Japanese.

I is a nephew of the King and grandson of the Tai-wön-kun. They were all dressed in European clothes and had their hair cut short, quiet, intellectual-looking men the two first. He said they were much perturbed at recent events, feared Russian annexation, would not England do something to help them. I said it might reassure them if they knew that we had sent some more marines to Söul. Of course there could be no question of our interfering to turn out the Russians, especially as the King had put himself in their hands voluntarily, and had right on their side. What I feared was lest the Japanese might think it necessary to do so, and then Corea would again become the battleground of other nations. But I did not think Russia wished to destroy the independence of Corea, only to prevent the Japanese taking possession. We had an agreement about Port Hamilton, Komundo, from which we retired on condition that Russia should not annex any portion of Korean territory.

In reply to a question about the new Cabinet, he said they were impartial on the whole, not exclusively Min Party, though the present Minister President Kun Phong-si might be regarded as such.[23]

Japanese-Russian Rivalry in Korea

The coup d'état and unrest in Korea remained a topic of public debate in Japan. Satow reported home:

The semi-official press is extremely guarded in its comments upon the *coup d'État* of the 11th instant. It affects to place confidence in the assurances said to have been received from the Russian Government that it had no knowledge beforehand of the step the King was about to take, and the general tone is one of enforced resignation to the turn affairs have taken. There is an evident desire to avoid giving any umbrage to the Russian Government, or to afford any pretext for troops being landed in addition to the sailors that have been dispatched to Seoul from the men-of-war at Chemulpo. Under all this, however, there is a feeling that Japanese diplomacy has been skilfully outwitted, combined with an earnest desire to arrive at an understanding with Russia as regards the future of Corea. It is difficult, how-ever, to see what form of compromise is feasible which would insure to Japan a joint influence in the affairs of the Peninsula.

It had undoubtedly been the wish of the Minister President to proceed to Moscow in the capacity of Ambassador Extraordi-nary on the occasion of the Emperor's Coronation, and to take advantage of the opportunity to discuss the Corean question much on the lines pursued in 1884, when he negotiated with the Viceroy of Chihli the Convention which regulated the policy of China and Japan in Corea for the ten years previous to the war. This project, however, has been laid aside in consequence of re-cent events and the opposition of some of his colleagues in the Cabinet, and Marshal Yamagata [Aritomo], distinguished more as a soldier than as a diplomatist, has received the appointment instead of Marquis Ito.[24]

In the House of Representatives the National Unionist party brought forth a resolution censoring the Government:

This House considers that the present Cabinet have committed many mistakes in the administration of both home and foreign affairs, and is of opinion that, more especially as regards the recent *coup d'État* in Corea, their action has been wrong, and not in keeping with the illustrious Imperial Proclamation of War. Therefore this House calls upon the Cabinet to bear in mind their high duty of assisting the Throne as Ministers of State, and arrive at an immediate decision, and hereby manifests its opinion.

The Government responded by obtaining an Imperial Rescript, suspending the session for ten days. Satow commented in a dispatch:

The Government, having thus triumphed even more conclusively than had been anticipated by their friends, have been greatly strengthened, and will be able to pursue the moderate policy they have adopted, unless their hand should be forced by some fresh development in the way of attacks upon Japanese subjects or the proscription of the Corean partisans of Japan.[25]

On February 27, Satow called on Hara. "He says Russians have landed some sailors at Fusan to go overland to Sŏul, about thirty, perhaps only to take the place of others who are to rejoin their ship. About two hundred at Sŏul. Thinks Japanese troops will remain to protect Japanese settlers. Only about twelve hundred at Sŏul."

On March 2, Satow met with Ito. All that Ito knew about Russian intentions regarding Korea was "that she had declared her intention of not occupying, but would maintain her right to assist in protecting Corean independence." Ito told Satow that Tani [Tateki, the general?] had asked him against what enemy all the armaments were directed. "He had replied against no one, but as Japanese possessions extended over 1800 miles, necessary to increase defensive preparations. All the Powers were constantly adding to their armaments, yet no one thought it was directed against any power in particular."

Later Satow spoke to Asaina who said that Japan would remain quiet. "Does not want to move again for another eight or nine years, till she is ready" [i.e. until 1904!].

On March 4, Satow dined at the home of Gerard Lowther, First Secretary of the British Legation. Among the guests there was Sannomiya, with whom Satow had a long talk about Korea afterwards.

He expressed his anxiety about presence of Japanese and Russian troops together in Corea, almost sure to lead to a row. What did

England mean? Did she not mind Russia becoming predominant there?

Replied that Japan could not withdraw troops because that would be a signal for massacre of Japanese population. . . . Lord Kimberley had cherished the idea of a joint guarantee by Russia, Japan and England, but he had since gone out of office, and Ito I heard was busily engaged in negotiating with Russia; as far as I knew he had said nothing to Great Britain. At this he expressed his disapproval.

On March 12, Satow went to Saionji. "He told me confidentially that Yamagata would be empowered to discuss Corean question if the Russian Government showed any desire: embodied all this in a despatch," Satow jotted down in his diary. The dispatch read:

The Acting Minister for Foreign Affairs informed me to-day, in confidence, that there is an understanding between his Government and that of Russia that instructions should be given to their respective Representatives at Seoul to avoid by all means in their power anything that might lead to a collision between the Russian sailors and Japanese troops quartered there.

He added that they had stated to Mr. Hitrovo, just before his departure on leave, and had also instructed their Minister at St. Petersburgh, that, if the Russian Government desired to discuss the Corean question, Marshal Yamagata, who, it is hoped, will be able to leave by way of America next week, will be instructed to state the views of the Japanese Government and to endeavour to arrive at a solution.

What the intentions and wishes of Russia were the Japanese Government had no means of conjecturing. All they knew at present was that, though the flight of the Corean King was contrived without the previous knowledge of the Russian Government, it seemed clear that the latter were disposed to approve of what had been done.

I have been told by one of my colleagues that the instructions given to Mr. Waeber and Mr. Komura are that they should act, as far as possible, in harmony, and communicate freely to each other everything that comes to their knowledge; but whether such a bond of mutual confidence is practicable, seems more than doubtful.

Marquis Saionji painted the situation as almost hopelessly complicated, owing to the existence of various hostile factions, pro-Japanese, pro-Russian, and pro-American. To this list, I imagine, may probably be added a pro-Chinese party.[26]

Suspended for ten days in March for attacking the Government's Korea policy, the Diet resumed its opposition upon reconvening. Satow reported to the Marquess of Salisbury:

On the 11th instant another interpellation was addressed to the Government demanding an explanation of the reasons why no answer had as yet been given to that of the 15th February. M. Kudo made a long speech explanatory of his question, in the course of which he again reminded the House of the declaration contained in the proclamation of war issued in 1894 that Japan's intention was to assist in maintaining the independence of Corea. In the furtherance of that policy a great war had been carried on against China at an expense of 400,000,000 yen, and at the sacrifice of several thousand lives of Japanese. But the result had been that Japanese influence in Corea was now much less than before the war, when they had only China as a rival. He therefore called upon the Government to declare what measures they intended to take in order to give effect to the intention expressed in the declaration of war. Since the flight of the King to the Russian Legation on the 11th ultimo, the nation had been anxiously looking for a statement of policy by the Government reassuring them that there was no danger of the peninsula being seized by Russia or falling back under the domination of China. If newspaper reports were to be relied upon, the feeling of the Japanese residents in Corea was one of insecurity, while the Japanese garrison had been exposed to the insult of seeing the corpse of the pro-Japanese Prime Minister treated with the grossest indignity before their very eyes. How different from the situation after the declaration of war against China. Then all the Coreans vied with each other in showing marks of respect to Japanese. But since the 11th February it was the Russian sailors who had become the popular favourites. Japanese residents in the interior had been compelled to retire under military escort to the open ports, in many cases having to abandon their property. What steps did the Government propose to take to protect their interests? They dispatched no men-of-war, apparently for fear of a collision with Russia. What was the use of a fleet but to defend Japanese subjects abroad. Already some twenty or more were stated to have been murdered. Where was the utility of an army? The Japanese garrison at Seoul had been removed from its quarters in front of the King's Palace to a distance of more than a mile in order to be out of the way. Clearly all this was the result of the want of a policy on the part of the Government. After the war they had asked from the nation authority to greatly augment the number of war-vessels and to increase the army. They had demanded taxes on alcoholic liquor, tobacco, and trade to a huge amount, all of which had been accorded to them. And what was the object of these enormous efforts, if Japanese subjects were to be murdered with impunity, and the national dignity to be insulted as it had never been before the war.[27]

On March 18, and again on March 26, Satow conferred with Saionji. "He says cannot get much out of Speyer who talks as if the Russian Government wished King to leave Legation, 'but of course cannot force him to go as long as he wishes to remain,' " Satow recorded in his diary.

On April 16, Satow conferred about Korea with Mutsu Munemitsu who had succeeded to the position of Foreign Minister. He recorded the substance of their conversation in a private letter to Lord Salisbury and in a dispatch. He wrote:

The opinion has been gaining ground here that whatever may be the intentions of the Russian Government with regard to Corea, no forward step is likely to be taken until after the coronation festivities are over. Meanwhile transports carrying troops to Vladivostock call from time to time at Nagasaki, and the *Rurik* and *Dimitri Donskoi* are on their way out to join the Russian squadron in Eastern Asia. The *Vladimir Monomakh* is on her way home.

The Russian Chargé d'Affaires told one of my colleagues recently that though he had taken a house at Chusenzi for the summer for his family, he did not expect to be much away from Tokio, as important negotiations regarding Corea would probably be going on then between the Russian and Japanese Governments.

Prince Lobanoff, it appears, recently observed to Prince Radolin, the German Ambassador at St. Petersburgh, that the Japa-

nese were unaccountably dilatory in withdrawing their forces
from Corea, and he contrasted their proceedings, I am told, with
the expeditious retirement of the Chinese. I confess that I do
not understand this allusion, unless it was meant as a hint that
as the Chinese were driven out by Japan, the Japanese would in
their turn be expelled by Russia.

In my No. 48, Very Confidential, of the 12th March, I reported that the Japanese Special Ambassador to the coronation
festivities was empowered to discuss the Corean question if the
Russian Government should desire to take advantage of his
presence at Moscow to enter upon an exchange of views.

On the 16th instant Count Mutsu, in answer to a question
which I put to him as to the general state of things in the peninsula, stated that he had told the Russian Chargé d'Affaires that
if Coreans went on murdering Japanese as they have been doing
lately, the opposition press would attack the Japanese Government, implying by this hint that the latter would be forced to
take some more active measures for the protection of their own
people. He had also told M. de Speyer not to attach too much
importance to the language of journalists, who, ignorant of European world-politics, busied themselves almost exclusively with
the affairs of Corea, a country close at hand, whither correspondents could be sent at a trifling expense. To keep a competent
staff of correspondents in Europe and America was beyond their
resources. Hence the exaggerated importance given by the press
to Eastern Asiatic questions.

His own earnest wish, he said, was to keep things quiet in
Corea. Of course, perpetual peace was more than could be hoped
for, but it was absolutely necessary for Japan to have peace for
the next five years and trust to the possibility of something turning up during that time in her favour.

His Excellency appeared to be somewhat disappointed at your
Lordship's language to Mr. Kato on the 17th February. Russia
would have no need to use violence, he observed, to obtain anything she wanted either in Corea or China, as witness her present
commanding position in Seoul and Kiaochau Bay.

I observed to Count Mutsu that people had talked of the possibility of a partition of Corea between Russia and Japan. That, I
thought, was quite impracticable. That a suggestion of this kind
was made to M. Hitrovo at the outbreak of the war by certain
unofficial Japanese speaking on their own account is, I have been
informed, a fact, and I thought it might be worth while to

obtain an expression of opinion as to the likelihood of such a scheme being entertained by the Japanese Government.

His Excellency answered that in any such arrangement Japan would, of course, require to hold at least the port of Fusan at the south-east corner of the peninsula. For that reason he did not think a partition satisfactory to both Powers was feasible. What he earnestly desired was to maintain the independence of Corea. Russia had made a similar declaration of policy, while Great Britain and other Powers also supported that view. He repeated his language about the necessity of peace for the next five years at least. However much clamour might be raised by the opposition papers, the men at the head of affairs were quite sensible of this, and there was no fear that they would allow their hand to be forced.

I said I entirely agreed with him that peace was necessary to enable Japan to develop her resources.[28]

Japan was building up her military might, however. As Satow recorded after seeing Asaina on April 21: "He . . . says that Japan is arming with greater rapidity and secrecy than she did for her war with China. (These are almost his *ipsissima verba*.)"

On May 4 Satow saw Mutsu to ask whether Japan would agree to a declaration of neutrality if such a proposal were made.

I told him Belgium was the model, to which he replied that there was this difference that Belgium could keep order, while Corea could not. However, if the neutralization were arranged, that could be discussed afterwards.

Evidently the Japanese Government have concluded from Balfour's Bristol speech and Lord Salisbury's reply to Kato on the 17th February that Great Britain meant to have nothing to do with the Corean affair, and that they must arrange direct with Russia, and it seems to me that they were justified in drawing this inference. Hence they do not quite know what to make of the present proposal, and wish to learn what grounds Her Majesty's Government have for expecting that such a proposal would be accepted by other Powers especially Russia. To me it seems that we are too late with our idea of obtaining a joint guarantee.[29]

On May 5, d'Anethan visited Satow. "Told d'Anethan that I had no knowledge of what the Japanese were arranging with Russians about Corea. He said that it was the same while Lowther was in charge. The Japanese would never tell him anything."

On May 7, Satow received Gutschmid, who told him as far as he knew what de Speyer was negotiating with the Japanese. In a dispatch Satow conveyed the points which de Speyer was believed to be discussing with the Japanese Foreign Minister and added his own appraisal of the negotations:

I understand it is to be stipulated that Japan may maintain two companies of 200 men each at Seoul and a company at each of the three ports of Chemulpo, Fusan, and Wonsan, besides a company for the protection of the telegraph line from Seoul to Fusan. There appears also to be a question of the purchase of this line by Corea from the Japanese Government, at whose expense it was constructed.

Russia, on her part, would agree to limit the number of her troops in Corea to 200 men.

It seems that the anxiety for this provisional agreement for a *modus vivendi* is all on the Japanese side, the Foreign Minister having urged its conclusion of M. de Speyer as being necessary in order that the Government should be able to show something accomplished in accord with Russia, and so satisfy Japanese public feeling. M. de Speyer is all amiability, and the only opposition to the scheme is supposed to come from M. Waeber. In any case, it is only a *modus vivendi* that is contemplated, to last until the result of Marshal Yamagata's negotiations takes a concrete shape, but it can well be imagined that M. Waeber is in no hurry to surrender the commanding position he has occupied since the skilful maneuvre by which the King fell under his exclusive influence.[30]

Later in the day the Korean Minister called on Satow. "Speaks English with American accent. Told him England earnestly desires the independence of Corea."

On May 7, Satow had a "friendly general conversation" with de Speyer. Later Mutsu told him all that Speyer and Harmand, the French Minister to Japan, had said to him about Satow's return and about newspaper reports of England being asked to help Japan in the *modus vivendi* negotiations. Denison, with whom Satow talked the next day, was glad to think the Japanese might get some help. "Does not believe the Russians would fight well at sea; there is too much corruption, the sums divided among officers being enormous."

On May 12 Gutschmid told Satow that "Speyer is nervous about a possible alliance between England and Japan and had a two hours' talk with Ito recently on the subject of Corea." Satow, meanwhile, informed the Japanese that England's interest in Korea was secondary to that of China, Japan or Russia, and that one of the latter should take the initiative in concerting with the other interested Powers to find a remedy for Korea's anarchy.[31] In a dispatch to the Foreign Secretary, Satow reported that in view of its negotiations with Russia, the Japanese Cabinet had promulgated an Ordinance restricting Japanese travel to Korea, lest its hand be forced by the "irresponsible and hot-headed patriotism of a small minority."[32]

On May 16 Satow called on Ito, Mutsu being ill.

Asked reason of proclamation forbidding Japanese subjects going to Corea. He said that there was some reason to think that the turbulents wanted to go back there, to look after investments, money lent to Coreans, etc. Did not want a row. This was third time it had been enacted, within powers of Government.

I observed that the practical result was that during the session of the Diet they could go, during its recess they were prevented. Perhaps in the end the Diet might get tired, and sanction the Government proposal.

He replied that in the last diet Upper House had sanctioned, Lower House thrown out the bill. The Jiyuto [Party] were willing, but Kokumin Kiokwai [Party] refused, because many of them connected with Corea. Therefore Jiyuto, not willing to risk being put in a minority had joined in refusing. These were the sort of difficulties one met with at the beginning of Parliamentary institutions.

I asked him what prospect there was of the *modus vivendi* with Russia being agreed to. He answered only in general terms

71

that before Hitrovo went off, he came and said Russia had no desire to appropriate Corea. Ito had replied that neither did Japan, nor did she wish to exercise more than her fair share of influence. Why then could they not get on together. He hoped they might. He made no allusion to the communications that had recently passed between Mutsu and myself.

In the afternoon Vice Admiral Sir A. Buller came to Satow.

Thinks that after the coronation the King of Corea will go back to his Palace with a guard of Russian sailors. The Russian officers made no secret that this was their idea. This seemed to him much more likely than that the King should be protected by a guard of Coreans under the command of Russian officers, which I had thought probable. Showed him the recent telegrams exchanged about proposal to guarantee Corean neutrality, and my despatch. He could not make out (any more than I) why Lord S[alisbury] should have said anything about it, if he had no intention of doing it, and his language to Kato was in contradiction of the suggestion. I told him my impression at first had been that Lord S[alisbury] was about to put his foot down here and take a strong line. That if we undertook to keep the Straits of Tsushima for the Japanese, they could pour soldiers into Corea at any rate they liked, quite enough to prevent the Russians coming in. We could account for the Russian fleet, and the Japanese would undertake the French. This estimate he agreed with, but he thinks the railway will be ready in three years, and that each train could bring a regiment. The Russians he says are constantly accumulating stores at Vladivostock.

On May 21, Satow discussed Korea with Mutsu.

Thanked me for note telling him Lord Salisbury's answer. When I was away at Kobe, thinking I might perhaps not come back at once, he had telegraphed to Kato in the sense of the communication he made to me after I returned, to take opportunity of seeing Lord Salisbury and speaking to him unofficially. He repeated what he had said before about Speyer and Gutschmid's curiosity and added that Speyer had also been to question Ito, who of course used the same language as himself. I replied that to the fishing inquiries of my colleagues I had given no answer. He told me that an understanding had been arranged at with Russia, and gave me the heads (put into a despatch). Evidently distrust of Russia is great.

Japanese-Russian Rivalry in Korea

In the above-mentioned dispatch Satow wrote:

Count Mutsu informed me to-day, confidentially, that an arrangement with regard to Corea has been arrived at between the Japanese and Russian Governments. The first point is the return of the King to his Palace. It has been agreed that the Russian Chargé d'Affaires and Mr. Komura should both urge on His Majesty the necessity of taking this step. Secondly, as long as the present disturbed condition lasts, Japan may keep 400 troops at Seoul, 200 at Wonsan, and an equal number at Fusan. Thirdly, they may have 200 gendarmes to guard the telegraph line from Seoul to Fusan, which is recognized as an international interest. The gendarmes may, under circumstances of necessity, be reinforced by troops of the occupying force. Fourthly, Russia may land, for the protection of her Legation, a number of armed men, not exceeding what Japan maintains in the country. At present, his Excellency said, there are only 150 bluejackets on shore, who are stationed at Seoul. Fifthly, the Russian Chargé d'Affaires and Japanese Minister are to give their advice to the King to prevent sanguinary proceedings against political offenders, and to insure the accused being fairly tried before a properly constituted Court. Sixthly, whatever changes are made in the Cabinet, the two Agents shall use their influence to procure the appointment of suitable persons. This last class of recommendations, his Excellency added, was likely to prove of a platonic character.

Count Mutsu also remarked upon the constant increase of the Russian naval forces in this part of the world. Now that the Liao-tung question was disposed of, for which this large squadron had ostensibly been assembled, there could be but one object for its remaining. It was unfortunate, he thought, that one result of the war with China had been to demonstrate to Europe the utter weakness of that Empire, and he concluded that the assemblage of the Russian ships was intended to support a policy of aggression on the Chinese mainland.

As he appeared to wish for an expression of opinion, I ventured to say that the establishment of Russian influence in Corea, to the exclusion of Japanese, was rather what was aimed at. One of the papers had recently published a conversation with a Russian official, who, I had good reason to believe, was a member of the Russian Legation, in which the latter had expressed the opinion that Wönsan or Sestakof Bay would be a more useful acquisition than either Kiao-chou or Talienwan Bays, because there would then be no danger of communications with Vladivostock being cut by an enemy cruising near Tsushima.

Count Mutsu admitted the intention with regard to Corea, which he said Japan would not attempt to oppose by force. He thought, however, that Russia had no idea of annexing Corea. With this view I expressed my concurrence, as her objects could be attained without attempting to govern such an unruly race as the Coreans have proved themselves to be.

On my inquiring his views as to the way in which the King's guard would be formed after His Majesty's return to the Palace, I found that he expects it will consist of Corean troops, drilled and commanded by the Russian military instructors who have recently arrived at Seoul, and that they will be armed with the rifles that have been sent from Vladivostock, apparently as a present from the Russian Government to the King of Corea. His Excellency thought this more likely than an alternative plan that is, I hear, spoken of freely by Russian naval officers, namely, that His Majesty should be protected by the blue-jackets from the Russian squadron.[33]

On May 27 "Tommy" (Nagano Keijiro), a Japanese businessman, called on Satow. "The day I met him he was going to Suyematsu to urge that Japan should insist with King of Corea and the Russians upon the King's immediately returning to the Palace. Told him that was impracticable."

At the end of the month ill health forced Mutsu to step down from his post. Saionji became Foreign Minister again, and Komura Vice Minister of Foreign Affairs.

On June 4, Viscount Fukuha had a lengthy conversation with Satow.

He observed that Inouye's work in Corea was an attempt to substitute the new civilisation that Japan had adopted from Europe for the Chinese form, but it would seem that Corea was not able to receive it. I said that the Coreans were intelligent enough but Inouye had been in too great a hurry. It must be recollected, that the first nine or ten years of Japanese intercourse with Europe had passed without any change. But perhaps one judged the Corean mind too favourably, from the superior specimens of that nation which visited this country. It was impossible I thought to predict the turn affairs are likely to take in Corea, with Japan and Russia contending for the mastery.

On June 16, Komura visited Satow. "Says he signed a memorandum with Waeber before leaving," On June 18, Satow asked Nakada about the memorandum signed between Waeber and Komura."

He . . . said parties had agreed to keep the memorandum secret. But Saionzi had charged him to say that it was a mere provisional arrangement of a very simple character, not in any way affecting British interests. The parties agreed to urge on King his return to the Palace, to recommend the selection of suitable functionaries as ministers; Japanese to be allowed to guard telegraph line by gendarmes, in interest of general communication, and they would not go outside zone of 2 *ri* [Japanese miles].

On June 19, Gutschmid told Satow "that de Speyer told him Aoki had some time back asked [Sir Frank Cavendish] Lascelles [the British Ambassador to Berlin] whether England would back up Japan about Corea, to which he had given a most decided negative. . . . Also de Staal [the Russian Minister in London] had put the same question to Lord Salisbury, who had given the same answer."

On June 25, Satow asked Saionji about Korea. "Said he could not tell me anything about Yamagata's negotiations, which did not appear to be of a definite and final character until his return. Said he would certainly tell me all he could at any time. Expressed my satisfaction."

On July 11, Watanabe Hiromoto of Takebu in Echizen called on Satow, and they had a general talk.

Says that he was against the [Sino-Japanese] war, which has had for its principal result the substitution of Russia for China in Corea. Tried to find out why Miura was sent. He says the idea was to send a soldier. Then he was a 'discontented general' like Tani and Soga, and he was a protegé of political personages. Great mistake however to appoint discontented people. Okamoto

75

and other people (*sōshi* [political bullies]) had previously maintained the necessity of getting rid of the Queen, but Inouye had prevented their action. His influence was not so great with the Corean Government as people had thought, and he was not able to hold in men like Pak. He went there with carte-blanche as he thought, and then the Cabinet did not adopt his ideas or approve his action. He is rather a man of impulse, but most 'serviable' to his friends; will do anything for them, even to procuring a *mekake* [mistress]. Miura was supposed to be a simple soldier, who would merely carry on Inouye's policy, a quiet sort of person. So he went there with no special instructions. Then he was got hold of by the opponents of the Queen, and at least countenanced (*dōi*) her murder.

On July 13, Satow went to see Ito.

Asked if Yamagata's visit to Moscow had been satisfactory. He made a grimace and said he supposed it must be so regarded, but though the Russians had accorded to Li Hung-chang [the noted Chinese statesman] the 'treatment' of a prince, they could not give it to Yamagata as Prince Fushimi was there. As to Corea, Japan desired its independence, and the Russians denied any intention of taking it, which came to the same thing. Of course all the Japanese wanted was to protect the large number of Japanese residents. The arrangement amounted to no more than this, that both sides would avoid the danger of collision. The King is going to live in a Palace close to the Russian Legation (Mrs. Bishop says Russian and British Legations back to back, with a door of communication in the wall).

On August 10 Satow talked with Saionji about Yamagata's mission.

He did not really arrange anything. Merely that the Coreans should have time given to them to form a body of troops in proportion to their resources, and that in the event of trouble in the Peninsula, neither side would act without consulting the other. I remarked that practically this amounted to a substitution of Russia for China, which was so far satisfactory that Russia was more easy to negotiate with.

He said it was not Waeber nor his wife who arranged the King's flight to the Russian Legation, but de Speyer, who was just the man for that sort of thing.[34]

76

On August 19, Satow wrote a dispatch describing the activity of Japanese railway projectors in Korea.[35] On August 27, he reported to Lord Salisbury he had reason to believe that the Russian Government was "endeavouring to urge upon that of Japan the necessity of withdrawing troops from Corea, and replacing them, if necessary by gendarmes."[36]

On October 2, Satow saw Okuma, who had replaced Saionji as Foreign Minister. Their conversation turned to Korea.

I remarked that this was a difficult question. He made a wry face, and said it was necessary to talk to Russia on the subject. She had declared that she had no desire to annex. It was to be hoped that the King would wish to go back to his Palace. Of course he was a very timorous person. I alluded to Miura at which he made another grimace. Japan, he said, to show her appreciation of the benefits she had derived from Foreign assistance was anxious to lead China and Corea in the same path. In the latter country there seemed to [be] no proper feeling about government, everybody snatching at power for himself and to fill his pockets. The best man they had was the Prime Minister who was murdered in February last, next came the other Minister who is now at the head of Government. De Speyer says he is only waiting for a successor to Lobanof to be appointed in order to go to his post in Corea, and denied that Waeber had been appointed there.

On October 16, Asaina visited Satow. "Asaina says that Okuma has sent Toda, a merchant, over to Corea to act as secret agent, and buy some Corean officials. The government will not follow the strong policy indicated by the papers, for that means war. Hara will probably return. (Speyer went to Okuma and objected to Oishi [Masami]).

On November 13 Satow talked to d'Anethan. "D'Anethan says de Speyer told him the Japanese will certainly not be allowed to get the railway from Fusan to Söul. That Waeber has given dissatisfaction to his government. The French have complained that he is too English: he is disliked also by the Coreans. Very wrong of Waeber not to be on good terms with Plancy [?]; e. g. he (Speyer) disliked English, but if his

Government policy required it, he should do violence to his feelings.

On November 14, Satow talked with Okuma about a recent railway dispute. As he reported in a dispatch:

The Japanese papers having stated that a note, in which the Corean government had expressed their regret for having given railway concessions in Corea to American and French Syndicates contrary to their engagements with this country, had been returned by Count Okuma to the Corean Minister at Tokio, I took an opportunity of asking his Excellency whether the report was correct.

Count Okuma said that it was quite true that Corea was bound by a Treaty negotiated in 1894 by Mr. Otori [Keisuke, the Japanese Minister to China] to give priority to Japan in railway construction, and though he did not think the moment opportune for claiming the execution of the engagement, it was necessary to insist upon the rights of Japan being duly respected. He had therefore returned the note in question, as its terms were not satisfactory. He explained to M. de Speyer that he had no intention of putting pressure on the Corean Government, but only wished to remind them of the irregularity they had committed. All that Japan desired was to aid in assuring the independence of Corea, which he felt certain was the object which the Russian Government also had at heart.

The Seoul-Inchhön line, he said, would pay well, but he believed the capital would be found in Japan and not in the United States, which does not make foreign investments. A line from Seoul to Fusan could not possibly be made a financial success, but one to Mokpho might. He had good reason to hope that this port, which gives access to the most fertile region in Corea, would shortly be thrown open to foreign commerce. He added that the relations between Japan and Corea had much improved of late, and Japanese traders were now able to carry on their business in the interior without running any risk of insult or injury. One of the Imperial Princes, the younger Komatsu, on a recent visit to Seoul, had been well received, and the King had left the Russian Legation for the purpose of giving him an audience. He had grounds for supposing that the King would transfer his residence from the Russian Legation to his Palace in another month or so.

In spite of the cheerful tone adopted by Count Okuma, it

seemed to me that he felt rather acutely the difficulties of contending against the preponderance of Russian influence in Corea.[37]

On November 24, Okuma talked to Satow again.

The arrest of the Corean officials reported is attributed to several causes: one that the individuals who do not wish the King
to leave the Russian legation are trying to frighten him into
thinking that it is not safe; a second that the former Chinese
Resident Yüan [Shih-k'ai] is at the bottom of it all; thirdly
that the officers of the old bodyguard are being laid hold of to
prevent interference with the formation of the new guard under
Russian officers.

He also went at length into the history of Corean difficulties
since 1882, and said that the murder of the Queen was contrived
by the Taiwönkun with the aid perhaps of a few *sōshi*, and
that the result had been to put all the foreigners in Corea
against Japan. I said she had been great favourite with foreigners
generally on account of her intelligence, and they had suspected
Japanese of being mixed up in the affair. Then he became more
frank, and introducing the name of Okamoto Riunosuke, a man
who he said had barely escaped execution for his share in the
mutiny of the guards in 1878, described him as having tried to
persuade the Tai-wön-kun that reforms could never be made
by bloodshed, 'and in spite of all that,' he added, 'he was probably the very man himself' (who killed the Queen understood)!

On December 9, Satow was visited by Ignatius V. Chirol,
Foreign Editor of the London *Times.*

Has just come from Corea, where he found Russian influence
paramount, but a certain current rising against it. Thinks if the
Japanese would undertake to employ Corean labour they might
have concession for Soul-Pusan line: the recent decree refusing
to grant any more railway concessions for a year was however
directed against them.

On January 1, 1897 Satow dined with the d'Anethans, the
Herods and Paul May. Afterwards he recorded in his diary:
"It would seem that the distribution of the pamphlet about
Queen's murder by Corean Minister before his departure was
not altogether uninspired by De Speyer, and that Prince
Wihwa and other Coreans get supplies thence also."

79

On January 24, I Chun-yong called on Satow with his Japanese-speaking interpreter.

He wanted to find out what the policy of Her Majesty's Government was with regard to Corea. I told him that I had heard nothing. Then he said that he knew our relations with Japan were very intimate, but how were they with China. I said that we were well disposed towards China, but that the obstinate opposition of Chinese officialdom to any kind of progress made it difficult to get on. He said that the Corean who went to the Russian Emperor's funeral is now to be sent on a general mission to Europe, but in reply to a question said he did not know in what capital he would principally reside. (As it is to be St. Petersburg this was very discreet of him).

On February 10, d'Anethan told Satow that telegrams had been exchanged between de Speyer and Petersburg about the publication of the agreement as to Korea. "The Japanese are going to publish it."

On February 18, Satow talked to Okuma.

Has given instructions to Kato to ask whether Great Britain will not establish a Legation in Corea like the other Powers. The commerce of Corea is growing and it has made quite as much increase in proportion as Japan in its earlier years. Besides the step would add to British influence in the East.

I said I had no instructions as to the views of Her Majesty's Government but speaking personally, I did not think Her Majesty's Government would be likely to fall in with the proposition. Since the year before last Japan and Russia had agreed to treat the Corea question as one interesting themselves alone, and had come to an arrangement which they had agreed to keep secret. I had heard what its nature was, but had never seen it. It would probably excite umbrage in the minds of the Russians if we suddenly without any apparent reason converted our Consulate General into a Legation.[t]

He admitted there was a protocol, signed by Yamagata and Lobanof last year, and he was about to communicate it to the Diet, after arranging with the Russian Government for its being published simultaneously or nearly so.[39]

[t] Count Okuma rejoined that increased commercial interests of Great Britain in the peninsula furnished a sufficient motive.[38]

On February 25, Satow reported to the Foreign Secretary that the removal of the Korean King to his new palace three days before, at least a month earlier than expected, had caught the Japanese Government by surprise. He observed: "It has naturally given great satisfaction to both the Cabinet and the nation, to the former in particular, because while publishing the Moscow Protocol, and the arrangements made at Seoul between the Russian and Japanese Representatives last year, they will be able to say that the principal article has already been carried into effect."[40]

On March 1, Satow forwarded to his Government translations of the Russo-Japanese Memorandum regarding Korean affairs, signed at Seoul on May 14, 1896, and of the Yamagata-Lobanov Protocol signed at Moscow on May 28 (June 9), 1897. He commented:

The first of these documents corresponds very closely with the account of its contents, which I had the honour to report to your Lordship in my despatch No. 109 of the 21st May last, on the authority of Count Mutsu.

In my No. 156 of the 19th August I had the honour to acquaint your Lordship that Marquis Saionji had stated to me that nothing but a verbal arrangement had been come to by Marshal Yamagata for the organization by the Coreans of a body of troops proportionate to their resources, and that, in the event of trouble in the Peninsula, neither Power would act without consulting the other. The Agreement, which now proves to have been in writing, also contains a stipulation that, in the case of Corea requiring a loan, the two Governments shall come to her aid, as well as a provision that Russia may construct a line of telegraph from Seoul to her frontier, Japan continuing to administer the lines already under her control; but Corea may purchase all these lines whenever she has the means.[41]

That day Satow also described in a confidential dispatch to Lord Salisbury how "extremely unpalatable" Count Okuma had found it to try to explain how circumstances had forced Japan to come to terms with Russia in regard to Korea:

It was evident from the manner of Count Okuma throughout

the sitting of the 26th February that the task of trying to explain how circumstances had forced Japan to come to terms with Russia in regard to Corea was extremely unpalatable to him, and that the taunts of the Opposition easily upset his equanimity. There can be no doubt that, during the progress of the war with China, he expressed himself somewhat too boastfully respecting the ability of his countrymen to carry through their policy in Corea in despite of European Powers, and that he advocated a "strong" attitude towards foreign Governments. The recognition of the necessity of coming to an understanding with Russia must have been a bitter humiliation for him, and it is difficult to understand how he brought himself to publish the documents inclosed in my immediately preceding despatch, unless he hoped so use them as a lever to force on the King's return to his Palace, and to prevent the projected loan from the Russo-Chinese Bank. Their value, however, was discounted by the removal of the King to his new Palace on the 22nd ultimo.

When asked by one Member whether this building was not close to the Russian Legation, he replied that it lay at a considerable distance. I have been informed, however, by one who has personal knowledge of the locality, that communication can easily be established by breaking a door in the wall of the Legation grounds.

According to correspondence published in a Japanese newspaper, the removal of the King would seem to have been brought about by strong representations made to him on the part of his Ministers, and that, when his Majesty informed M. Waeber of his intention, the latter replied that he could not be answerable for His Majesty's safety outside the walls of the Russian Legation, to which the King rejoined that his Ministers would provide for that.

The story wears the appearance of having been manufactured for Japanese consumption, as does also the alleged incident of Madame Waeber being induced to go for a walk with a Russian-speaking Corean whilst the Decree was being presented for the King's signature.

On my remarking to M. de Speyer that the Moscow Protocol was of a comparatively insignificant character, he replied that Marshall Yamagata had made proposals of a far more extensive kind, involving the partition of Corea, which Prince Lobanow had declined, on the ground that Russia did not desire any Corean territory. This is probably a fact, for the proposal was certainly discussed by Marquis Ito's Government, and I am assured that about the time of the outbreak of the war in 1894, M. Hitrovo was sounded on this point by an unofficial agent. On his expressing his readiness to entertain the idea, and proposing that some official person should be appointed to discuss it with him, the suggestion was dropped.

The real significance of the Protocol and Memorandum which have now been published, seems, however, to be that Japan henceforward stands committed to a recognition of the right of Russia to intervene in the Peninsula, and the only advantage gained by the Japanese Government is that by this move they have succeeded in discrediting the policy of their predecessors.[42]

On March 3, Asaina visited Satow. "Thinks publication of the Russian agreements a sign of weakness. The strong man simply refused to open his mouth. The object was simply to pacify the Diet. It is reported that the secret agent sent over to Corea by Okuma some time ago turned out a failure: he got drunk at Inchhon and let out his secret to the Coreans; has been recalled."

On March 11 Satow talked with R. L. Thomson. "Has had talk with Takashima [Tomonosuke, Minister of the Army] about Corea. The latter says Corea ought to be neutralized under the guarantee of the Powers. I made no remark as to the feasibility of this."

On March 14, Satow talked to Okuma about "the foolish proceedings of Corean reformers, acting with the approval of Japanese, who had introduced the hair cutting ordinance and thereby excited popular hatred."

Happily things were going better. The murder of the Queen was got up by the Taiwönkun, who employed Japanese for the purpose. I interposed my profound regret for the sake of Japan that Corean affairs had been so mismanaged. He went on to say that the suspicions of the King with regard to Japan were now quite dispelled, and the people behaved much better to Japanese peddlers in the interior. Quite "couleur de rose."

On April 29, Satow went to Okuma and had a talk on the general situation. Okuma stated that all the efforts of the Japanese Government were directed toward the maintenance of peace, but that difficulty might be apprehended, if "a Power he would not name" should endeavour to disturb the existing balance of influence in Korea.

Recently the relations of the Corean Government with that of Japan had much improved, and the agreements negotiated at Moscow and Seoul last year had contributed to their stability. Suddenly, however, reports had reached him that the King of Corea contemplated engaging a large body of Russian officers and men for the ostensible purpose of drilling the Corean troops. A certain number of officers had already been brought to Corea for that purpose, and he had not felt himself in a position to offer any objection.

Some time ago, when the question of the King's return to his palace was being discussed, it had been suggested that his leaving the Russian Legation would be greatly expedited if he was allowed to have a guard of Russian soldiers, but to this proposal he had given a decided negative. The large increase of Russian officers and men now proposed was believed to have been negotiated by Min Yonghwan at Moscow last year, but no effect had followed in consequence of the understanding negotiated by Marshal Yamagata with the late Prince Lobanoff. It had now been revived under the following circumstances. Baron [Roman] Rosen having been appointed Minister to Tokio, the departure of M. De Speyer to replace M. Waeber was imminent. Count Okuma believed that the latter was desirous of effecting a *coup* before his departure, and had therefore influenced the King to prefer a request for this large body of so-called military instructors. As soon as this was reported at Tokio, the Japanese Government had sent instructions to their Minister at Seoul to present a protest to the King, and at the same time remonstrances had been made at St. Petersburgh.

It could not, of course, be maintained by Japan that their engagement would be a violation of Article II of the Moscow Protocol, but it was quite contrary to the spirit of Article IV, by which the two Governments bound themselves to discuss any further points needing common action which might arise in the sequel, and this was certainly one of those contemplated. He felt sanguine that the Russian Government would listen to the representations that had been made to them, and that M. Waeber's plan would be without result, all the more because of the change in the higher personnel of the Russian Foreign Office, which now included a chief of the Asiatic Department, who is believed to be much more friendly to Japan than his predecessor.

Count Okuma also informed me that M. Waeber, rather than proceed to his post at Mexico, had asked permission to retire and enter the service of the Corean King, but his Excellency had caused a representation to be made to Count Mouravieff to the effect that such an arrangement would certainly not conduce to harmony between Japan and Russia, and Count Mouravieff had replied that he concurred in this view. Consequently M. Waeber had been informed by his Government that he would not be allowed to remain at Seoul in any private capacity.

I gathered from the way in which Count Okuma expressed himself that there is great risk of complications arising in this part of the world should Russia endeavour to strengthen her hold over Corea, and to play in that country the part which China had assumed previous to the war of 1894. The arrival of the two battle-ships, *Fuji* and *Yashima*, which have recently been completed in England, will no doubt greatly strengthen the confidence of the Japanese Government in their belief that time alone is necessary to render this country a match for Russia at sea, as they already hold themselves to be more than able to cope on land with the army of Eastern Siberia.[43]

On the occasion of Queen Victoria's diamond jubilee Japan sent a congratulatory mission, headed by Prince Arisugawa. Satow accompanied the mission, sailing on the *Empress of India* from Yokohama on May 7.

In England Satow talked to Lord Salisbury at the Foreign Office about Korea (October 7):

Does not think the Russians wish to be very active there at present, but they are trying to oust McLeavy Brown [the British Director of Korean Customs]. Emperor of Russia more bent on developing Siberia. I said that Brown being a neutral gave no umbrage to Japan, but the latter would be annoyed if a Russian were put in his place. Lord Salisbury agreed, but said we could do nothing to hinder it. He went on to say that Germans wanted a port out there. I replied that no port in Corea could be of use to any one. That I did not believe the Russians would take Port Arthur, as it would divide their forces, and the Japanese would lie between them. Nor did I think Japanese would be pleased to see them at Port Lazareff.

Lord Salisbury said as long as the Russians only looked for commercial advantages out there, we should not interfere, but if they contemplated any military movements, we should have to take corresponding measures. In the meantime we should not egg on Japanese against them, but rather counsel them to get on happily with the Russians. I replied that the Japanese could easily be stirred up by their own Government at any moment, but Port Lazareff in Russian hands would cause great popular commotion.

He went back to the Germans, and said they wanted us to let them have Chusan, over which we have certain rights. I replied Admiral Buller had told me the tides were bad and place much infested by fogs. For his part if we were to have a base there, he would prefer Port Hamilton.

Lord Salisbury said this had been given up at the instance of Admiral Elliott, who said it could not be defended.

I replied I had heard it said that an enemy outside could shell a British squadron lying in the harbour, but I did not quite see how British ships could be lying there to be shelled.

He said he was not quite of Admiral Elliott's opinion.

On October 12 Satow talked to Sanderson at the Foreign Office and repeated part of Lord Salisbury's talk. "[As for] Corea [and the removal of] J. M. Mc Leavy Brown," he recorded in his diary, "Jordan [the British representative at Seoul] has been told he may say that dismissal would annoy Her Majesty's Government and the Japanese too have protested."

On November 21, Satow returned to Japan. On November 25 he went to see Komura, the Vice Minister of Foreign Affairs. "In reply to a question [about the appointment of Kir Alexeieff in Corea] he said Japan does not take a very lively interest in Corea just at present. The newspaper report that there had been negotiations between Rosen [the Russian Minister to Tokyo] and Okuma about drilling Corean troops was incorrect. At the utmost they may have had one or two friendly talks."

On November 26, Satow saw Asaina: "Says the hope of the Japanese is that the Coreans will get tired of the Russian domination. England and Japan. Told him we thought the moment had not come for joint action, and till then a formal alliance undesirable, but in meanwhile to cultivate the closest possible understanding."

On December 16, Satow went to see Nishi Tokujiro, the new Minister of Foreign Affairs, whom he regarded "as taciturn as most Satsuma men." Nishi knew nothing about Russian ships being sent to Korea. "Apropos of the [Yamagata-Lobanov] Moscow agreement, he remarked that Russian deeds do not correspond with Russian words." Commenting on this remark in a dispatch, Satow wrote to the Foreign Secretary:

As your lordship is no doubt aware, Japan had for some time past observed an attitude of something resembling indifference to Russian proceedings in Corea, in the expectation that, sooner or later, the Corean people will become tired of their new protectors, and turn again to Japan for assistance. But I cannot think that they seriously believe in the probability or success of an anti-Russian movement in the Peninsula, and that they must have some other hopes of recovering their lost influence by means which it is thought prudent to make no allusion to at present.[44]

On December 23, Satow saw Nishi again. As he informed Lord Salisbury in a dispatch, the Japanese Government had received a communication from the Russian Government to the effect that Port Arthur had been lent to Russia "only temporarily as a winter anchorage."[45] The question arose whether other powers would seek ports in China or Corea. "We certainly should not be found occupying any place, but our squadron was going to look [and] see, and might possibly be found in Corea, demonstrating against McLeavy Brown's being turned out," Satow told Nishi. "Something would be known by the end of the month."[46]

On January 6, 1898 Nishi asked Satow what the British squadron was doing in Corea. "The story went that the Russians were going to double their guard, because we had sent one. I said I did not think this true, but really I had no information, except about the displacement of J. McLeavy Brown and the negotiations that had ended in his retaining the Chief Commissionership of Customs."

On January 10, Satow received a letter from Admiral Buller, to the effect that Lord Salisbury was "thinking of acquiring a port somewhere about Gulf of Pecheli." On January 12, Asaina came to Satow. "Says Russia has offered to give King of Corea 500,000 *yen* annual allowance, if he will become a Russian vassal."

On February 4, Satow was visited by two Koreans, Riu Seinam and Shen Ong-hi.

Riu had been a Vice Minister at the time the Corean King had taken refuge in the Russian Legation; Shen was an officer in the Kunrentai. The latter has been in America and speaks English fairly well, but we talked Japanese. He was one of those who fled from Corea after the failure of Kim Okkyun's attempt to kill Min Yong-ik in 1884. The object of their visit was to ask me to suggest to Jordan to advise the King to recall Pak Yong-hyo. The King and others are tired of the Russians, and Cho Pyöng-sik has been turned out; the English and United States Ministers have been asked to help in selecting men to form a ministry. Said I had not seen Pak for so many years, that I could not well interfere. Besides when he was in power before, he made himself obnoxious by introducing petty sumptuary regulations. Shen said he would not do that again. When he was in office, the peasants were contented. The people would be glad to get him back. Then he talked about [Kir] Alexeieff having turned out McLeavy Brown, who had done so much good by placing the finances on a good basis [as Director of Korean Customs].

On February 7 Satow saw Ito, who had become Prime Minister again. "I tried to interest him in Corea and the retirement of Cho Pyöng-sik," Satow wrote, "but he seemed

quite indifferent, even when I said that Cho's going would deprive Speyer of his chief instrument."

On March 2, the Korean Pak Yong-hyo called on Satow.

Looks very civilized, in an irreproachable frock-coat. Told him
how the news of the squadron coming to Chemulpho reached
Jordan just after McLeavy Brown's new agreement was signed.

He said the fickle character of the King, who is only 47, is
at the bottom of all the evils of Corea. If he could be got to
abdicate in favour of the Crown Prince, the latter might reign,
helped by Wi-hwa who is intelligent and a Cabinet composed
of capable men. Otherwise there is no hope.

He asked whether England would not take a more active part
in Corea. I said that England had no direct interests there.
Only Russia and Japan had. But the latter neither spoke nor acted.
Coreans must be patient for a few years. France of course (in
answer to a remark of his that the Russian and French Chargé
d'Affaires were constantly bullying the Coreans and extorting
concessions) merely worked in the interests of Russia.

On March 17, Satow saw Nishi.

Russians were very active last night in sending off telegrams.
Poklevsky [Stanislav Poklevskii-Kozell, first Secretary of the
Russian Legation] and Chichkin [Ivan Chagin, the Naval Attaché?] left this morning for Nagasaki by train in a sudden
manner. But perhaps about Corea. Nishi would not tell me
anything about Corea, pretending to think it a very troublesome
country. Remarked to him as a draw that the Russians having a
good prospect of getting Manchuria did not care so much about
Corea, a country difficult to govern without an army of occupation. He said yes, there would always be small insurrec-
tions here and there.

On March 19 Asaina informed Satow that "communication
of some sort" had been received, but that he had been unable
to find out the content. "Nishi keeps his mouth closed (*kuchi
ga katai*) and does all the translations from Russian himself,
instead of sending them down to the translators' department."

That day Satow received telegrams from the Foreign Office briefing him on the exchange between it and Jordan about the withdrawal of Russian instructors and financial adviser from Korea, and asking him if he knew anything about it, notably about the reasons for the withdrawal.

So went to Ito, and . . . said as he had asked me the other day about Corea, I had something to tell him. Then I briefly communicated what [Count Mikhail] Mouravieff [the Russian Foreign Minister] said to [Sir Nicholas R.] O'Conor [the British Ambassador to Russia],[g] and asked if he could tell me the explanation. After a moment's hesitation he said Mouravieff had told Hayashi that they were going to withdraw the advisers, and he hoped it would be agreeable to the Japanese Government as this would restore the balance of influence.

On March 23 Riu Seinam and Shen Ong-hi called on Satow again.

Their principal object was to get me to suggest to Jordan that he should advise the King to recall Pak Yong-hyo to power. Told them I had done so after their previous visit, and that Jordan would do it if he saw an opportunity. That the state of affairs seemed hopeful in Corea. The new Russian Chargé d'Affaires [Nikolai Matiunin] would probably not pursue the violent policy of de Speyer. Coreans were said to be so torn by party dissension as to be unable to maintain their independence without the assistance of some foreign power. This was a disgrace to them: they should sink their own quarrels, and unite together for the good of their country. .

Told them Russian Government had informed Her Majesty's Government that the military instructors and financial adviser would be recalled, and that they were willing to modify the last clause of Article 8 of the Agreement between Speyer and the

---

[g] Count Mouravieff informed O'Conor that if the Yamên granted a lease of Port Arthur and Talienwan to the Russian Government, foreign trade would have free access to both these ports similar to the other ports in the Chinese Empire, that Russia had no intention of infringing the treaty rights and privileges of foreign countries in China, and that he trusted that Her Majesty's Government would abstain from an announcement in Parliament of these undertakings, in view of the negotiations still pending in China.[47]

Corean Government which declares that none but a Corean or Russian shall be financial adviser.

That day Satow attended a farewell dinner for Lowther. "Cartier saw Poklevsky today and chaffed him about Corea, to which Poklevsky replied that it was not easy for any one to penetrate the profundity of Russian policy, but he would not tell him any more as he was too English."

On March 25, Satow conferred with Okuma.

I said the Russians had probably withdrawn the financial adviser and military instructors as a sop to Japan, to prevent their objecting about [Russian lease of] Port Arthur. But he said what did we go to war for? To establish the independence of Corea. But the other was our property and they made us give it up. We ought to make a strong protest. I rubbed it into him about the "mere spectator" policy of the Japanese.

On March 28, Asaina came to see Satow. "The Russians seem to have said to Japan that they may do what they like in Corea," Satow recorded afterwards.

On March 31, Satow talked to Komura. "[As regards] my telegram [No.] 16 [dated March 19], the phrase about the equality of influences [of Russia and Japan in Korea being restored] and hoping it would please Japanese Government was not part of the original communication," he reported in a dispatch; "probably said by Russian Minister [Mouravieff] unofficially to Hayashi. . . ."[48]

On April 5, Satow went to Inouye. "It seems the verbal note and the Russo-Corean convention (question about financial control) occupied their time," he wrote.

On April 12, Asaina came to Satow and repeated that the Russians "seem to have said Japan may do what she likes in Corea, but the latter is not likely to take advantage of it."

On May 4, Satow went to see Komura.

As to Corea he says Japan did not cease to protest against financial adviser and military instructors, but the motives of Russia

91

in withdrawing were various, one being the desire to devote all her available resources and attention to Port Arthur and Talien-wan Bay. The protocol signed 25 April may perhaps be published: they can do it when they please. When I come to see it I shall be disappointed. I asked Why? Because, he said, there is nothing in it; it is merely a recognition of the status quo, disturbed by the engagement of Alexeieff and the Military Instructors.

On May 9, Komura called on Satow and gave him a copy of the [Nishi-Rosen] protocol about Corea, signed on the 25th of April.[49]

Said it was a more valuable document than from its size it seemed and congratulated him. He asked if Her Majesty's Government would see anything to object. I said no, Her Majesty's Government had always recognized that the interests of Japan and Russia [in Korea] came first; ours were only commercial and secondary, which was what I had always told the Coreans who came to see me.

On June 25, Ye Ha-yung, the Korean Minister, visited Satow, "and unbosomed himself of a greal deal."

Seems to be far more intelligent than one is usually inclined to take him for. Thinks he will be sent for to take post of Minister for Foreign Affairs, but dislikes the idea. Japanese much disliked by Coreans; nevertheless necessary to make friends with them. That was what he had been aiming at ever since he came here as minister. No doubt about murder of Queen by two Japanese of whom one was Sugiyama, the Secretary of Legation, and Miura must have been cognizant of the plot. Talked a great deal about de Speyer and Waeber, the two together arranged flight of King to Russian Legation. Speyer wanted to go too fast.

On July 2, Satow told Okuma, now Premier and Foreign Minister, that he thought Russia had withdrawn from Korea only temporarily.

On July 26, Satow called on Komura, who informed him that Ito was going to Peking, "but will be only twenty-four hours at Chemulpho, and so will not go to Soul." Komura told Satow that the Japanese were trying to get the Korean

Government to agree to a Soul-Fusan railway, "but do not think it will be easy." The Japanese "also are demanding compensation for murdered Japanese." On July 27, Satow conversed with Okuma. "Ito *is* going to Soul. We talked about the necessity of China reorganizing her defenses, and he said Chang Chi-tung [now Governor General of Wuchang] was sending 150 students over here."

On October 6, Satow went to see Okuma. "It seems that Japan sent (i.e. paid for) Prince Wiha and I (the grandson of the Tai-won-kun) to United States and England. The former is clever, but the latter is a better and more able man," Satow recorded.

On December 7, Satow went to Aoki Shuzo, who had succeeded Okuma as Foreign Minister.

Told him how de Speyer had talked of his trying to divert Japanese attention away from Corea to the South and that this was merely a continuation of the policy which had allowed Japan to retain Formosa and the Pescadores, though contrary to French wishes. I had always said to everyone that Egypt occupied our attention in the first place, and till that was settled we could do nothing in the Far East. Now Fashoda had been arranged for, but there were other details yet undecided. We had several disagreements with France, about Newfoundland and Siam. However Japan would not be ready till 1903, and by that time our hands also might be free. He implied that Japan could not sit still and see Corea absorbed by Russia.

On January 25, 1899 Satow saw Aoki again.

He suggested that Russia might promise to give them a free hand in Corea in return for recognizing their position in Manchuria. Asked about [the Korean General] An Kyong-su. He said An was an unreliable man, though clever. I told him that An wanted me to ask Jordan to advise the King to come to terms with the reformers, and I had promised to send Jordan anything he might write. But as to Corea, Great Britain had only secondary interests, and that Japan and Russia were nearer. Aoki observed as to this that Japan would arrange direct with Russia without

English intervention, to which I rejoined that we should observe a disinterested attitude, but that Japan had our sympathy.

On February 15, Satow congratulated Ito.

He said that when the Rosen-Nishi protocol was being negotiated, the Russians offered the clause about Japanese commercial development, and he had insisted on adding industrial. I told him their position there was now much better than four years ago, and that showed what a good thing it was to keep one's head cool. He replied: "I always keep my head cool." According to him what Matutine [Matiunin, the Russian representative in Seoul] said to Kato about the Rosen-Nishi protocol was that it ought to be got rid of, but that it could not be helped.

On March 30, Satow went to Aoki.

He spoke very strongly about Russia in Corea. There is an idea of bringing a railway from Vladivostock through north Corea to a port on the Gulf of Pechili. If Russia has Corea Japan cannot sleep in peace. Unfortunately the interests of England there are not sufficient to make it worth the while to support Japanese policy. But if Russia gets command of the peninsula she will have a great and damaging position as regards commercial nations. I observed that Japan would not be ready till 1903. He replied she might be obliged to act before. I said there was no likelihood of her finding money for the Soul-Fusan railway, which he admitted. He does not like the Russians obtaining land for nominal whale fishery, and Japan must follow her example. Om, the King's Concubine, is ambitious of becoming Empress, and the Russians back her.[h]

On May 18, Satow spoke with Aoki again. "Kato returns from Corea, because the military men are dissatisfied with him. They say he is slow."

On June 22, Satow asked Aoki about the throwing of bombs into the residences of various high officials in Korea. He reported in a dispatch:

It is believed in Tokio that a Japanese named Tsuneya, who has been for years past in the service of Pak Yong Hyo, one

[h] A recent change of ministry at Seoul had brought the pro-Russian party to power.[50]

94

of the Corean refugees in this country, is in some manner mixed up with this affair, and the Government have consequently issued an Ordinance empowering the Japanese Representatives in Corea to deport any suspected persons, and prohibiting Japanese subjects from proceeding to that country without a passport.

Viscount Aoki, whom I asked for information, told me today that the complicity of any individual Japanese was not actually proved, but the Government knew that three Corean refugees had recently returned home with two Japanese companions, and that there were hot-headed young men in Kinshin ready to take part in any revolutionary movement in the Peninsula. They had thought it wise rather to err on the side of caution, than to run any risk of international complications arising out of the acts of Japanese subjects.

I contented myself with expressing an opinion that the step taken might in Europe be interpreted as indicating something much more serious than the facts related by him would seem to necessitate.[51]

On September 8 Satow saw Aoki again.

We spoke about dispute between Russians and Japanese at Masanpho. When the matter was referred to Hayashi [Gonsuke], their Minister at Seoul, the latter replied that he had had no control over Japanese private persons. Aoki now understood the Russians wished to exchange their establishment at Nagasaki for the disputed ground at Masanpho, where they desire to build a dock.

On October 5, the German Minister, Graf von Leyden, came to Satow. "He shares my opinion that the Japanese [Aoki] will give way about Masanpho; it will cost him his portfolio but his successor will be able to reply that it was a '*fait accompli*' for which he is not responsible."

On October 12, Satow spoke about Masanpho with Aoki.

He told me the same story as last week, with the addition that he was at Nasu at the time, and Rosen saw Takahira. He says Rosen is a nice fellow to deal with, but the Russians are always trying to grab something. I remarked that they were like a tree that was always putting out branches over the neighbour's wall. Then sounded him about Deer Island, Masanpho being merely a blind, and suggested they were like the bamboo, that sends its rootstock along under ground, and then suddenly comes up where you least expect it. . . .

On October 13, Satow told Ercole Orfini, the Italian Minister to Japan, his impression about Masanpho. "He asked whether Japanese would not try to get something in Fuhkien. I said that I felt persuaded they would rather, if they saw their way, put the pot on as regards Corea." On October 15, Satow told Aoki who came to him to talk about his idea of a port in Fuhkien, that the British Government would not approve of any aggressive measures against China. "I added," Satow reported to the Foreign Secretary, "that I should have thought that the interests of Japan in Corea . . . must far outweigh any objects that could be attained in Fuhkien. To this his Excellency assented, remarking that the interest of Japan in Fuhkien was merely nominal."[52]

In his diary Satow noted: "According to what [Evgenii] Stein, the Russian Chargé d'Affaires at Soul told Jordan, there is no danger of a row between Japan and Russia over the land at Masanpho, he having found another site which will do quite as well." Satow added, with Aoki as his source: "The Japanese Chargé d'Affaires was told by Muravieff that the Russians had no 'intention' of acquiring a port in Corea (Koje Island). He seemed however to doubt whether this assurance could be trusted."

On January 10, 1900 Satow talked about Masanpho with Aoki.

He saw [Alexander] Pavloff [the Russian Consul General at Seoul] whom Rosen introduced to him with the words 'you see he is not such a jingo after all.' Of course the purchase was a private matter, with which the Japanese Government had nothing to do. I suggested Pavloff might buy out the Japanese purchases, to which he answered they were so fanatical that though they might sell to English or Americans, they would not sell to Russians. Hinted at the possibility of Russia fortifying Masanpho, but this did not draw him. He said the Russians talked of withdrawing their hospital from Nagasaki, and I do not doubt that this was offered as an inducement to the Japanese. His tone altogether was much less bellicose than formerly.

Speaking to Aoki on January 18, Satow obtained further information about Russian activity. "It appears that the Russian Naval Department did not actually say they had presented a demand for the island, but talked about its being desirable. Hayashi the Minister in Corea who was here a few days ago, did not know of any such demand being made. Aoki had received telegram from Petersburg that Russia was sending troops to Herat. Pavloff talked to him about Masanpho but he had said it was a private purchase. The utmost he could do was to tell the Consul he might try to influence the Japanese purchaser."

On January 23, Satow talked with Leyden, who was of the opinion that the Japanese "would resist Russia taking possession of Corea, as they could never feel safe otherwise."

When Satow saw Aoki on January 25, the latter "seemed to regard Yamagata's story of the Russians on Corean frontier as a bit of a maresnest." Satow reflected:

Leyden told me another thing he heard from Rosen last Thursday, namely that the row between naval officers and Japanese at Fusan having been brought to the notice of the Emperor Nicholas, His Imperial Majesty caused instructions to be sent out here to express his deep personal displeasure. Then it would seem the Japanese began to arm and the Russians to get irritated. (Then Aoki gave assurances, as he told me in December).

On January 28, while in Atami, Satow talked to Ito, who came to see him when he sent over his card.

Russian dissatisfaction about Masampho, and rows at Mokhpo and Fusan between Japanese and Russians. He had scolded Aoki for letting the Russians, who were in the wrong, be the first to complain; he should have anticipated by sending the

Chargé d'Affaires to complain to Mouravieff. There had been also a complaint about Chaghin's [the Russian Naval Attaché Chagin's] treatment by Yamamoto, and the Japanese naval attaché at Petersburg had been told that till it was altered, nothing would be shown to him. However, everything had now been smoothed over.

I suggested that Rosen's recall was connected with these matters. He thought on the contrary that Rosen had asked for a change. Anyhow, even if [Alexander] Isvolsky [who was to suceed Rosen as Russian Minister to Japan] were the active personage he was represented, that would not matter, just as in the case of Hitrovo, whom they had not found difficult to deal with. At the beginning of the war in '94, Hitrovo had told them they ought not to attempt anything on a large scale, as China had a great reserve of power, and they would get the worst of it in the end. The Russians finding their advice was not taken were at first angry, but afterwards, on suitable explanations being given, they changed their tone, and said it was quite satisfactory to them!

In a conversation with Aoki on March 22, Satow asked about Masanpho.

At first he was rather inclined to be costive till I showed him I knew about the choice of a site made by the Russians, then he admitted that he had heard privately about it. He supposed the Coreans would be forced to yield, as the Russians had sent eight ships there. Told him the story of Pavloff's pretending to know that Jordan had signed a cheque for the payment through the British Admiral of the purchase money of the lots acquired by Japanese forestalling Russians. He exclaimed "unverschämter" [shameless]. Also told him that Pavloff reported him to have said he knew who paid the money, but was not at liberty to tell. Same exclamation.

On March 29, Satow talked with Aoki.

He had heard from Söul that the Russians had demanded a piece of ground outside the limits of the Foreign concession at Masanpho, six English miles to the South, but the precise locality he had not yet heard; he supposed the Coreans could not resist. It was a serious question. The Russians spoke of removing their hospital from Nagasaki there, and having a coal store, but what might not that grow to in later years. Japan might have to acquire an equivalent.

I said the only real equivalent would be a coaling station on one of the Islands in the Baltic, opposite the Neva.

He remarked that the establishment of a Russian naval station there would be threatening.

On April 4, Okuma called on Satow.

Said there was no trouble about the Masanpho affair; but the Japanese people, the army and navy would not allow the Government to stand quietly by and see Corea fall into the hands of Russia.

On April 5, Satow went to see Aoki about Masanpho.

The question is not quite settled. The Russians have undertaken to content themselves with a piece of ground within Treaty limits, but wish to couple it with a condition that the island they had previously demanded shall not be given to any one else. The negotiations were being kept very secret. I remarked that agreements of the nature proposed by the Russians were often construed into a right of pre-emption or refusal in the behalf of the party to whom the declaration was made.

On April 12 Satow and Aoki talked about Masanpho again. "He feigned to know very little of what is being done between Coreans and Russians, the negotiations being secret, but he understood Pavloff had asked for the exclusive right to carry on mining, which would mean a monopoly opposed to the interest of other nationalities."

In May of 1900 Satow left Japan. On May 2, he had his final conversation with Ito.

He said in reply to my observation that all seemed quiet in the Far East, that one could not tell how long it would last. . . . As to war, I said no one could suppose it was to the advantage of Japan to fight Russia. Yet many people talked about it. Japan and Russia as to Corea like England and France as to Siam, a pretty woman with two suitors; no need however to come to

99

blows. One thing however seemed clear, Russia regarded Japan as the only obstacle to her designs in the Far East. All this he agreed with, but seemed to imply that there was a strong sentiment in Japan in favour of fighting among the non-responsible classes.

Upon his return to England, on May 31, Satow hastened to the Foreign Office. St. John Brodrick, the Secretary of War, was anxious to know whether Japan would fight Russia about Masanpho. "I give it as my opinion," Satow recorded in his diary, "that she would not act in any case before 1903, when her fleet and army will have attained their full expansion, and even then only if England backs her up. . . ."

The Liaotung Peninsula

Russia, Germany, and France had intervened when Japan, in the Treaty of Shimonoseki that ended the Sino-Japanese War, tried to obtain a foothold on the Asian continent. The three powers insisted that the Liaotung Peninsula in Southern Manchuria, occupied by the Japanese and ceded by the treaty, be returned to China. China was to compensate Japan for Liaotung with an increased war indemnity.

When Satow went to see Prime Minister Ito on August 1, 1895, they discussed the tripartite intervention.

He said that the European triple alliance was not quite so solid as previously. Asked him if he knew why Germany had joined Russia and France. He said it was with the object of preventing their too intimate union. I said that Germany's action being prompted by a political necessity, she was probably not actuated by unfriendliness to Japan, and might therefore be counted on for an arrangement with regard to Corea. He remarked that apparently the Foreign Representatives were not all of them in close touch with their governments. For example, on April 20, Gutschmid [the German Minister] had telegraphed congratulations to him at Shimonoseki [on the signing of the treaty], and yet two days later had joined him in the protest about the [Liaotung] Peninsula. I said I had not yet seen Gutschmid, but supposed him to be friendly, though perhaps less hearty than Italy. On this he said that Italy had exhibited a friendly disposition throughout; she had been invited to join in the protest, but had declined.

On August 5, Satow called on Saionji Kinmochi, Acting Minister of Foreign Affairs, and discussed with him the indemnity Japan wanted for withdrawing from the Liaotung Peninsula, as demanded by Russia, Germany and France.

Ito had told him what he had said to me on the subject, and he had also telegraphed to Lord S[alisbury] [who had become Prime Minister and Foreign Secretary following the collapse of the Rosebery Government] through Kato for his advice. As to Liaotung, Lobanof [the Russian Foreign Minister] had informed Nishi [the Japanese Minister in St. Petersburg] that they were not satisfied with the last answer, that 50,000,000 was too much, and they wished Japan to hasten the withdrawal of their troops. The German Government apparently did not share this view, but he thought France desired to join [?]. Lobanof had added that a communication would be made to the Japanese Government through Hitrovo. I said 50,000,000 was a sum the Chinese would have difficulty in raising, as the 16,000,000 would be absorbed by the two payments of 50,000,000 demanded. Saionji observed that this was what we had frequently suggested to them before. Then I told him the Russians are supposed to suspect them of wishing to hold on to the peninsula permanently. Saionji said he thought they should take measures to remove these suspicions. The number of troops now left in Manchuria is only about *ichi shi dan* (1 Division), though nominally there are two, one having gone to Formosa, the garrison of Wei-hai-wei having been supplied from Manchuria. This was a small force for so large a territory. I remarked that hitherto they had only exchanged verbal declarations, but perhaps what was necessary was an exchange of notes.[53]

On August 19, Satow called on Ito. He had heard nothing about the Liaotung Peninsula since the 9th. "Nishi saw Lobanoff, who said he was expecting a telegram from somewhere. It could hardly be France or Germany, probably China that caused the delay [in replying to the Japanese proposal regarding the retrocession of Liaotung]."[54]

On August 21, Satow dined with Freiherr von Gutschmid at the resort of Chiuzenji. "Agrees with me that Japanese are rather flattered than otherwise that in the Liaotung question, though forced to retrocede, they have been treated as if they belonged to the European concert," Satow noted in his diary.

Upon his return from Chiuzenji (August 29), Satow found a telegram from Sir Nicholas O'Conor, the British Minister in China, asking him to urge the Japanese to demand the opening of Wuchow in their negotiations for a commercial treaty with China, and the following day (August 30) went to see Ito. "He seemed at first to think that Wuchow was up the Yangtze, but called Komura Jutaro (Chargé d'Affaires at Peking when the [Sino-Japanese] war broke out), who put him right. After some talk got him to agree to what I asked." But the next day (August 31) Ito called on Satow. "Says it all hangs on the reply of the three Powers to Japanese conditions about Liaotung," Satow jotted down in his diary. "Is very anxious to get it speedily. (Yesterday when he told me this, I suggested unwise to display too much anxiety)."

In a dispatch to the Marquess of Salisbury, the Foreign Secretary, Satow elaborated:

Though he had been told that Germany assented, he was inclined to believe that she would not dissociate her action from that of France and Russia. On the 19th instant Mr. Nissi had pressed for an answer, but all he had been able to extract from Prince Lobanoff was that the latter considered 25,000 taels would be enough, and that he was awaiting a telegram (presumably from Peking) in order to give a definite reply. Since then the Japanese Government had heard nothing further. They were especially desirious of having the point settled, because it would be necessary to make arrangements with regard to the troops in occupation of the peninsula, if they had to remain there over the winter. From what he heard from Peking he was led to infer that France and Russia were encouraging China in refusing to pay the price demanded for the retrocession. When asked at the beginning of this negotiation whether they would use their influence with China to insure the acceptance of the Japanese conditions, the three Powers had preserved a discreet silence.

I inquired whether China might not perhaps be willing to let the peninsula go rather than pay a large sum of money to recover it.

Marquess Ito replied that he thought this very likely. The

total revenue, including customs, which it would yield to the Chinese Government he estimated at 2,000,000 taels, out of which the military expenditure of the province would have to be paid for. It was not a valuable piece of territory, and the maintenance of order would be a very troublesome matter for the Chinese. However that might be, the negotiations for the Commercial Treaty could not take place until Japan knew what she was to get for the retrocession, as any commercial concessions beyond those stipulated in the Treaty of Peace would have to be obtained by way of compensation for lowering her price for the Liao-tung.[55]

Satow had telegraphed the gist of his two talks with Ito to the Foreign Office and to O'Conor. The latter replied on September 1, that the Chinese could not pay the 50 millions that the Japanese wanted for Liaotung, "and *if* they pay will demand reduction of amount." Satow cabled back that he felt Japan would be willing to reduce the amount, and asked O'Conor whether he thought that if they acted together, they could bring China and Japan "into direct communication in the matter."[56] On September 10, Satow told Ito of O'Conor's telegram and of a telegram received from Lord Salisbury. He found that Ito had received "similar information" from Berlin, St. Petersburg and Peking. In a dispatch, Satow elaborated:

I have not yet learnt the terms of this communication, but Marquess Ito, on the 11th instant, informed me that he had heard from Berlin, St. Petersburgh, and Peking that the three Powers would propose a reduction of the special indemnity to 30,000,000 taels; and he was also led to expect that they would also object to the conditions making the evacuation depend on the payment of that indemnity and the conclusion of the Commercial Treaty. Japan would probably be reminded that a guarantee for the Commercial Treaty was provided for in Article VIII of the Treaty of Peace by the occupation of Wei-hai-wei.
His Excellency did not say what would be the attitude of the Japanese Government with regard to the expected proposals, but, from the manner in which he spoke, I am inclined to think that he will not make any strenuous objection to the reduction of the Liaotung indemnity to the amount named. I pointed out

to him the difficulty China must encounter in raising an additional 50,000,000 taels, and observed that increased commercial facilities, which would be of a continuing character, would be much more profitable to Japan in the end than the interest on a possible 20,000,000 taels. The opening of Wuchow, I urged, would be certain to lead to a considerable development of trade, of which Japanese merchants would have their share.[57]

On September 13, Satow discussed the Liaotung question with Saionji.

He said the three colleagues [the Ministers of France, Russia and Germany] had said the indemnity [for Japan's retrocession of Liaotung] should not exceed 30,000,000, and that the question ought to be arranged independently of Treaty of Shimonoseki, consequently could not be made to depend on payment of indemnity or conclusion of commercial Treaty. They asked that a definite date should be fixed, the evacuation to take place as soon as the special indemnity was paid.

"If the Japanese agree to this," Satow observed in a dispatch, "I am afraid that it will not be possible to demand the opening of Wuchow as a part consideration. For this reason I suggested the acceptance of 30,000,000, and a reply that, besides this, additional facilities commercially would be asked for and that Japan would carry on further negotiations in the matter with China direct."[58] Later Satow added in his diary that O'Conor had telegraphed that the evacuation must not depend on the payment of an extra indemnity.

On September 25, Saionji informed Satow that "it was clearly understood between himself and the representatives of the three Powers that the extra indemnity for the retrocession of the Liao-tung Peninsula would be entirely paid by China before the evacuation by the Japanese troops."[59]

On September 26, Ito told Satow his position about the abandonment of the Liaotung peninsula.

He had made up his mind to accept the 30,000,000 taels to which the three Powers had suggested the original demand should be reduced; but, of course, he was not suing to Russia to obtain a settlement for Japan. All he had done was to inquire whether the Powers could give an assurance that China would agree to the amount proposed by them. That was the only condition on which Japan would consent to surrender her acquisition of the mainland; and if it were not accepted, then, of course, Japan would remain in possession. [Viceroy] Li Hung-chang [Senior Grand Secretary and leading Chinese statesman] had said that his fellow-countrymen would never forgive him for having surrendered so much in signing the Treaty of Shimo-noseki, and that he could not exercise any influence in the matter. This convinced him that by direct negotiation Japan would obtain nothing.

I replied that I had learnt from Sir N. R. O'Conor that the Chinese were ready to close for 15,000,000 taels; and also that they would be disposed, if asked, to open the West River. But it was evident from the way in which his Excellency received this information that he was bent on getting the larger sum, in comparison with which the necessity of having to negotiate through the three Powers was a matter of quite secondary consideration, and that he cared nothing for Wuchow.

It also seemed to be quite clear that his Excellency had also resolved to abandon the two points previously insisted on by him, namely, the payment of the first instalment of the war indemnity, and the negotiation of the Commercial Treaty. As to the latter, indeed, he professed a certain measure of indifference; because, as he remarked, the principles on which it was to be elaborated were already embodied in the Treaty of Peace and the enjoyment by Japanese subjects of all the commercial privileges conceded as a consequence of the war was entirely independent of any further negotiations.[60]

On October 3, Satow discussed the Liaotung Peninsula with Gutschmid, who had called on him. "He thinks the Liaotung business will soon be settled. China will be induced to pay 80,000,000 taels on 8 November, taking the 30,000,000 out of what was subscribed in Paris and Petersburg."

That day Satow went to Saionji. "He confirmed my idea that the Japanese Government had made up their mind to agree not to insist upon the payment of the instalment of war indemnity and conclusion of commercial treaty before evacuating Liaotung," Satow recorded in his diary. "They had not yet heard what was the 'serious guarantee' which the Russian Government proposed to offer, and had consequently not given their final answer. . . ."

On October 7, Satow called on Ito to talk about the contents of a private letter which he had received from O'Conor.

Mentioned the article in *Blackwood* which is being reprinted in the *Japan Gazette*, which affirms that Li Hung-chang agreed to the cession of Liaotung because he knew the three Powers would interfere. Ito combatted this, on the ground that they did not know beforehand long enough what the Japanese terms would be. I said that the press had for some time before talked on Liaotung, Formosa and an indemnity, and everyone knew that whatever the people wished the government could rely on their thorough support for, as had been shown by the unanimity with which the Parliament voted the supplies. So the Powers certainly expected that Japan would make those demands. Besides, the correspondence (of the *Times*) from Tokio to London papers said the same thing.

In a dispatch Satow added that he had voiced to Ito his concern at the fact that Russia, Germany and France had emerged as arbitrators between China and Japan.

Their prestige had thus enormously increased while that of Japan had declined in a corresponding degree, which appeared to me of serious import for the future of Eastern Asia. . . . Was it not worth while to sacrifice a portion of the extra indemnity in order to put an end to this constant intervention of a humiliating character to both countries? Marquess Ito replied that the intervention of the three Powers must be regarded as a misfortune, but China had at no time shown any readiness to treat, and Japan had therefore been compelled to accept their intervention. . . . I observed that the three Powers . . . constituted themselves into a sort of Protectorate over China, as far at least as concerned her engagements towards Japan, and that it looked as if their interference would continue to increase and extend. Was it not possible to avoid this by dealing directly with China even at the sacrifice of a portion of the indemnity?

His Excellency replied that it was now too late. If at the commencement China had approached Japan, either by sending a special Envoy or by instructing their Minister at Tokio to negotiate, the present state of things would not have come about. China was no doubt anxious to shake off the burden of the tutelage under which she had placed herself, but he had no confidence in the good faith of any Chinese statesman with the exception of Li Hung-chang, and he had yet to learn that the latter possessed any real power. He might perhaps be made temporary use of as negotiator, but as soon as his usefulness in that capacity had been profited by to its full extent, he would be thrown on one side, and Japan would then be left without assurance that his agreements would be fulfilled. China, he considered, was unable to manage her affairs alone, and he preferred, under the circumstances, to rely on the three Powers. Of course, it was thoroughly well understood by the three Powers that if China failed to pay the amount demanded, Japan would remain in possession.[61]

On October 17, Satow called on Privy Councilor Soyeshima Taneomi, who was very anxious about the negotiations with the three intervening powers. Satow told him that he understood it had been settled that China should pay an indemnity, and when it had been received the Japanese troops would be withdrawn.

On November 19, Saionji told Satow that the Liaotung indemnity had been received by Japan and that she intended to evacuate by December 25.

On January 14, 1896, Satow wrote two lengthy dispatches on the efforts of politicians in Japan to make use of the foreign intervention and the resultant retrocession of the Liaotung peninsula and of the Korean fiasco to topple Ito. Satow reported:

The agitation assumed such dimensions that it seemed at one time possible that he might be forced to retire; but having strengthened his position by forming an alliance with the Lib-

eral party under the leadership of Count Itagaki, he was enabled to present a bold front to his opponents, and to meet them
at the opening of the Diet on the 28th ultimo. I have already had
the honour to acquaint your Lordship with the speech delivered
by the Emperor at the opening ceremony. The deliberations of
the Diet having been adjourned until the 8th instant, a motion
of censure was brought forward and discussed on the following
day. Its supporters belonged to the Progressive and Reform
parties ("Kaishinto" and "Kukushinto"), and it was framed not
without some ingenuity, so as to contain a censure of the Government for their management of the negotiations relating to
the cession and retrocession of the Liao-tung Peninsula, as well
as the less important question of the diplomatic errors of Japanese Agents in Corea. The motion dwelt on the fact that
within three weeks from the announcement by Imperial Rescript of the acquisition of the peninsula, a pledge for its retrocession was given to the intervening Powers, and blamed the
Ministers for being unable either to foresee or prevent the formation of a hostile alliance between France, Russia, and Germany,
or to confront that combination with a counter-alliance. The
attention of the Government had been drawn by the Diet to
the increase of the foreign squadrons in Eastern waters, but
they took no notice, and shut their eyes to possibility of an
intervention. In the debate that followed, these topics were enlarged upon by the Opposition speakers, one of whom asserted
that the German Minister had asked for an interview with the
Minister for Foreign Affairs on important business, but no notice had been taken of his request, and the Rescript announcing
the acquisition of the peninsula was issued on the following
day. Had the Cabinet been more attentive, the Emperor would
have been saved the indignity of issuing two inconsistent Re-
scripts within a few weeks of each other. He also expressed
his regret that the Cabinet had not taken the courageous course
of defying the Powers and accepting their challenge.

He was followed by a supporter of the Government, who
vindicated their prudence in not risking a foreign war at a
moment when the greater part of the troops were in China,
the fleet weakened by incessant work during a whole year, and
the Reserves at home indifferently armed. With whom could a
counter-alliance have been formed? (A voice, "With England").
Very well; but England had other matters to attend to, and she
might not have thought her interests sufficiently involved to

justify a combination with Japan against the three Powers. Japan feeling herself unable to cope with them had been obliged to abandon their acquisition, but had established an indisputable right to interfere in the event of any other Power attempting to seize it.

After a long debate, the closure having been moved and carried, the motion was rejected by 170 votes to 103—a result which had been foreseen from the beginning.[62]

In November of 1895, before the Liaotung indemnity had been received by Japan and prior to her evacuation of the peninsula, rumors had reached Satow of a secret treaty between Russia and China and of Russian designs on the very region, which she had denied Japan. He had recorded his first reaction to such a step on November 16, after a visit to Gutschmid.

Talked with him after dinner and expressed the belief that the Russians have no secret treaty with China about Port Arthur [on the Liaotung peninsula] etc. and he thinks so too, that it would have been indecent under the circumstances of their joint action with Germany and France.

Rumors about a secret treaty between Russia and China persisted, the *North China Daily News* actually publishing the text of the alleged treaty. Opinions differed whether it was genuine. Asaina, who came to Satow at his request on March 10, 1896 thought it was not genuine. On March 14, Satow reported the concern of Japanese legislators regarding Russo-Chinese relations in a dispatch to the Foreign Secretary.

The supposed Secret Treaty between Russia and China recently published in a Shanghai journal has naturally excited a good deal of interest here, but, as far as I can learn, the Japanese Government do not believe that the understanding which evidently exists has as yet been reduced to writing, and that the document in question, though in agreement with facts to a certain extent, must be regarded as a fabrication.

The matter has been taken up by the House of Representatives and was made the subject of an interpellation on the 11th instant in the following terms:

"The 'North China Daily News' has published what purports to be a Secret Treaty between Russia and China. What appears in a newspaper may not be entitled to be hastily accepted, but the action of a certain friendly and neighbouring power since the conclusion of the Treaty of Shimoneseki, the guaranteeing of the Chinese indemnity loan and the loan of Kiaochau Bay would be sufficient as omens of such a report as that which has appeared in the journal alluded to. I wish to ask whether the Government has ascertained whether such a Secret Treaty between Russia and China exists or not, what has been the result of their investigation, and, in case it should prove to be a fact, what steps do they propose to take in regard to it."

In addition to this, a question was put asking how it comes about that while the Government had not publicly communicated to the Imperial Diet the details of their proposals for the defence of the country, a foreign newspaper should have been already able to publish the whole scheme, which evidently must have been revealed by some one in authority.

In the course of a speech, explanatory of these two interpellations, Mr. Takagi made an allusion to the occupation of Port Hamilton by Great Britain in 1886, from which she was induced to retire in consequence of the representations made to her by Russia. In return, however, she obtained an undertaking from the latter never to occupy any portion of Corea.

It must be remarked in passing that the questions whether Russia is bound, under the changed circumstances, by the undertaking she gave to China, and through her to Great Britain in October 1886, and whether Great Britain will hold her to it, possess the greatest interest for Japan, as has been remarked to me by several Japanese belonging to the political world, and the telegraphic summary of Mr. Curzon's answer in the House of Commons on the 19th February has consequently given great satisfaction here.

The speaker went on to observe that the intervention of the three Powers in regard to Liao-tung was justified by them on the ground that its retention by Japan would disturb the balance of power and so be a danger to the peace of the Far East. Consequently Liao-tung was abandoned. If Russia, however, acquires such a preponderant influence as is manifestly bound to be the result of recent Russo-Chinese action, quite apart from

111

the question of the genuineness or otherwise of this document, the danger to the peace of Eastern Asia will not be less great. It was no longer merely a Corean question, but a Chinese question, and he did not hesitate to say that the very independence of Japan was at stake. What the Government were doing to meet this grave state of things, he did not know, but he called upon them to give such assurances as might satisfy the anxiety of the House.[63]

Japan concluded a commercial treaty with China. Okuma, whom Satow saw on October 22, spoke about the ratification of the treaty with China and about the "necessity of preventing the downfall of that country." As Satow reported in a dispatch:

The principal motive by which he had been actuated was to evince friendly feeling towards China, and so pave the way to a reconciliation by effacing from the minds of the Chinese the resentment caused by the late war. It was of supreme importance that Japan should be on good terms with China, and so be in a position to assist in preserving the Empire from dissolution.

I took this opportunity of assuring his Excellency that the rumours which had found currency in certain newspapers of an understanding between Great Britain and Russia for the partition of China were absolutely devoid of foundation, and that Great Britain, equally with Japan, desired to maintain the integrity of the Chinese Empire.

Count Okuma responded that he did not know what the aims of Russia might be. No doubt to conquer China would not be difficult, and Japan by herself might accomplish its subjugation, if there were no (? external) opposition to be reckoned with. But, in his view, it was indisputably to the general advantage that China should remain independent, and discharge the function for which she was so well fitted, that of a market for the commerce of the whole world.[64]

On November 5, Satow called on Okuma again. "He talked very freely about the military and naval preparations. I said to him that the half-million of men might excite suspicion as to Japanese intentions in certain quarters, as it was too large for mere self-defence, and he replied that it was in view of eventualities in China and Japan."

On November 13, Satow saw Okuma once more. "Okuma said the opinion at Peking was that the secret Russo-Chinese treaty published in China was not genuine, and his consul at Newchwang telegraphs that French syndicate have got concession for railway from Talienwan Bay to join the Russian line in Siberia. I said that probably the Treaty was concocted by those who knew there was a secret agreement, but were not acquainted with its contents."

On April 13, 1897, Lt. Col. Waters, Military Attaché at Petersburg, called on Satow.

He says Siberian railway will be completed in 1901, including the line through Tsitsihar and Kirin across Manchuria. About 10,000 troops are annually sent to Vladivostok by sea, in addition to those that come overland. This year the latter number will be 7,000. The East Siberian troops are of good quality, and the Russians are confident that they could give a good account of the Japanese. What they fear is English action, to be taken in support of the Japanese. There is a rumour that they are negotiating for a coaling station in the Philippines, which have been visited lately by a Russian general officer.

On April 15, Waters inspected the Japanese guard barracks. "Waters says Russians have 50,000 men in Eastern Siberia and two and a half years hence 80,000. Thinks with 25 of them he would knock the 136 Japanese guards into a cocked-hat."

On April 29, Satow talked with Okuma. He wrote in a dispatch the following day:

On taking leave yesterday of the Minister for Foreign Affairs, I observed to him that, at the time of my arrival here in August 1895, some anxiety was still felt with regard to the situation in the Far East arising out of the war with China, but that, owing to the prudence displayed by the Powers interested, peace had been preserved, and every month had given addi-

113

tional tranquility to this part of the world. I expressed the hope
that nothing was likely to occur to disturb the present condition of things.

His Excellency replied that all the efforts of the Japanese
Government were directed towards the maintenance of peace,
and that trouble could only arise from two possible quarters.
As far as he could judge, China had learnt little or nothing
from her experiences of 1894 and 1895, and, if left to herself,
was not likely to develop warlike tendencies. It would only
be in the case that some other Power egged her on to make
preparations for a war of revenge. He was very anxious, consequently, to avoid all possible occasion of friction and to cultivate friendly relations with China, and with that object had
urged Prince Kung to arrange for the immediate payment of
the balance of the indemnity, so that the occupation of Wei-
hai-wei might be terminated. As long as Japanese troops continued there it was to be expected that complaints would be
made from time to time that the Japanese were violating the
Treaty of peace by crossing neutral ground and taking sur-
veys in Shantung. China would also be a gainer by paying the
balance of the indemnity at once, as she could easily borrow at
5 per cent, and, moreover, would receive back all that she had
already paid to Japan on account of interest. He hoped, therefore, that the report from Peking that Sir Robert Hart was
engaged in negotiating a loan of 100,000,000 taels might prove
to be correct. The other point where difficulty might be apprehended was Corea, if a Power he would not name should
endeavour to disturb the existing balance of influence. . . .[65]

On December 23, Satow called on Nishi. "Japanese replied
to Russia's communication about Port Arthur that they believed the assurance that it was only temporary, and would
take note of the declaration," Satow reported to Lord Salisbury. "Lobanof always declared Russia could keep Vladivostock open, and did not want Port Arthur."[66]

On December 27, Sannomiya came to Satow.

"Sannomiya very anxious to know whether I had heard anything more about the project of Russia lending China money
to pay off indemnity and so get Wei-hai-wei freed," Satow
noted in his diary. "Replied that it was a newspaper report,

and where was Russia to get the money from except from France."[1]

On January 8, 1898, Russel L. Dunn, a mining engineer who had recently been at Vladivostok, came to see Satow, to tell him that he had discovered within twenty miles of Vladivostok a vast coal field on the railway line, and that he would be able to put coal on board in Vladivostok.

If no war breaks out he will be able to furnish coal this summer. Russia which has hitherto depended on Japanese coal will then be independent. Close by is the province of Manchuria with 25,000,000 of hardy Chinese, the best physique in the country. When these resources are developed the position of Russia on the Pacific coast will be as strong as that of the United States on the west of the Atlantic. She will not care what ports other Powers may have acquired, and the South of China will be a matter of indifference to her. The proposed railway across Manchuria is only a blind, the real line will come to Kiakhta. The construction of the line West from Stretensk [?] is being proceeded with energetically, and probably has got to Chita. Later on, when established in Corea and with 100,000 Russian troops in Eastern Siberia (she has now 50,000) arming and disciplining the Manchurians, she will probably attempt the acquisition of Kiushiu. He does not take the Japanese at their own valuation, but they have done wonders in the last thirty years and will make further progress. He has no fear however of their industrial competition. Very anxious the Russians should not know he has been to see me. Vladivostock can be kept open with the ice-breaker they have.

On February 7, Satow saw Ito.

As to Russian troops having marched into Kirin he was not very clear. (Probably the Intelligence Department had not told him.) But he thought it quite possible. The Russians are entitled to guard their railway lines, which indeed is necessary. They are to bring it down to Talienwan, and the whole of Manchuria will be theirs.

[1] Satow has a question mark after "from," with "except from France" as an afterthought.

115

On March 10, d'Anethan came to Satow "to ask whether the news that China had been asked by Russia to lease Port Arthur and Talienwan Bay was true. I told him it seemed so." On March 11, Komura told Satow that [Sir Claude] Mac-Donald [the British Minister at Peking] had said to Yano Fumio, the Japanese Minister to China, that "Russians had declared the object of the proposed lease and railway was to prevent foreign aggression, and they asked him to get Lord Salisbury to give an undertaking that he means no aggression, which could then be alleged as a ground for refusing the Russian demand." Satow noted that it seemed the Russian demand had been presented on the third, "with a request for an answer in five days."

On March 12, Asaina came to Satow. "I told him to try and find out whether the Russians have informed his government of their desire to lease Port Arthur and Talienwan Bay, and whether the Cabinet have made any observations to Russia on the subject."

Komura came to Satow that day. "Asked him whether Russia had informed them of plans in regard to Port Arthur, and whether they had remonstrated. He replied in the negative to both questions, but I am not confident that he spoke the truth."

On March 16, Ito asked Satow whether Russia had got Port Arthur and Talienwan Bay, and whether Great Britain opposed her getting them.

I said I did not know how the negotiations were proceeding, but it was difficult for us to offer effective opposition, because of Russia's advantageous position by land, but that Great Britain would have preferred that no one should acquire ports, only we could not undertake the world [whole?] world as our antagonists at once.

On March 19, Satow conferred with Ito.

I asked if there had been any interchange of views as to Port Arthur etc. to which he replied no.[67] I asked whether Russia would certainly get that. He thought she would, China being unable to resist. I expressed my regret at all this. . . . I rose to go, and added what a pity it was that Japan had not insisted with China on her stipulating not to cede to any other power, to which he replied that he had not expected the present development to take place.

On March 25, Satow went to see Okuma.

He says that when the Russians notified their going to Port Arthur, they said it was because of Kiaochou [which Germany had leased], and did not give any undertaking about leaving again; and that the Japanese Government simply said 'very well.' (But I think he is wrong). That the people, electors are indignant about the Russians taking Manchuria; if any people have a right it is the Japanese.

On March 26, Satow reviewed the course of Far Eastern international relations in a very confidential dispatch to Lord Salisbury. He wrote:

Since the intervention of the three Powers in 1895, which resulted in the retrocession of the Liaotung Peninsula, Japan seems to have taken up an attitude of present resignation to the inevitable, accompanied by strenuous efforts to place her military and naval establishments on such a footing as to enable her in the future to resist any attempt at intervention of the same kind. It was Russia that Japan feared most of the three Powers, and her resolve to avoid a collision extended also to her position in Corea, a disposition that the unfortunate murder of the Queen, in which Japanese officials were implicated, strengthened still further.

The gradual acquisition by Russia of a preponderating influence in the peninsula, especially after the flight of the King to the Russian Legation, led to the negotiations carried on almost simultaneously at Moscow and Seoul, the ostensible effect of which was to place the two Powers in a position of equality.

This balance of power was, however, disturbed by the engagement of a large number of Russian military instructors, and finally, by the Convention of November last, which put the finances of the country under Russian control.

As your Lordship is aware, the Japanese Government remonstrated against the engagement of military instructors; but they were told that the promise to lend these officers was prior to the Convention of Moscow, and that they could not be withdrawn.

It would appear that Japan silently acquiesced in this answer, nor did she, as far as I have learnt, oppose the engagement of M. Alexeieff otherwise than by endeavouring to put pressure on the Corean Government through the Japanese Minister at Seoul.

The Japanese Government trusted to time to produce a spontaneous revulsion of Corean feeling against the too active interference of the Russian Chargé d'Affaires in the affairs of the kingdom, and this expectation has recently been realized, with the results that the Russian Government have withdrawn the military instructors and the financial adviser.

Whatever the ostensible reason for going to war with China may have been, there can be little doubt that the main object was to anticipate the completion of the Siberian Railway and to prevent Russia gaining free access to the Pacific Ocean.

The Treaty of Shimonoseki accordingly gave to Japan the Liaotung Peninsula, including Port Arthur and Talienwan Bay, with the whole coast of the Gulf of Pechili from the Corean boundary to the Treaty Port of Newchwang.

By this stipulation the object aimed at was held to have been attained.

Then followed the intervention of the three Powers, on the ground that the permanent occupation of the Liao-tung Peninsula by Japan would be detrimental to the peace of the Far East, and the submission of Japan.

Russia now asks from China, under the form of a lease of Port Arthur and Talienwan Bay, coupled with permission to construct a branch from the Siberian Railway to these ports, a grant of the very territory from which she summarily ejected Japan, on the ground that her possession would be a standing menace to the independence of the Peking Government.

In spite of the feeling which this news has aroused in Japan, as evinced by numerous and repeated articles in the press and the conversation of Japanese outside the Cabinet, it seems that the Japanese Government have remained passive, just as they were silent when the occupation of Kiao-chau by Germany was announced, and as they simply 'took note' of the Russian Government's communication last December that they had obtained the permission of China to use Port Arthur as a temporary anchorage for their squadron.

If Marquis Ito has addressed any observations to the Russian Government on the phase that this temporary occupation has now assumed, he certainly has not taken the outside world into his confidence; and the answer given by him by Baron Nishi and by Mr. Komura, to my questions, has been that no communications have passed between the two Governments. I think it, however, very possible that in informing the Japanese Minister at St. Petersburgh of the intention to withdraw M. Alexeieff and the military instructors, some intimation may have been given that, in return for the restoration of equality of influence in Corea, Japan would be expected to acquiesce in the recent demands on China in respect of Manchuria.

I do not think that, under the circumstances, Japan would openly oppose the action of Russia on her own account; and though she doubtless would be pleased to see Great Britain place a check on Russian progress, the Government would be unwilling to associate themselves with the action of Her Majesty's Government direct to this end. The exclusion of Russia from Port Arthur, while that Power was at liberty to lease Talienwan Bay and to bring a branch of the Siberian Railway to that place, would seem to them a result of comparative unimportance, especially as they have been informed that what Russia is aiming at is a naval base; and they moreover hold that the construction of the railway will eventually be followed by the acquisition of Manchuria.

I understand that your Lordship thinks it possible that Japan may have obtained some undertaking from Russia that Port Arthur should not be used as a naval base in return for allowing her to occupy Wei-hai-wei; and the question put to me in your Lordship's telegram No. 18 of the 23rd March, was whether, if the Japanese Government were made acquainted with the policy of Her Majesty's Government, they could be prevented from committing themselves to such an engagement.

In spite of the inquiries which I have made, I cannot detect any indications of such an understanding being contemplated; and it seems to me unlikely that the Japanese would regard the presence of Russia at Wei-hai-wei as in any way compensated by Port Arthur remaining unfortified.

They would rather see it in the possession of any other Power, even of Germany; but if China cannot maintain hold of

119

it, they would prefer to see it occupied by Great Britain. An undertaking such as that offered in your Lordship's telegram No. 90 to Her Majesty's ambassador at St. Petersburgh would not seem to them to go far enough, because they would think that Talienwan Bay could be hereafter fortified, in spite of present promises.

The Japanese Government, and especially the present Minister-President, are anxious to avoid any kind of foreign complication.

They have the appearance of being thoroughly disheartened, and they do not seem to appreciate the value of diplomacy, except as a preliminary to the use of force.[68]

On March 30 d'Anethan visited Satow. "Told him we had strongly opposed Russia's taking Port Arthur, and offered to keep out of the Gulf of Pechili if she would abstain." That day Satow also talked with Ito and Inouye.

Ito told me that Russia had communicated officially the cession in usufruct of Port Arthur and Talienwan Bay, also that China at the beginning of the negotiation had asked Japan for a declaration that she had no aggressive intentions. He refused to give this, and said they could quite well give the assurance themselves. Told him that the same request had been made to us. . . . Inouye. . . remarked that Russia neither mentioned the term of years, nor extent of territory. Only said 'adjacent.' That might mean anything.

On March 31 Satow talked to Komura.

He confirmed what Ito told me. They have not yet returned any answer to Russia. The Russian Chargé d'Affaires at Peking told Yano that Talienwan would be partly used as a naval station. Yano has telegraphed nothing about term of years or extent of territory. They have nothing but press telegrams.

On April 1, Satow received a telegram from the British Foreign Office authorizing him to communicate to the Japanese Government that Russian occupation of Port Arthur had forced the British to demand from China the lease of Wei-hai-wei whenever the Japanese evacuated that fortress.[69]

The Japanese, who had agreed to this beforehand, were delighted, fearing that Russia or Germany would move in if Great Britain did not. When Satow saw Ito about this matter that day, Ito "said he thought unnecessary to give any answer to Russian communication about Port Arthur etc., as it had not taken the form of a consultation."

On April 5, Satow visited Inouye. Afterwards he recorded in his diary:

Japanese naval and military preparations not ready yet; though the scale had been enlarged, the body has not been filled up. Five years hence when the Siberian railway is finished, a great struggle will take place. Then with the coal supplies under the control of England and Japan, the three Powers will be able to do nothing. They did not wish to excite the suspicions of the three Powers. I said that such suspicions did more good than harm; it made the three Powers hesitate. The Emperor of Russia had made a speech in which he said that he had been very anxious about Japan, but that his mind was now relieved. That meant, I said, that as long as there was an idea that Great Britain and Japan had an understanding, he was afraid, but relieved of that anxiety he had at once laid hands on Port Arthur and Talienwan Bay.

As the instability and weakness of the Chinese government raised the possibility of the break-up of China, Russian influence at the Chinese Court worried the British and the Japanese. On February 15, 1899, Ito told Satow about his talk with Li Hung-chang.

He had told Li Hung-chang he was accused of being pro-Russian. The fact was that when he was in Moscow he was consulted about the concession for a railway through Manchuria, but did not himself take any part in negotiating the Treaty, but of course this made it impossible for him to oppose it afterwards. He had said to Li, "Of course you see Manchuria will become Russian." "No," said Li, "only they have permission to build a railway." Ito said, "No one will believe you do not see what the result is, and that is why people accuse you of being pro-Russian."

121

Ito then showed Satow the draft of his letter to Lord Beresford, in which he asserted that the Chinese could not be governed except by people of their own race.

I objected that this was historically incorrect [Satow recorded in his diary]. They had been conquered and ruled by the Golden Horde, by the Mongols and Manchus. To this he replied that the conquerors were of the same race. I said that the Russians aimed at acquiring the whole of China North of the Yellow River. "Dreams," he answered. "But Manchuria," I said, "they will absorb." "Yes," he replied, "because the population is thin, but it will take them a long time, and they cannot bring millions from Russia to fill it up."

On April 20, Satow met with Aoki.

He said the Consul at Newchwang had told their men that the Russians demanded the whole of China North of the Yellow River; no concessions, land or anything else to be given except to Russians; that as a condition of recognizing our sphere of influence to be the Yangtze valley. . . . I replied that privately I had long been of opinion that China would not hold together. . . . Russia he observed had force on the spot, and could enforce her own will, but how could we over such an enormous area as the drainage basin of the Yangtze. He wished he knew what Lord Salisbury thought. I rejoined that I did too.

On October 27, Asaina came to Satow.

Says the Japanese fleet is in full fighting order. Nishi goes to Peking to counteract Russia. Aoki annoyed with the military people, because they do not give him full information as to what their spies discover. He generally tells both Army and Navy Ministers that their departments and forces are not up to the mark; hence ill-feeling. . . . Asaina thinks that perhaps the state of things in April next may be such that I shall be unable to go on leave. But, he added, Japan can do nothing alone. The naval people would like to go in at the Russians.

On December 6, d'Anethan visited Satow. "Seems much interested in the possibility of complications between Japan and Russia in the spring. . . ." On January 10, 1900 Asaina came. "He says both Japan and Russia are desirous of peace, and that Japan will submit to anything rather than make a row." On January 24, Satow talked with A. G. Churchill, the British Military Attaché, and with Whitehead about the likelihood of war between Japan and Russia.

Churchill thinks the Japanese will stand almost anything rather than go to war with Russia, and doubts whether Russia wants war with Japan, unless she thinks the navy of the latter is getting too strong and that it would be wise to crush it without delay. The strategical value of the Siberian railway has been exaggerated; it could be used to mass troops previously, but would not suffice for transport of provisions and munitions during a war. The Japanese might perhaps succeed in a first campaign, but it would be only a campaign, as Russia would go on, and never make peace until she had defeated them. [The Russian Military Attaché Boris] Vannovsky's cue while here was to depreciate the Japanese army. Though he thinks any alliance between Japan and England is greatly to be deprecated, he sees that a war between Japan and Russia at the present moment might be to our advantage. Whitehead thinks a badly beaten Japan would weaken our position at Peking.

Satow added in his diary:

With d'Anethan I had a little talk yesterday. He sees no reason to suppose that the union of the three Powers against Japan has ceased to have effect. I said some thought it had faded away, others thought it still subsisted. Germany did not get out of it what she had expected, and was annoyed when the Russians and French effected a loan to China to her exclusion. On the other hand, the acquisition of Kiaochou was made after exchange of private telegrams between the two Emperors, their Foreign Ministers being kept ignorant.

On the whole I think Ito, Yamagata and Matsugata between them will try to keep from going to war, and I do not see the man who is capable of turning them out and heading a warlike cabinet.

On February 22 Clements came to Satow. "Clements brought the *Chicago Record* with an absurd letter from

123

Petersburg signed Ivan Ivanovitch [Chagin?], about Russo-Japanese relations, cooperation of England with the latter, winding up by saying that I daily had conferences with the Japanese Ministers at the Palace and asked for audience of the Mikado. Told him it was pure invention; that I did not believe in war between Japan and Russia, and had done nothing to stir up strifes."

On March 4, Satow told George Ernest Morrison, correspondent of the London *Times*, about the tension between Japan and Russia in November and reiterated his belief "that the Japanese would not take the initiative, at any rate not before 1903."

PART TWO
1900-1904

The Manchurian Convention between Russia and China

RUSSIAN ARMIES overran Manchuria during the Boxer Rebellion and overcame Chinese resistance. On November 5, 1900, Sir Ernest Satow, now British Minister at Peking, was informed by Shiba Shiro, a Japanese writer and politician, that "a day or two ago the Russian Minister informed Prince Ch'ing [I-k'uang, chief member of the Foreign Office and Chinese Plenipotentiary] that Manchuria being now pacified, the Russian Government desired to have new Chinese Governor appointed." Baron A. d'Anthouard, the French Chargé d'Affaires, stated: "Russian policy in Manchuria is to induce the Chinese officials to return and administer the country for them, as they find it impossible to do. This is the meaning of nonannexation, a sort of unofficial protectorate." (11/11)

The withdrawal of Russian forces from Manchuria was not necessarily to China's advantage. Satow talked to Baron Moritz Freiherr von Czikann, the Austro-Hungarian Minister to Peking: "As to the Russian withdrawal, he thinks they [the Chinese?] have badly blundered: they partly need them to suppress trouble in Manchuria, partly to put pressure on the other Powers to withdraw." (11/10)

On January 2, 1901 Satow forwarded to Lord Henry Charles Keith Petty-Fitzmaurice, the Marquess of Lansdowne, the new Foreign Secretary, a copy of the temporary Russo-Chinese agreement, signed at Port Arthur on November 22, 1900, and awaiting final ratification in Peking.

Korea and Manchuria Between Russia and Japan

His Majesty the Emperor of Russia, desiring to preserve for ever unimpaired the friendly relations between Russia and China, has consented to allow the Chinese Tartar General and the officials under him to return to their various posts in the Province of Fêngt'ien [the southernmost of the three Manchurian provinces, and containing the Manchu capital Mukden] which have been occupied by the Russian troops, and there to resume their former admirable government. Accordingly, His Majesty the Emperor has appointed Admiral [Evgenii] A[lexeieff] Governor of the territories leased to Russia in the Liaotung Peninsula, placed in general control of the land forces and commanding the Pacific Squadron, to be his Plenipotentiary, and to hold conferences with the Tartar General of Fêngt'ien with a view to effecting a speedy settlement.

Tsêng [Chi] the Tartar General of Fêngt'ien, has appointed as his Plenipotentiaries Chou Mien, the Taotai, Jui An, the Sub-Prefect, and Chiang Wên-hsi, the District Magistrate, with authority to discuss the matter in all its bearings, and we have now arrived at Port Arthur.

Admiral A[lexeieff] has appointed Kúo, Resident at Port Arthur, for the control of all matters affecting the two countries, as his Representative to confer with the Representatives of China and draw up a temporary Agreement.

We have now respectively affixed our signature to an Agreement in nine clauses, which we respectfully submit to Admiral A[lexeieff] and the Tartar General Tsêng for their indorsement and due affixing of their seals.

The clauses are as follows:

1. Upon the return of the Tartar General Tsêng to his post he must undertake to protect his province and take steps to pacify it, and must further see that no resistance be offered to the construction of the railroad.

2. Russia having occupied posts in Mukden and other places with a view to protecting the railroad and pacifying the province, the Tartar General and local officials must treat the Russians kindly and render them every possible assistance, e.g., in providing them with lodging or provisions.

3. Throughout the Province of Fêngt'ien rebellions have occurred on the part of the soldiery, and the railroad has been destroyed. It is therefore the Tartar General's duty to disband his various troops and dispossess them of their arms. Those who accept these conditions will be exempt from investigation re-

specting their former errors. The munitions of war in arsenals not occupied by the Russians must likewise be delivered over in their entirety to the Russian military officials.

4. Places in Fêngt'ien which have not been occupied by Russia where forts and barricades were erected must be inspected by Russian and Chinese officials in conjunction, and in their presence dismantled. Arsenals for the storage of gunpowder when not required by the Russians must be dealt with in the same manner.

5. Ying K'ou [the port of Newchwang] and other places are being administered by Russian officials pending the time when the Russian Government shall be completely satisfied as to the pacification of the country upon which it shall be permitted to the Chinese officials to resume their functions.

6. The various cities and market towns throughout Fêngt'ien Province must carry out the instructions of the Tartar General of Fêngt'ien respecting the maintenance of bodies of cavalry or infantry for police purposes and for the protection of merchants. The villages of the province are likewise entirely under the Tartar General's orders, and it will be for his discretion to determine how many men are to be dispatched and the nature of their equipment, and act accordingly.

7. It is expedient that a Russian official with general powers of control should be stationed at Mukden for the settlement of all questions affecting the two countries between the Tartar General on the one hand and the Governor of the Liaotung Peninsula on the other. The Tartar General must give the official Resident at Mukden full information respecting any important measure he may make.

8. Should the police force maintained by the Tartar General at Mukden and elsewhere be insufficient for some particular emergency, the Tartar General will immediately communicate with the Russian official Resident at Mukden—no matter whether the place concerned be on the sea coast or in the interior of the province—and invite Russia to dispatch reinforcements to his assistance.

9. Should any dispute arise in connection with the interpretation of any of the above eight clauses, the Russian text is to be accepted as the standard.

The above temporary Agreement shall be put into operation immediately after the return of Tsêng, the Tartar General, to Mukden; but should the Tartar General, in conjunction with the

Governor of the Liaotung Peninsula, subsequently agree upon any additions or alterations that would conduce to the advantage of both nations, it will be open to them to put such into operation if found feasible.[70]

Satow forwarded also the petition of Chou Mien, who had been delegated by the Tartar General Tsêng Chi to affect the settlement with Admiral Alexeieff, the commander of the Russian land forces and the Pacific Squadron, to Li Hung-chang, Chinese plenipotentiary and Viceroy of Chihli. "Now that a temporary Agreement in nine clauses has been drafted, your petitioner's grief pierces his very soul, but what alternative has he," Chou wrote. "Now that the Hu rebels overrun the country the people have no resources left, and if the villagers are forbidden to carry arms the life of every soul in the province is in danger."[71]

On January 8, Satow reported that Alexeieff allowed the Chinese Imperial Maritime Customs to keep a recognized Chinese Department on the spot, and, "as regards revenue collected, what is eventually to become of it depends on the settlement of the Russo-Chinese question, and does not necessarily raise any international question, unless or until China defaults."[72]

On January 25, Satow met with Li, who expressed concern at the Russian attempts to extend control over railroads.

They were now offering to take over portion of line outside Great Wall in part payment for damages to the Manchurian line, but he (Li) had refused. I said he should stick to that, and I knew he was strong enough to refuse sometimes what Russians asked. He gave me quite clearly to understand that the Chinese had borrowed the money from the bondholders to construct line to Shin-ming-ting and Newchwang to keep the Russians out. If Russia gets possession of the line to Peking, China is done for. (1/25/1901)

On February 5, Satow telegraphed to the Foreign Secretary that he had learned from Komura Jutaro, the Japanese Minister, that the Russian Government insisted upon the immediate ratification by China of an agreement with Russia and demanded the following conditions for permanent settlement:

1. The leased territory in the peninsula of Liaotung shall include the city of Kinchow.
2. Provides for the appointment, only after Russia's consent has been obtained, of the Governor-General of the Manchurian Provinces.
3. Agreement as to the strength of police force which the Chinese shall maintain will be made between Russia and China.
4. The supervision of the above police force will be intrusted to a Russian officer on the staff of each Governor-General.
5. Adjustment of the indemnity for military expenses will be made here; the damage to the railway is, however, not included.
6. Russia is anxious of purchasing the railway to the north of Shanhaikwan, the purchase-money to be deducted from the amount to be claimed as war indemnity. The balance and interest of this is to be paid from the Customs revenues in Manchuria.
7. Custom-houses in Manchuria to be controlled and managed by Russia.
8. Manchuria to be evacuated by Russian troops by degrees.[73]

Russian reluctance to withdraw from Manchuria without first obtaining special rights in that region, aroused the opposition of the other Powers. On February 5 Komura had expressed the wish of his Government "that an effective opposition should be made to the proposed arrangement by a combination of the Powers."[74] On February 15, he spoke to Satow again. "Said England, Japan and Germany were giving the same advice to China about Manchuria," Satow recorded in his diary. "Showed him what I am going to say to Li and Ch'ing on this point. He has instructions to take similar step, and will send an interpreter up."

From Hankow the Acting Consul-General E. H. Fraser reported to London that the Viceroy was advising the Court not to sign the Agreement on Manchuria, while Russia was

131

pressing upon the Chinese Minister at St. Petersburg, and that the Viceroy was "anxious to know how far His Majesty's Government will go in supporting China in her refusal to sign." Fraser wrote:

I have reported to Sir E. Satow the terms of this Agreement, which secures Russian occupation of Manchuria until the completion of the railway, and gives Russia control of the Chinese military and police forces in the three provinces.

Foreigners other than Russians are excluded from employment in the military or naval forces in Northern China; nor may China, without Russia's consent, grant in her territories bordering on Russia any railway, mining, or other concessions; China may not even herself build railways in those territories unless Russia assents. In addition to the right to build a railway to Peking as far as the Great Wall, the Agreement further guarantees to Russia, the Manchurian Railway and its employés compensation for losses which may take the form of modifications of the present contracts or further concessions.[75]

Meanwhile Sir C. Scott, the British Minister at St. Petersburg, reported from the Russian capital after seeing Foreign Minister Count Vladimir Lamsdorff: "As regards the eventuality of the conclusion of a special arrangement or Convention, with regard to conditions for the evacuation of Manchuria by the Russian troops, he was only able to assert *for the present* that there existed a *modus vivendi* concluded between Russian military authorities and the Chinese local authorities to regulate certain conditions of the provisional administration of Manchuria."[76]

On February 26, Satow forwarded the substance of an additional agreement concluded at Port Arthur on January 31 by the Russian Commander-in-chief and the Chinese Military Governor of Moukden.

1. All official residences in Moukden to be handed back to the Chinese officials, who will act in accordance with the terms arranged.

2. Chinese officials to be allowed to go to their posts in all

those towns taken by the Russians. They may establish police forces, in large places to the number of 500 men, in medium sized places to the number of 300 men, in others, 200. These police may carry arms, but must be provided with distinguishing badges stamped by the Russian and Chinese authorities.

3. Robbers and rebels taken by the Russian soldiers are to be handed over to the local officials to be dealt with by Chinese and Russian law (sic).

4. Yingkow customs duties and *li-kin* are to be collected temporarily by Russia, and the Imperial commands awaited as to the application of such funds after a Treaty has been made between Russia and China. All other sources of revenue are to be under the control of the Military Governor.

5. The western roads of the province are at present disturbed and unsafe. Russian troops to be withdrawn from those parts, so that traffic may be resumed. Yingkow being now closed by ice, the products of the northern roads—tobacco, hemp, beans, and grain—have no exit. The rail to Port Arthur can be used for their transport.

6. Russia may establish a Resident at Moukden, and two Deputies for international affairs, who will transact such business in co-operation with Chinese Deputies.

7. The duty of the Taotai of Yingkow is to control the customs. The Russian authorities are at present collecting the revenue of the foreign custom-house. The Military Governor may order the Taotai to return and act in co-operation with them.

8. The disbanded Chinese troops for the most part took their weapons with them in their flight. The Russian Military authorities need not send to search them out. The Military Governor will dispatch officials in all directions to find them, and so obviate any alarm to the populace.

9. The Military Governor has no plenipotentiary powers. The result of the negotiations of Prince Ching and Grand Secretary Li must be awaited. Russia is desirous of a lasting peace.

10. The Military Governor Tsêng Chi is to remain for four years in office in this province to reorganize public affairs after the late disturbances.[77]

H. E. Fulford, the British Consul at Newchwang who had sent the text to Satow, noted that its wording was not exact, having been written down from memory. "Certain of its provisions point to its being intended for more than a temporary arrangement," he added.

The following day Satow forwarded a telegram he had received from the Acting Consul-General at Hankow. It read:

The Viceroy's Secretary came by instruction to see me yesterday, and showed me a summary the Viceroy had received by telegram of the Treaty which is being pressed at St. Petersburgh upon the Chinese Minister. His Excellency urges that the signature of this Treaty means granting exclusive privileges, and inquires how far His Majesty's Government would support China if she refused to do so.

The following are the provisions:

1. Manchuria to be restored.

2. Until the last four provisions of the Treaty are carried out, Russia will maintain an additional force for the protection of the Manchurian Railway.

3. Assistance to be given to China by Russia in keeping order.

4. No army to be maintained by China until the completion of the Manchurian railway, and then Russia is to be consulted as to the strength of the army. No munitions of war are to be imported.

5. If Russia complains of any official, however high his rank, he shall be cashiered. The strength of the police is to be settled with Russia; they are not to possess artillery, and no foreigners other than Russians are to be employed in it.

6. No foreigners are to be employed in connection with the sea or land forces in North China.

7. Abolition of Chinese administration in the town of Chinchou.

8. China is not to grant any mining, railway or other rights without the permission of Russia in the territory upon the Russian border, i.e., Manchuria, Mongolia, Ili, Yarkand, etc., and Russia's permission is to be obtained before China builds railways in these. No lease is to be granted to any but Russians outside of Newchwang.

9. The indemnities of the Powers and the expenses incurred by Russia in Manchuria are to be dealt with on the same footing.

10. With reference to the damages suffered by the Manchurian Railway and its employés, these shall be made good by the . . . (here the meaning is obscure).

11. Instead of this, Concessions may be accepted or existing contracts modified.

12. Building of a railway line, on the same terms as the Manchurian Railway, from the main or branch line in the direction of Peking up to the Great Wall.[78]

Satow added:

Confirmation is given to this information by what I ascertain here. Pressure is being brought by the Russian Legation on Li Hung-chang to obtain his consent. The whole question has evidently been referred to the Court.

I have sent a message to the Viceroy through Mr. Fraser, saying that, in the event of China agreeing to this Treaty, Russia's example will form a precedent for other Powers, and that China should refuse these terms if it is desired to prevent her disruption.[79]

The next day Satow clarified articles 10 and 11 of the Manchurian Agreement:

Article 10 provides that compensation shall be settled with the Railway Company with regard to the damage done to the Manchurian Railway and suffered by its employés.

Article 11 states that the form such compensation may take is the granting of new Concessions or modifying of contracts now existing.[80]

Satow telegraphed also that he had been informed by his Japanese colleague, "that Li Hung-chang told him yesterday that he did not consider that the proposed Manchurian Convention impairs the sovereignty of China in that region, and has, therefore, pretty well decided to accede to it."[81] Komura had made "strong remonstrances," but to no effect.

On March 1, the Marquess of Lansdowne communicated to Satow that the Chinese Government had requested by Imperial Edict the mediation of Great Britain, Germany, Japan and the United States in regard to the proposed Russo-Chinese Agreement. He had replied to the Chinese Minister that Great Britain had not yet the full text of the agreement and must confer with the other Powers before acting, but "assumed that China could not commit herself in the meantime, and that she would await the answer to her request for mediation before she took any further steps."[82] In a confidential letter Lansdowne added that Prince Ch'ing and Li Hung-chang felt that the agreement would not deprive China of any part of her territory or financial rights. "They therefore hoped that the foreign Powers would not oppose it, as if they did there might be a rupture of the relations between China and Russia which might prove detrimental to the interests of the Powers, and the temporary Russian occupation might become a permanent one."[83]

Meanwhile Fulford reported from Newchwang, and Satow sent on to London, the assurances of Vice-Admiral Alexeieff that the Russo-Chinese Agreement concerning Manchuria "was merely a temporary measure for providing provisional government of the country."

Russian assurances notwithstanding, Great Britain sought to encourage Chinese opposition to Russian demands. On March 4, Lansdowne instructed Satow to "strongly urge upon Li Hung-chang that he should not commit himself further in regard to Manchurian Agreement until he has received the replies of the four Powers, whose mediation has been formally applied for by the Imperial Government."[84] Satow telegraphed to Fraser at Hankow:

Li Hung-chang has telegraphed to the Chinese Minister in London saying that he hopes the Powers will not oppose the Agreement, which, he considers, will not deprive China of any territorial rights.

Inform Viceroy [Chang Chih-tung] of this, and point out that it will immediately place Manchuria entirely in the position of a protected State, i.e., Russian, and that, by interdicting to China construction of railways in Mongolia and the New Dominion, it lays the foundation for the future absorption of these regions in the same manner as Manchuria, where also the Russians began by getting China to agree to let no other Power construct railways in that province but Russia.

You should endeavour to discover how Li's attitude is viewed by the Viceroy.[85]

In reply to Lansdowne's telegram Satow reported that the following telegram was sent on March 2 to His Majesty's Consul at Nanking:

The effect of the Convention proposed by Russia for the future government of Manchuria will be to deprive China of her sovereignty over that region, and the prohibition to construct railways in Mongolia and Turkestan is equivalent to abandoning those regions into the bargain.
This Treaty will form a bad precedent, and will probably lead to the partition of China. You should therefore urge the Viceroy to memorialize the Emperor against it, and add that, unless prevented by orders from the Throne, Li is about to sign.[86]

He received the following reply from Mr. Sundius:

The Emperor has already been memorialized by the Viceroy to refuse assent to the Russian Convention, and his Excellency earnestly begs that China's refusal will receive the strong support of the British, Japanese, and United States' Governments.[87]

That day Satow telegraphed the full text of the agreement— an English translation of the Chinese text, "which is evidently translated from the Russian."

1. The Emperor of Russia, being anxious to give evidence of his friendly feeling towards China, is willing to forget the hostile acts committed in Manchuria, and to hand back the whole of that country to China—its administration to be carried on as heretofore.
2. Under Article 6 of the Manchurian Railway Agreement, the Administration is authorized to maintain troops for the protection of the line. The country, however, being at present in an unsettled condition, and such troops few in number, a body of soldiers must be retained until order is restored, and until China shall have carried out the provisions of the last four Articles of the present Convention.

3. In the event of grave disturbances the Russian garrisons will afford China every assistance in suppressing the same that lies in their power.

4. In the recent attacks against Russia, Chinese troops having taken a prominent part, China agrees, pending the completion of the line and its opening to traffic, not to establish an army (in those provinces). She will consult with Russia as to the number of troops she may subsequently wish to establish there. The importation of munitions of war into Manchuria is prohibited.

5. With a view to safeguarding the interests of the territory in question, China will, on representations being made by Russia, at once deprive of office any Military Governor or other high official, whose conduct of affairs may prove antagonistic to the maintenance of friendly relations.

A police force, consisting of mounted and unmounted units, may be organized in the interior of Manchuria. Its numbers shall be determined after consultation with Russia, and from its armament artillery shall be excluded. The services of the subjects of any other Power shall not be employed in connection therewith.

6. In conformity with the undertaking given by China at an earlier date, she will not employ the subjects of any other Power in training Chinese soldiers or sailors in North China.

7. The neighbouring local authorities will, in the interests of peace and order, draw up new special Regulations with reference to the neutral zone (see Agreement of the 27th March, 1898) treated of in Article 5 of the Agreement relating to the lease (of part of the Liaotung Peninsula).

China's autonomous rights in the City of Chinchou, secured to her by Article 4 of the Special Agreement (of the 7th May, 1898) are hereby abrogated.

8. China shall not, without the consent of Russia, grant to any other Power, or the subjects thereof, privileges with regard to mines, railroads or other matters in conterminous (i.e., with Russia) regions, such as Manchuria, Mongolia, and the sections of the new Dominion known as Tarbagati, Ili, Kashgar, Yarkand, and Khoten. Nor shall China, without Russia's consent, construct (rail)roads there herself.

Except as far as Newchwang is concerned, no leases of land shall be granted to the subjects of any other Power.

9. China being under obligation to pay Russia's war expenses and the claims of other Powers, arising out of the recent troubles,

the amount of the indemnity presented in the name of Russia, the period within which it will have to be paid, and the security therefore will all be arranged in concert with the other Powers.

10. The compensation to be paid for the destruction of the railway lines, for the robbery of property, belonging to the Railway Administration and its employés, as well as claims for delay in carrying on the construction of the line, will form subject of arrangement between China and the Administration.

11. The above-mentioned claims may, by agreement with the Administration, either in part or in whole, be commuted for other privileges. The grant of such privileges would involve a complete revision of the previous Agreement.

In conformity with the undertaking previously given by China, it is agreed that a line may be constructed from either trunk line of the branch line (of Manchurian Railway) in the direction of Peking up to the Great Wall, its administration to be governed by the Regulations at present in force.[88]

Satow commented:

China's liberty of action is infringed by the prohibition to employ foreigners in Articles 5 and 6.

Article 8 is contrary to possible interests of other Powers, and lays the foundation for future treatment of those districts in the same way as Manchuria.

The railway indemnity is withdrawn from the purview of the Powers by Article 10. (An arrangement in regard to money indemnity for damage to Shantung railways has already been made with the Governor of that province by Germany.)[89]

The argument advanced by Fraser to Viceroy Chang Chih-tung in response to the telegram from Satow, was as follows:

His Excellency the Viceroy has deigned to consult me more than once on China's position and policy, and is, I hope, convinced that I have China's interests at heart. I venture, therefore, to suggest to his Excellency that China can gain nothing by the acceptance of the terms. Their acceptance will not be followed by the withdrawal of the Russian forces in Manchuria; on the contrary, the acceptance of the terms will enable Russia to plead China's consent in reply to any protest raised by other Powers and will give China's enemies a good excuse for charging her with bad faith in making a separate Treaty behind the backs of the Powers. If China refuses to sign this Treaty and publishes the facts to the world, what can Russia do? She can only brave the public opinion of the world and try to take by force what the Treaty would have made China give her voluntarily. And even Russia has hitherto shrunk from such open rapine. The Treaty gives Russia a lien, or rather practically a Protectorate, over not only Manchuria but all Chinese territory outside the eighteen provinces, and what more could she get by a successful war? Perhaps she holds out promises of supporting China in obtaining mitigation of the terms demanded by the other Powers; but, even if she were capable of carrying out such promises (which in my opinion she is not), the price she demands is out of all proportion to the promised benefits, to say nothing of the certain fact that her example will be followed by France in the south, Germany, Japan, Italy, and perforce England in the centre and west.[90]

Chang Chih-tung was in agreement. He himself protested the proposed Treaty. As regards the question why Li Hung-chang acted the way he did, Chang felt that "the only explanation of Li's conduct was that he had sold himself to Russia, that is, that for his personal aggrandizement, Li had promised to back Russia's demands."[91]

Satow continued to bolster Chinese opposition to Russia. He telegraphed to Fraser at Hankow:

Have an interview with the Viceroy at Wuchang and inform his Excellency that the Powers, whose assistance has been invoked concerning the Manchurian Convention, are co-operating in Europe.

It would be well that Prince Ch'ing and Li Hung-chang should be instructed by the Emperor to forward a separate copy of the draft to each foreign Representative here, with a written request to submit it to the Peace Conference, and ask the foreign Representatives to notify their views upon the clauses to which His Imperial Majesty objects as likely to interfere with the independence of China.[92]

But Russia resented the foreign interference. As Lansdowne informed Satow, the British Government had asked Russia for the text of the Manchurian Agreement.

Count Lamsdorff, in his reply, said that in his opinion it would not be compatible with the character of an independent State, when negotiating with another, to communicate to a third party the details of such negotiations.

The questions which the Powers were negotiating in concert with China were, he maintained, quite separate from the Manchurian question, and Russia has the right to make whatever conditions seemed necessary to her for evacuating Manchuria, and the occupation could be continued if those conditions were not accepted by the Chinese Government.[93]

The Russian attitude was reflected in China, where Li Hung-chang had impressed on the Court that "the communication of his Secret Treaty to any other Power would be resented as an insult by Russia."[94] The problem was the more complicated because China feared to reveal the text unless first assured of British mediation, while Britain first wished to see the text before deciding on mediation.

On March 11, Satow reported that he had told Prince Ch'ing "that the indemnity to the Manchurian railway ought to be placed on a par with other claims for indemnity instead of serving as a lever for fresh demands without limit to be extorted by Russia."

I pressed him to communicate to the foreign Representatives the draft Convention. Prince Ch'ing replied that he would desire to invite the opinion of the foreign Representatives as soon as the draft had assumed a more definite shape, and added, in confidence, that his co-Plenipotentiary, Li Hung-chang, required careful watching, as he was on very intimate terms with the Russians.[95]

Yet Li's motives were not certain. On March 13, Lansdowne wrote to Satow:

The Chinese Minister told me to-day that Li Hung-chang's telegram, which he had communicated to me on the 1st instant, and which rather conveyed the impression that Li was in favour of complying with the demands of Russia as to the Manchurian

141

Agreement, was in reality written with a different object. Li was just as much averse to such an Agreement as the Imperial Court and the Yang-tsze Viceroys, and had only suggested that China should accept it if it became clear that such a course was absolutely inevitable.[96]

On March 15 Satow called on Prince Ch'ing.

He said Yang-ju [the Chinese Minister to Russia] had told Lamsdorff that rather than sign the proposed convention, he would leave Petersburg and ask the Emperor of China to appoint another representative [Satow recorded in his diary]. Lamsdorff thereupon said he would consult with [General Aleksei] Kuropatkin [the Minister of War] and [Count Sergei] de Witte [the Minister of Finance]. I told him that China need not fear Russia breaking off negotiations, and that if he remained firm the articles impairing Chinese sovereignty would be taken out. That His Majesty's Government was using very firm language at Petersburg, and though Germany from her position was unable to take quite so strong a line, yet she took a lively interest in the matter; and the United States and Japan, both sea-powers like England could also speak firmly.

On March 17, Satow reported in a secret telegram, that Li Hung-chang's coadjutor, Chou-fu, had informed him that Russia had made the following modifications in the Manchurian Agreement, "satisfactory to China":

There will be no interference by Russia in Manchuria with regard to the appointments of Chinese officials, nor with the customs or *li-kin* collection there.

The article relating to Mongolia and Turkestan is to be eliminated.

China is only to grant mining and railway concessions in Manchuria to foreigners after she has referred to Russia.

Russia withdraws her stipulation respecting foreign instructors for the army and navy.

The Chinese Administration in Kinchow is to remain.

Signature of the Agreement must take place within fourteen days. It may be made known afterwards.[97]

Satow added: "I am also informed from an equally good source that the cession of Newchwang Railway will no longer be claimed by Russia, who, however, stipulates that she may have the right to construct a branch up to the Great Wall from the Manchurian line."[98]

Two days later Satow telegraphed that the 6th article of the Russo-Chinese Manchurian Agreement had been omitted. As for the others, he reported:

Article 4. The number of troops and military posts in Manchuria is to be determined with Russia. In accordance with common agreement to be made with the Powers, prohibition of importation of arms and ammunition. Meantime, prohibition to be made by China.

Article 5. Any Governor-General, or other high official, complained of by Russia as having acted in an improper manner in matters which affect foreign policy is to be transferred at once. China may maintain a police force of cavalry and infantry, determining its strength in consultation with Russia. This body is, however, not to have cannon until the pacification of the country, and only Chinese are to be enrolled.

Article 7. The local authorities in the neighbourhood of the neutral zone, provided for by Article V of the Convention relating to the lease of the Peninsula of Liaotung, are to frame a set of special Regulations suitable to the circumstances.

Article 8. Without previous consultation with Russia, China shall not grant to any other Power, or its subjects, railway and mining concessions and commercial advantages throughout Manchuria.

Article 10. The principles agreed upon by the Representatives of the foreign Powers and approved by their Governments shall be used to adjust the indemnities for the destruction of railways, of the Railway Company employés' property, and for losses due to delay of work.

Article 12. It is stated that China has contravened a previous Russo-Chinese Agreement by constructing a railway line direct into Manchuria, from Shanhaikwan to Newchwang and Sinminting, with money borrowed from a private Company. On the 28th September, 1898, China is to give compensation for this by conceding the right to the East China Railway Company to

143

build an extension line of its main railway to the Great Wall, on the Chihli-Manchurian boundary.

The other Articles, as they were in the original draft, remain unaltered.[99]

On March 19 Satow discussed the revised agreement with Li. "Told him they ought not to sign the last article, as it makes China confess that she had violated an agreement. He was anxious he said to obtain a delay of ten to twelve days, in order to get rid of this and other objectionable features, which might induce other Powers to follow Russia's example." (3/19) In a secret telegram to Lansdowne Satow commented: "No previous agreement between Russia and China exists. It is not fair to China nor to His Majesty's Government to force China to sign such an Article as is contemplated."[100]

Reviewing his conversation with Li, Satow recorded in his diary:

As to Manchurian agreement he found [Mikhail] de Giers [the Russian Minister to China] had no authority to agree to anything, but was very angry and very urgent. Li complained that Fraser had told Chang Chih-tung on my authority that he (Li) had already signed, but I must know very well that he was not the negotiator. At first it was in the hands of Prince Ch'ing and himself, but now the Court was running the show, and did not always consult him. I replied that I had not told Fraser so, for though it was rumoured all over Peking, I had telegraphed to Lord Lansdowne that I did not believe it. But I told him about Lo going to Lord Lansdowne and saying that the Plenipotentiaries wished His Majesty's Government and other Governments to mediate, and then next day went back and said it was not the Plenipotentiaries but the Court. He also said their Minister at Berlin had telegraphed that Germany could not interfere, because of her land-frontier, but that England and Japan were in a different position. A curious echo this of what I said to Prince Ch'ing a day or two ago. (3/15)

On March 19 Satow had another interview with Grand Secretary Li. J. W. Jamieson, officiating Chinese Secretary of the British Legation kept notes:

A great deal of preliminary fencing took place before business commenced.

His Excellency endeavoured to extract what the views of the Great Powers in regard to the proposals were, a point on which Sir Ernest declined to enlighten him until he had been furnished with further particulars as to the stage which negotiations had reached.

The Grand Secretary stated that it was impossible for him, and, moreover, contrary to etiquette, to divulge the terms of a diplomatic Agreement until it had been signed. Russia, too, had the strongest objection to any discussion of the matter with outsiders; her reply to China's suggestion that the draft Treaty be laid before the foreign Representatives at Peking being in the form of a decided negative.

On being asked whether the objectionable terms in the original Agreement had been modified, his Excellency admitted that they had; the claim for exclusive rights in Mongolia and Turkestan had been abandoned. The prohibition against engaging non-Russians in training land and sea forces in the North had been removed. The stretch of the railway between Shanhaikwan and Newchwang was to be handed back to China, and Russia intended to build a separate line to connect her own railway systems with a point on the Great Wall.

Sir Ernest said he understood that this latter provision was accompanied by a statement that Russia claimed this as a penalty for "the signature of a contract with a private Company for building a line outside the Great Wall, such signature constituting an infraction of a previous Agreement."

His Excellency asked if any such previous Agreement existed.

The Grand Secretary was at much pains to explain that the so-called Agreement was a one-sided pretension put forward by Russia that China, in signing the contract with the British and Chinese Corporation, had infringed a previous understanding. This, Russia had asserted time after time, but China had never admitted, and declined to admit, that she had ever agreed to refrain from building railways beyond the Great Wall. Besides, the contract having been entered into with the cognizance of the British Government, it could not be called a private one.

Sir Ernest then said that it seemed to him that China would stultify herself by putting her signature to such a statement. His Excellency was of the same opinion, but found himself in a difficult position. Russia had conquered Manchuria by force of arms; she was willing to hand it back to China, but not unnaturally expected some consideration in exchange. China was willing to meet her as far as lay in her power, but was being unduly pressed to sign before details had been fully discussed. As matters stood the draft Constitution, to which in general neither China nor other Powers could offer any objection, but one or two points required modification, among which the most important was the inclusion of this accusation against China of bad faith. Russia, however, was of opinion that she had reached the extreme limit of concession, and that it was only the friendly feeling towards China by which the Emperor was actuated which had induced her to abate her original demands.

From her present demands she could not recede. M. de Giers was exercising the greatest pressure, but his Excellency had observed that he was kept somewhat in the dark by his Government as to what they had conceded in St. Petersburgh, and he was hopeful that, could time be gained, matters could be placed on a satisfactory footing. Russia had, however, demanded that the Treaty should be signed within six days and the time was very short. He would like, therefore, to know if Sir Ernest could induce His Majesty's Government to make representations to Russia, pointing out that a report had reached them that China was being forced to subscribe to a mis-statement of facts and that it was obviously unfair to make her do so, at the same time intimating that the contract was one executed with Russian cognizance and approval. It was with the greatest relief that he received the British Minister's assurance that he would telegraph to London in this sense.

On being asked if, when this clause had been dropped, the Agreement was otherwise unobjectionable, he replied that there were one or two other points he wished to have altered, "as he was afraid that their retention in their present form would lead others to imitate a bad example." What these points were he was not at liberty to say, but he thought that given an extension of time—say ten days or more—the Chinese Plenipotentiary at St. Petersburgh could arrange matters. If no extension could be obtained, Chinese interests would be prejudiced. When asked what would happen were China not to sign on the day appointed, his Excellency replied that negotiations would be broken off and the draft Convention torn up. Sir Ernest then asked whether it was Russia from whom the proposal to hand back the Manchurian provinces emanated. The reply was in the affirmative.

That being so, Sir Ernest said, confirmed him in what he had heard, namely, that Russia, finding herself unable to govern the provinces properly, was only too anxious to get rid of them, and that, were China to hold out a little longer, she would possibly discover that the threats were empty ones. The Grand Secretary was not inclined to share this view.[101]

On March 20 the Foreign Secretary telegraphed to Satow confidentially a slightly different version of articles XI and XII, obtained from the Japanese, and added:

I was informed by Baron Hayashi [Tadasu, the Minister of Japan] that the Japanese Government regarded this special Convention as modified, though less objectionable than the previous version, as the most dangerous, both on account of the nature of its contents and on account of its having been negotiated by Russia behind the backs of other Powers, with whom China was negotiating as well as with Russia. Such separate Convention would materially lessen the capacity of China to meet her obligations towards the Powers, and it was against the principle of solidarity uniting the Powers. It was the wish of the Japanese Government that His Majesty's Government should unite with them in again advising the Chinese Government not to sign the draft Convention as amended. He said the Japanese considered that it would be very effective if such advice were renewed by the two Governments, and possibly also by the German Government.

In reply, I informed the Japanese Minister that the warning already given in regard to the conclusion of separate Agreements with individual Powers would be repeated by His Majesty's Government, and China would be advised by them not to sign the draft Convention in its amended form.

I request you to give to the Chinese Government, through the Yang-tsze Viceroys, the necessary warning and advice, and also to the Chinese Plenipotentiaries if you consider it desirable to make such a communication to the latter.[102]

That day Lansdowne further informed Satow of a meeting he had had with the Chinese Minister. "I told him that although His Majesty's Government understood that the Russian Government had consented to the introduction of certain amendments in the text of the Manchurian Agreement, we nevertheless considered that China should on no account commit herself to such a bargain without the full knowledge of the Powers."[103]

On March 22 Fraser forwarded the modified terms of the Manchurian Agreement. Articles 1-4 remained unaltered.

5. If Russia complains of an official, high or low, he shall be transferred away from Manchuria. The number of police and guards in Manchuria shall be settled with Russia; they shall have no artillery, and only Chinese shall be employed to drill the police or guards.

6. Without reference to Russia no railway, mining, industrial, or commercial rights in Manchuria may be granted to foreigners. Apart from Newchwang no special lease shall be given to other foreigners.

7. Same as original Article 9.

8. The losses of the Manchurian Railway Company and its employés shall be treated on the same footing as the indemnities claimed by other Powers.

9. Same as original Article 11.

10. To atone for China's breach of the former Treaty in making the Newchwang Railway, Russia may build a railway in the direction of Peking, starting either from the main or any branch line of the Manchurian Railway, as far as the Great Wall, on the same terms as the Manchurian Railway.[104]

Byron Brenan, the British Consul-General at Shanghai, conveyed an explanation of Chinese willingness to sign the agreement with Russia. The Director of Railways, Shêng Hsuanhuai, had come to see him. Brenan wrote to Satow: "Shêng explained to me that it was feared at Court that Russian seizure of Manchuria would be made a pretext by some other Power to seize Chihli. In his opinion, China would refuse to sign if she could receive a satisfactory assurance on this point, but if her refusal to sign was to be followed by the loss of Manchuria and then by the occupation of Chihli by some other Power, she would have to sign as the less dangerous course."[105]

On March 20 the Chinese Government had requested that of Great Britain "(1) to help the Chinese Government out of their difficulty, or (2) to ask Russian Government that time stipulated for signing the Agreement may be extended." Great Britain replied on the 23rd that an extension of time would serve "no good purpose" and that "to enter into such an Agreement will be a source of danger to China." To reinforce its advice Lansdowne warned the Chinese Minister that it might be necessary to consider what "compensations" Great Britain should require in the event that China made separate agreements detrimental to British interests.[106] That day Satow telegraphed to Lansdowne:

The Viceroy, through his Secretary, has made a statement to the effect that Chinese Minister at St. Petersburgh telegraphs that the Russian Foreign Office has stopped intercourse with him, and returns his letters unopened. The apprehension of the Court has been increased thereby, so that, in his opinion, on the expiration of fortnight, the Court is almost certain to accept the Manchurian Agreement unless other Powers intervene within the next three or four days to insist on extension of time being granted for signature.[107]

On March 24 Satow conferred with the Japanese Minister. "Went to tell Komura of Sheng's lie about my having, as he said, informed Kiu Kunyi and Chang Chih-tung through the respective consuls that the Manchurian Agreement was satisfactory, and that Li still wanted ten or twelve days grace before instructing Yang-ju to sign," Satow noted in his diary. "Li had been with me to ask whether there was any answer from Lord Lansdowne about the delay asked for. Told him I had none, but would send it to him as soon as it came."

On March 28, Satow telegraphed to the Foreign Secretary:

A telegram dated yesterday from His Majesty's Consul at Nanking states that the Viceroy has received a telegraphic communication on the 28th instant, from the Chinese Minister in Tōkiō, reporting that the Russian Government had received a summons from the Japanese Government to withdraw their demands respecting Manchuria. The Court has simultaneously informed the Viceroy, by telegraph, that it is not their intention to sign any Agreement with Russia.

According to a telegram from the British Acting Consul-General at Hankow, I learn that strict instructions not to sign Manchurian Agreement have been issued to the Chinese Plenipotentiaries by the Court. I have informed His Majesty's Minister at Tōkiō of the contents of the two above telegrams.[108]

Several days later Fraser wrote to Satow describing a visit by the Secretary of the Viceroy:

Mr. Liang had, as I telegraphed on the 27th March, written that the Court had given strict orders to the Chinese Plenipotentiaries not to sign the Manchurian Agreement. He now informed me that the Emperor had at one time actually empowered Li Hung-chang, if he were sure that the Agreement would not prove dangerous to China, to act on his own discretion, that Li had already ordered the Chinese Minister at St. Petersburgh to sign, when the Yang-tsze Viceroys sent Yang Ju a telegram warning him that, if he signed, he would incur personal danger, and that Yang happily hesitated long enough to enable the Viceroys and their friends to sway the Court. The Emperor of China then about the 20th March ordered his Minister to Russia to forward to the Emperor of Russia a letter explaining that China was most anxious to retain the friendship of Russia, but could not disregard the admonitions of the other Powers against making separate Agreements with any individual Powers while the whole situation was under discussion at Peking with the Powers as a body. This Imperial letter the Russian Foreign Office refused to receive, and the Chinese Minister, in order to avoid further responsibility, now reported himself seriously ill. Two days before the fortnight expired the Russian Foreign Office asked whether the Chinese Legation had received orders to sign; since then no communication had come from the Russians. The Chinese Court, having listened to the representations of the Wuchang, Nanking, Foochow, and Canton Viceroys, together with the Governors of Anhui, Shantung, and Shensi, now called upon them to move the foreign Powers, whose protests against the Agreement they laid such stress upon, to keep Russia from breaking off friendly relations or taking hostile action.

I reminded Mr. Liang that you did not think there was any

danger of a rupture with Russia over the Agreement. He said that the Viceroy was not himself very apprehensive, but felt the necessity of calming the nervousness of the Court, on which the refusal to receive the Emperor's letter had made a great impression. His Excellency Chang wished to know whether, if specially requested, England would bring the Emperor's letter to the knowledge of the Czar. I pointed out that while I would lay the point before you and Lord Lansdowne, His Majesty's Government was averse to any action which might imply the propriety of China's entering into any separate Agreement with Russia.

Mr. Liang explained that the Viceroy feared lest Russia might go so far that she could not retreat without loss of prestige, and his Excellency was therefore anxious to receive advice from Her Majesty's Government as to the proper steps to be taken in this crisis so as to keep the Court from surrendering to Russia in a panic, and also to save China from suffering on account of her refusal to accept the Agreement.

I suggested that the communication of the text, with China's views thereon, to the foreign Representatives at Peking, as proposed by you on the 8th March, would justify China's action before the Powers. Mr. Liang thought that under pressure this course might be adopted, but inclined to the opinion that a request in general terms that the Ministers would consider at the Conference the restoration of Manchuria to China would serve the same purpose, and leave Russia a way of withdrawal from her present position. For he told me that to Japan's request that the Agreement might be referred to the Conference, Russia replied courteously that, while anxious to come to an agreement on the question with Japan, she could not admit that the European Powers had any concern with Manchuria.

He added that the Court was so much afraid of Russia that the Viceroy considered it useless to expect China, eager as she certainly is, to throw Manchuria open to all nations, unless the Powers urged this step upon her. . . .

On my again expressing my inability to understand Li Hung-chang's course of action, Mr. Liang reminded me of the Viceroy's remarks on Li's pride and self-importance, and suggested that the explanation of his conduct might be found in the fact that, while the other Ministers snubbed Li on his arrival in Peking, the Russian Representative treated him with the utmost consideration and flattery. Li had also reported to the

Throne that on his telling M. de Giers that China would of course expect Russia's support against the pressure of other Power, the Minister assented as he left.[109]

Three days later Fraser reported an interview he had with Viceroy Chang, who "expressed his warm sense of England's support in the present crisis, and his personal anxiety to follow the advice given him."

It was, however, impossible to overcome the nervousness of the Court induced by Li Hung-chang's constant and strenuous warnings of the truculent intentions of Russia, who would, Li had convinced the Court, consider the communication of the text of the proposed Manchurian Agreement to the other Powers a *casus belli*. The Viceroy himself did not look upon the official communication of the text as essential, seeing that it was already known to all the friendly Powers. It seemed to him, also, that such communication to the foreign Representatives in conference at Peking would imply that the Agreement might, if modified, become capable of acceptance, whereas England and other Powers had warned China against entering into any separate Agreement with any individual Power so long as the general Treaty was under consideration. Moreover, the draft Agreement, even as altered by Russia, was, as he explained at length, so full of objectionable stipulations that satisfactory amendment was impossible. China was, among other hardships, deprived of the right of selecting her foreign advisers and assistants, and of exploiting her own resources, while her officials in Manchuria were to hold office at the pleasure of Russia. As explained in the Yang-tsze Viceroy's telegram of the 22nd March to the Chinese Minister in London, the provinces of the south and east, which withstood the Boxer frenzy, are ready to accept the arbitration of the Powers on the Manchurian question; but the Court is too timid to authorize the submission of the Russian proposed Agreement to the judgment of the foreign Representatives lest by this course Russia be incensed into violent action. Russia's declaration forwarded by Li Hung-chang, that, if the term for accepting her amended proposals were exceeded, she would drop the question of the restoration of Manchuria, seems to his Excellency to suggest a way out of the difficulty, which will also save Russia's pride should she desire to yield to the Powers. His Excellency's idea is to let the Agreement be ignored, and simply to ask the Ministers at Peking to include the settlement of the Manchurian question in the deliberations of the Peace Conference. In this way Russia would not be subjected to criticism, and could not find any colourable pretext for venting her ill-will on China. The Viceroy felt sure, that, if His Majesty's Government approved of his suggestion, he and the Viceroy Liu could obtain from the Court a Decree, ordering the Chinese Plenipotentiaries to address to each foreign Minister at Peking the requisite official request. . . .

His Excellency remarked that Russia was crafty and her declarations untrustworthy, and that Li Hung-chang persisted in warning the Court that Russia would not listen to the decisions of the Powers, none of which would dare to oppose her seriously.

I reminded him that, after her war with Turkey, Russia, even though victorious, had accepted the settlement of the Powers at Berlin.

The Viceroy asked whether Japan was likely to be moved by Russia's professed desire to act in close harmony with that country. I said that, so far as my personal knowledge and opinion went, Japan would not desert the concert of the Powers—a view with which his Excellency expressed his strong concurrence. He was much more doubtful of Germany's policy, although she had also advised China to make no separate Agreement. He was puzzled, too, as to the absence of any news from France on this question. Would she support Russia, irrespective of right or wrong? I could only declare that I myself believed that both Germany and France would join with the other Powers in striving to attain a just settlement of the whole Chinese question.[110]

On April 5, Lansdowne telegraphed Satow confidentially that he had learned "the Russian Government does not intend to insist further on the Manchurian Agreement being concluded."[111] In another telegram of the same day Lansdowne noted that "the strength of the Chinese Government lies in sitting still."[112] On April 6 Satow recorded in his diary: "[William W.] Rockhill [the American Commissioner Plenipotentiary] had a story this morning that the Russian Legation had broken off all relations with the Chinese Plenipotentiaries and returned their letters, and he wondered whether de

Giers would withdraw from the conference. [Freiherr] Mumm [von Schwartzenstein, the German Minister] and I had however later on telegram that the Russians had dropped the whole negotiation, in a 'dignified' manner, and would await events." But on April 7 Satow reported the following information, communicated to him from Hankow:

> The Court have received a telegram from Li Hung-chang, stating that the Russian Foreign Office threaten that, unless the Manchurian Agreement is signed, Russia will no longer support China as before against the demands made by other Powers, and that she will become the harshest of them all. This, Li stated, was China's last chance; but the Court has had it pointed out to them that this threat proves there is no danger of war, and that China has not gained anything whatever by the support of Russia. The Viceroy is in hopes that the effect of the Russian message on the Court will be to give them courage rather than alarm them.[113]

On April 9, Lansdowne sent Satow a copy of a telegram from Lew Kwun Yih [Liu K'un-i] the Viceroy of Nanking, stating that the Chinese Government, "relying on the assurance of the British Government's moral support" in resisting Russian pressure had refused to sign the Convention and that in consequence "the Russian Minister of Finance and the Russian Minister for Foreign Affairs have announced to the Chinese Legation in St. Petersburgh that, as China has listened to the calumnies of England and Japan, friendly relations between China and Russia must cease, and that Manchuria would have to be converted into a Russian province."[114] Lansdowne still doubted that "at the present moment anything was to be gained by making such representations to the Russian Government with reference to Manchuria as the Viceroy suggested."[115]

When Lansdowne talked to the Russian Ambassador on April 17, the latter "expressed his regret at the difficulties which had arisen with regard to the Manchurian Agreement, which, he said, had been pressed upon the Chinese Government by Russia solely with the object of enabling her to put an end to the military occupation of the province—an occupation which he feared would now be indefinitely prolonged."[116]

The refusal of the Chinese to sign delayed any possible Russian withdrawal from Manchuria. Yet the pressure of the Russians, or more correctly, Russian domination, vexed other foreigners. Thus Admiral Sir Edward H. Seymour complained to Satow that the need for Russian occupation of Newchwang, a treaty port, had passed now that the immediate neighborhood was quite peaceable, and suggested that "the Russian Government might be courteously approached on the subject, thanked for their past protection, and congratulated on its success, which leaves now no longer any necessity thus to tax their military resources."[117]

On July 4, Satow forwarded to London another letter from Fulford, asking that some effort be made to induce the Russians to withdraw from Yingkow, the port of Newchwang. "I have little doubts that without some external stimulus the Russian occupation of this port will be as prolonged as possible," Fulford wrote.[118]

But the indemnity question and many other issues were then being negotiated and Lansdowne did not want to endanger his position. As he telegraphed to Satow on July 15 "privately": "Care must be taken not to admit that we have pledged ourselves to obtain the withdrawal of the Russians from Manchuria."[119] On August 31, according to his diary, Satow talked with the American Minister, Edwin H. Conger, who said his Government had instructed him to sound out his colleagues as to the continuance of the Russian occupation of Newchwang.

On September 7, the Final Protocol was signed between China and the Powers, bringing the state of war officially to an end. With eleven months of bickering among themselves about the punishment of Chinese and Manchu "war criminals," reparations and the division of spoils behind them, the Powers could focus on the position of Russia in Manchuria.

On the very day that the Final Protocol was signed, Satow sent a confidential dispatch to the Marquess of Lansdowne in which he reviewed the Russian occupation of Newchwang. He noted:

It would appear from the most recent information that the Russian authorities have drawn up a financial scheme for the local administration of Newchwang, with a view to some years to come.

My United States' colleague informs me that he has been requested by his Government to obtain exact information from his colleagues as to the position of affairs there, and to report what steps may be advisable to take in order to bring about a resumption of Chinese authority there. So far he has only spoken to the Japanese Minister and myself. He considers that it would be of little avail to endeavour to enlist German support, inasmuch as the German Government has taken up, with regard to exclusive rights of railway construction and mining enterprise, exactly the same attitude as the Russian Government, in the draft Convention of some months back, assumed in respect of Manchuria.

The Japanese Minister informs me that he considers we ought first to replace the Chinese civil authorities in the administration of Tien-tsin and its district, before calling upon Russia to renounce her Provisional Government at Newchwang; but he suggests that it might be useful, now that the signature of the Final Protocol has taken place, to intimate to the Russian Government that the Native Customs at Newchwang, which form one of the sources of revenue assigned for the service of the indemnity bonds, must be placed under the Imperial Maritime Customs, and that the revenues of the latter institution must henceforward be applied to their proper purpose, as they likewise are pledged for the payment of the foreign debts of China.

I am inclined to agree with Mr. Conger in thinking that we shall not obtain much support from our German colleague in any efforts to obtain the withdrawal of the Russians from Newchwang, and with Mr. Komura's suggestion that the liberation of Imperial Maritime and Native Customs revenue should at once be asked for.[120]

On October 25, after a talk with Sir Robert Hart, Satow noted in his diary. "Rumour at Newchwang of Russia annexing the northern portion of Manchuria, so as to own territory on both sides of the main line, with a capital at Harbin, the rest being restored to China. He thinks quite possibly true. It would be given out not as a Russian demand, but as an offer of the Chinese. He is anxious to get Newchwang freed as soon as possible."

On October 2, Satow transmitted to London a dispatch from Consul Alexander Hosie at Newchwang to the effect that a Russian military movement was taking place along the road from the city of Liao-Yang to Feng-Huang Ting and the frontier of Korea.[121] Hosie reported that the movement "must have some other object in view than the pacification of Manchuria," and noted that "the general impression in Liao-Yang is that the movement or expedition is intended as a counterpoise to an alleged massing of Japanese troops at Chemulpo."[122] In an Intelligence memorandum, which Satow also enclosed, Major Wingate wrote:

So far as it is possible to ascertain, there is no reason to suppose that relations between the Russians and the Japanese are other than friendly at the present time. There is no news here of any massing of Japanese troops at Chemulpo.

It is well known that the Russians have for obvious reasons been steadily improving their military hold on Manchuria and the Liao-tung Peninsula, and have been collecting there all the arms, ordnance, and ammunition they can lay hands on, even to the somewhat antiquated materials which they took from the arsenals and armouries of Chihli. Knowing, as they well do, what a broken reed their railway is likely to prove for many years to come in case of war being suddenly declared, they are now doing everything they can to get into a state of defence. The pacification of the districts bordering on the Yalu River is a part of this programme.[123]

In response to repeated demands by Englishmen in Newchwang, the British Government decided to send a warship to that port for the winter. On November 17, Satow transmitted a secret memorandum from Reginald Tower, about a conversation he had had with the new Russian Minister, Pavel Lessar, on this subject.

M. Lessar, the Russian Minister, called at this Legation on the morning of the 8th November, and asked whether I knew why His Majesty's naval authorities were constructing a dock at Newchwang. He said that Admiral Alexeieff had sent him the definite information that His Majesty's Government had decided to keep His Majesty's ship *Algerine* there during the forthcoming winter, and that such a course would necessarily greatly embarrass the Russian authorities established at Newchwang, the intentions of the Russian Government having been so clearly defined to restore the province and the Treaty port to China as soon as the pacification was completed, but that the state of things had unfortunately not yet been reached, though they were doing their utmost to bring it about. M. Lessar said that, if His Majesty's Government sent a vessel of war to Newchwang for the winter, the Russian Government would be obliged to be similarly represented, and that this would entail a possible conflict of authority, and embarrassment to all parties concerned from the presence of the Russian naval officers as well as of officers from the British ship. He emphatically hoped that Sir Ernest Satow would telegraph to Lord Lansdowne saying that he had made this communication, in the hope that His Majesty's Government would not insist on sending the *Algerine*. He said that the information received from Admiral Alexeieff as to the construction of the dock left no room for doubt as to the present intentions of His Majesty's Government. I answered that, in the first place, it was no more strange that we should keep a vessel at Newchwang for the winter than that we should have one at many of the other Treaty ports of China, and no more than that we should have been represented on previous occasions latterly by a British ship at that port. I could not speak positively as to the intentions of His Majesty's Government on the subject, but I could readily understand that His Majesty's Goverment were unwilling to subject the officers and crew of one of our ships to the rigours of a winter in the north.

On the 10th instant, I received a telegram from Mr. Hosie, His Majesty's Consul at Newchwang, informing me that a dock for the *Algerine* was practically completed, in accordance with instructions from the Senior Naval Officer at Taku, dated the

27th October. I had received no other intimation of the intentions of His Majesty's Government, except Lord Lansdowne's telegram No. 321 of the 2nd November, stating that the Admiralty had strong objections to leaving a ship at Newchwang for the winter.

In my conversation with M. Lessar, I made no mention of this information.

I took the opportunity, however, of saying to him that, as he had broached the subject of Newchwang, perhaps he would forgive me if I spoke, unofficially and privately, on the point of view which presented itself to us British. I said that, since the signature of the Protocol on the 7th September, the position of affairs at Newchwang had materially altered. One could not help being struck by the anomalous procedure which continued at that Treaty port, the evidence of which I had myself seen during a recent visit. He asked what I meant. I replied that, in the first place, the Russian flag flew over the Imperial Maritime Custom-house and on all the boats in the service of the Customs; secondly, that the Native Customs were administered solely and exclusively by the Russians. Now that the revenues of the Native Customs were to be placed in the hands of the Inspector-General of the Maritime Customs, to serve, as well as the Maritime Customs, as security for the indemnity payable to all the Signatory Powers by China, was it not strange that no effort was being made by Russia to restore the former condition of things in this respect, viz., by handing over the Customs service, both Maritime and Native, to the unfettered administration of the Inspector-General? He said, "Perhaps the Chinese do not require the money. Why do you suppose they do?" I thought, with my limited knowledge of China, that the Chinese Government were hardly open to an accusation of a superfluity of wealth, even in more prosperous times, and that, especially at the present moment when additional taxation was being imposed all over the country, such an idea could hardly be seriously entertained. M. Lessar then said, "But I dare say an arrangement has been already made for the restoration of the Customs to the Chinese." I said that, if that were so, it was quite unknown to us, and that I thought we could hardly have failed to hear of it. He protested that it was only a supposition on his part, but asked what Russia could be expected to do in the matter. I rejoined that the provisions of the Final Protocol, which had been signed by all the Plenipotentiaries, including the

159

Russian, on the 7th September last, was a sufficient answer to that question. The Native Customs being security for the indemnity, one would think that Russia would be the first to settle matters as far as she could by restoring the Administration spontaneously to the Chinese in accordance with those provisions. M. Lessar replied that he would be too glad to assist in any way towards such restoration, but that he must have a peg on which to hang any proposal in that direction. He said that, if the Chinese made a request to him personally for the restoration of the Customs, he would very willingly further it to the best of his ability. On my asking him in what manner this could be done without embarrassing the Russian Government, he said that, if the Inspector-General would write to him on the subject, he would act. He especially appeared to wish to avoid the matter being dealt with by the Powers at St. Petersburgh, but completely ignored my suggestion that Russia should act spontaneously in the matter.

I told M. Lessar that I could certainly not accept the position of intermediary between the Russian and Chinese Governments, more especially as I was in no way authorized to act in the temporary absence of Sir Ernest Satow, but that I had spoken to him in a purely unofficial manner, without any instructions, in order to explain the reverse of the medal, as seen from our side. On his again stating the genuine desire of Russia to effect a complete pacification of the province with as little delay as possible, I replied that it was far from my intention to discuss with him any general question of the occupation of either the Treaty port or Manchuria by Russia. This was altogether beyond my sphere.[124]

In accordance with instructions Tower had kept in touch with the representatives of Japan and the United States. He reported:

Since the departure of Mr. Komura to assume the duties of Japanese Minister for Foreign Affairs, Mr. Hioki, First Secretary of the Legation, has acted as Chargé d'Affaires, and has frequently spoken to me respecting the continued occupation of Newchwang and the desirability of restoring the Customs to the Chinese Administration, though he had received no definite instructions. He thought that the initiative should certainly come from the Chinese. Mr. Uchida [Yasuya] who has now

come to Peking as Envoy Extraordinary and Minister Plenipotentiary, in succession to Mr. Komura, has expressed the strong
desire of the Japanese Government to effect a solution of the
present difficulty.

Mr. Conger, the United States' Minister, informed me on the
16th instant that the United States' Government had decided to
send the United States' ship *Vicksburg* to Newchwang for the
winter, and that orders had been already sent to prepare a dock
for her immediate reception. He said that should M. Lessar make
any remark to him on the question, he would reply that he
had pressed his Government to send a vessel, chiefly in consequence of a statement made to him by M. Lessar himself
some weeks ago, that the Russian Government had every intention of evacuating Newchwang "very soon, very soon," as
Mr. Conger quoted the words. The United States' Government
were already, Mr. Conger said, apprehensive lest the Russians
might suddenly evacuate Newchwang during the winter
months; that a state of anarchy might then ensue, to the serious
detriment of United States' interests at the Treaty port, and with
only one possible result, viz., the enforced return of the Russian
military forces to restore tranquillity.[125]

On November 21, while visiting Chinkiang, Satow conferred with Viceroy Liu K'un-i about Manchuria. As he recorded in his diary:

Told him that Russia having an agreement with China to build a
railway through Manchuria, was entitled to place troops there
to protect it. As to mining monopoly and the demand for an
indemnity for repairing northern railways, those ought not to be
allowed. He said the latter had been left out, or had not been in
it; Li Hung-chang must have been misinformed. I said Lamsdorff had admitted it to Scott. Liu said Li sent home a telegram from Moscow recommending permission to Russia to construct Northern Manchurian railway, but Liu and Chang were
kept in ignorance of this. It was a great loss to China. I told
him they could not get out of it. He said both he and Chang
had memorialized against the signature of the present draft, and
he had telegraphed to both Prince Ch'ing and Wang Wenshao
urging them not to negotiate separately. Li's death removed a
serious obstacle. I suggested that the Chinese Government should
insist on bringing the Manchurian question before the Powers.

161

He said Russia objected to this. Told him of my reply to the Viceroy of Fuhkien when he expressed fear of Russia's breaking off relations if the de Giers draft were not signed, that Russia would talk big but do nothing. He laughed, and said that he had telegraphed the same.

On November 25 Satow visited Wuchang and accompanied by Fraser, Hewlett and four naval officers called on Viceroy Chang Chih-tung, "a short slender man with a long white beard and an open countenance."

I found him much brighter and ready to enter into what was said than Liu, but in the latter's case his vile dialect and Sundius' deafness were distinct disadvantages [Satow noted in his diary]. I urged that if they could not obtain satisfactory terms unaided they should ask the Great Powers to take up the question. As Liu did, he too wanted England and Japan to take the trouble for the Chinese, but I said they must do the best for themselves before asking us to enter the arena on their behalf. He explained that the Court is persuaded that Russia and Russia only is their friend and of the Manchus, and they prefer therefore to trust to the chance of getting some kind of terms. (This explains why the Yangtze Viceroys have always asked us to intervene, while the Court has not, and as the latter are the negotiating Power, it is useless our taking such a course unless asked by them). He regards Prince Ch'ing and Wang as equally weak, and Junglu not much better. Lu Ch'uanlin is the only man at Court with any firmness of character, and is the one through whom he works. Finally he asked me to telegraph to Prince Ch'ing to delay concluding anything till my return to Peking, and to write himself a private letter of advice, upon which he could base a telegram or letter to the Court embodying the advice of His Majesty's Government. He spoke with a good deal of contempt of Li Hung-chang, who in his belief had an arrangement with the French as well as with the Russians.

As Satow continued his journey, he met General Sharratts, the United States Tariff and Commercial Tariff Commissioner.

[The American Secretary of State John] Hay and [the British Ambassador, Baron Julian] Pauncefote were in accord the whole time, in spite of the newspaper penny-a-liners [Sharratts told Satow]. The interests of the two countries were coming closer every day, and the time would come when the English speaking peoples would have to combine to resist the encroachments of Russia and Germany. I agreed with him, and remarked that the latter was compact and active, the other large and molluscous. It reminded me of a plant in Japanese gardens that if not constantly grubbed up, eat away the fine leaf of the turf. He thinks Russia will not clear out of Manchuria till she is told to go. (11/28)

Upon his return to Peking Satow went to Uchida Yasuya, the new Japanese Minister. "Spoke about Manchurian convention. Prince Ch'ing has half promised to show him the convention before he signs. Is anxious United States should join us. Told him we could not expect any help from the 'triplice,' but after all it was Powers who could actually exercise influence out here (in a military or naval way) that really counted." (12/3)

On December 6, Satow discussed the Manchurian agreement with Prince Ch'ing. The following day he saw Uchida again. "Told him result of my conversation of yesterday with Prince Ch'ing. He agreed with me that the latter had not been quite satisfactory about the mining concessions given to the Russians in Kirin and Hei-lung-chang, but that he was more open than Li, which he attributed to China being no longer afraid, and that his promise to keep us *au courant* was good." (12/7)

On December 9, Satow conferred with the American Minister. "Conger has got instructions to warn Chinese Government against concluding any convention with Russia which would put it out of their power to fulfil their Treaty engagements with foreign powers and also not to agree to anything diminishing the integrity of the Chinese Empire," he recorded in his diary.

On December 11, the British Minister in St. Petersburg reported about the negotiations of Marquis Ito Hirobumi with the Russian Government which "understood that the Japanese Government had been lately placing obstacles in the way of the conclusion by the Chinese of the necessary agreement with the Russian Government for the evacuation of Manchuria, on the ground that some of its alleged terms were of a nature to further Russian designs against the independence of Corea and the interests of Japan in that kingdom."

Advantage was therefore taken here of the Marquis Ito's visit to convince him that there was no connection whatever between the questions of the evacuation of Manchuria and of Corea, and that Russia had no designs of any description against the independence of Corea or Japanese interests there; that the Russian Government intended to adhere faithfully to the understanding arrived at in 1896 and 1898 with Japan on this question, and that they were anxious to hasten on as much as possible the evacuation of Manchuria, although it would probably now be necessary to await the return of the Chinese Court to Pekin before proceeding further in the matter of the conclusion of the agreement, but that, in the opinion of the Russian Government, Japan was not advancing her own interests by offering any opposition to the conclusion of an agreement which did not affect any of her interests.

My informant added that the Russian Government had evidently not succeeded in obtaining an admission from the Marquis Ito that there was no connection between the Corean and Manchurian questions, and that the inference drawn by the Russian Foreign Office, from his persistency in connecting the two questions together, seemed to be that, either in his own personal view or that of his Government, the opposition offered by Japan to the conclusion of the Russo-Chinese Agreement was a useful lever to employ in order to get the Russian Government to acquiesce in the cession to Japan of some additional rights or advantages in Corea, of a commercial, not territorial, nature, besides those she already possessed there or which were contemplated in the understanding with Russia.

The Russian Government were not prepared to enter into a bargain of this kind, and the Japanese statesman had therefore not obtained more from his visit than a renewal of professions of a sincere desire on the part of the Russian Government for a cordial understanding and conciliatory relations between the two Governments on all questions affecting their mutual interests in the Far East.[126]

On December 17 Satow discussed Manchuria with Uchida. "He believes the Russians have been negotiating for 'prior rights' in commercial matters and mining through Russo-Chinese Bank, and he has told Prince Ch'ing this will not do, as it amounts to monopoly."

On January 5, 1902, Satow saw Lessar, who complained that the consuls had not called on the new Russian Administrator at Newchwang, and produced a copy of Hosie's letter to Eberhard in reply to his on the subject of the *Algerine*. In his diary Satow recalled:

He wanted me to instruct Hosie to call on Russian Admiral, which I refused to do. "If he wrote to me on the subject would it be any use," he asked. I said that having no instructions, I should refer the question home. As to the *Algerine* I had no instructions that it was proper to give notice beforehand; the claim seemed to me without foundation. Admiral Alexeieff had written to him. The Russians objected to being "treated like the Chinese." I objected to the use of this phrase, which was an insinuation that we were uncivil to Chinese; a parallel to the German press accusing our troops of barbarity, and then turning round and abusing [Joseph] Chamberlain [British Secretary of State] for saying that we should be justified in adopting greater severity, after the example of the Germans in France and other modern civilized nations. My opinion was that the Russian authorities were temporarily administering in the place of the Chinese authorities like the Tientsin Provisional Government, and were not entitled to any other precedence. He on the other hand maintained that it should follow precedents of Europe; this I could not admit. Finally he said he would write to Admiral Alexeieff and say that he had spoken to me privately, and that I could do nothing about the calls, unless by instructions. As to the *Algerine* he tried to make out that she was a "stationnaire" and therefore different to a ship merely visiting the port, and raised a question whether in Europe men of war visited a foreign port without giving notice. (It is unfortunate that the Foreign Office gives one no written instructions, and the telegraphed ones are too short to be of use).

On January 6, Conger came to Satow.

Lessar had been to him and tried to frighten him into believing there was danger of bloodshed at Newchuang between United States sailors and Russians. Repeated to him my conversation with Lessar yesterday about the calls and notification of intention to send ships. He says that Christie [Khristofor Kristi], Russian consul [secretary] at Newchuang, freely admitted quite recently that Eberhard was wrong in not calling, and that Lessar himself had previously seemed uncertain on the point. When Christie left Newchuang, the instances of violence on the part of United States sailors of which Lessar complained had already occurred, and yet he did not mention them. Conger seemed to me to be very doubtful of the truth of what Lessar had communicated to him.

On January 11, T'sên Ch'un-ming, the Governor of Shansi, called on Satow with an interpreter who stuttered in English and another who spoke French.

He talked about Manchuria, and said the Russian proposals amounted to its complete acquisition, and if that took place it was felt by the Emperor and Empress-Dowager that they could not safely remain in Peking [Satow recorded]. I said the Russians were particularly anxious to have the Court here within their grasp. The only thing China could do was to bring the matter before the Powers if she could not obtain satisfactory terms. Something she must concede, as the Russians had obtained the right to construct railways, but she must not give away the Treaty rights of other Powers. On his objecting that Russia refused to allow them to put the matter before the other Powers, I said China need not fear. As in the spring the refusal to sign had not been followed by any of the dire consequences threatened, neither would they now. He also talked about Tientsin [which the Russians had occupied too], and asked whether its restoration depended on Manchuria being given up. I said that in my personal opinion Newchuang ought to be given up before Tientsin, there had been much less reason for taking it, in fact none, whereas Tientsin had been used as a base for attacking the foreign settlements, but I did not know that one was connected with the other.

On January 13 Yüan Shih-kai came to Satow and pressed for the return of Tientsin. Satow replied that the Russians held Newchuang and the railway to Shanhai-kwan. "If we gave up Tientsin and the railway which was sure to be demanded later, there would be an empty space between the Russians and Peking; would they like that? He must not suppose we had taken the northern railway for ourselves. We had stepped in, and taken it out of Russian hands for the benefit of the Chinese." Yüan said that he was told "by people outside" that Mumm and Satow were the only ministers who opposed the restoration of Tientsin. "I replied that I could see them doing it with my mind's eyes and was sure they were the very people who were opposed to giving up Manchuria," Satow noted in his diary and continued:

As to the latter [the evacuation of Manchuria] I could not get from him any admission that the Russians had replied they could not abate or modify their terms, as is reported. He assured me China would stand firm, and not give up any of our rights. Asked if our giving up the Tientsin Provisional Government would facilitate restoration of Manchuria, he said it would be deprecated, the one being linked with or made dependent on the other.

On January 14, Sir Robert Hart came to Satow to talk about Manchuria.

I got out the text of the four articles which Fraser sent us, and read them [Satow recalled]. They were he said just what Prince Ch'ing had shown to him through [Vice Minister] Nat'ung. The first about the Russo-Chinese bank was the one they most objected to, because it was giving to them treaty sanction for a mere commercial arrangement. The Russians wanted to have all enterprises in Manchuria reserved to them. The Chinese wish to stipulate that they shall do them, if unable they will in each case offer the refusal to the Russo-Chinese bank, which has five million taels of Chinese money. [Dmitrii] Pokotilov [Manager of the Russo-Chinese Bank and Director of the Russo-Chinese

Railway] has come out hastily to press this. Perhaps it is only bluff, and he may have got authority from de Witte to push for this clause if he can get it. The Chinese also object to the prohibition against cannon. Hart understands the Russians to insist on the limitation of troops in Manchuria, in order to diminish their own military charges on the frontier. I said that I thought as far as His Majesty's Government were concerned, they did not wish to be put in a parliamentary difficulty, as would happen if the Chinese gave a formal promise of monopoly of mines and railways to the Russians. We should not help any British subject who went prospecting for mines in Manchuria, any more than we would in Shantung. The fourth article stipulating for the observance of the Scott agreement and the Hong Kong and Shanghai Bank loan agreement was very satisfactory. I thought perhaps Lessar had suggested to them that they should divulge it to us, to allay our opposition. If so, why put in the first one about the Russo-Chinese Bank which could only excite our suspicions. As to the bridging of the Liao river etc., that seemed rather of an academical nature. Hart said he had been told by Lessar early in the month that no answer had come from St. Petersburg, so it is evident they discuss together. The Chinese want to content everybody. I said all we really cared for was freedom of commerce, but if the Chinese openly gave away what would conflict with the most favoured nation clause, we should ask for compensation.

On January 24 Uchida came to Satow to say that he had heard that the Manchurian convention was to be signed in a few days, and that the Russians were to get preferential rights in mining and so forth, by an agreement to be signed with the Russo-Chinese Bank. "I repeated to him that we must not allow anything to be done which interfered with our rights, and we agreed to speak to Prince Ch'ing."

On the evening of January 24 Campbell obtained the draft of the proposed agreement with the Russo-Chinese Bank and the following day Satow sent it to the Foreign Office and to Tokyo. The text of the separate arrangement read:

The Chinese Government, in view of the unprosperous condition of trade in Manchuria ever since the Boxer outbreak, desires to organize the resources and industries of that country.

168

The co-operation of an institution commanding capital and experience is required, and the Russo-Chinese Bank, which has undertaken on behalf of the Chinese Government, the railway, financial, and other important engineering and commercial enterprises, is suitable for the purpose.

It is now specially agreed that mining and railway enterprises undertaken by the Chinese Government, or by Chinese Companies or subjects authorized by the State and employing their own capital, shall in the future be made known to the Russo-Chinese Bank, which may finance such enterprises. In the event of the Chinese Government or Chinese subjects being unable to undertake a work, the Russo-Chinese Bank shall have the first refusal of an offer of participation, and if the bank refuses such an offer, any other person or Company can be allowed to undertake the work.

This Agreement is an unimportant matter concerning the commercial relations of Russia and China. It does not affect the Treaty ports, and it involves no detriment to the privileges, industrial or commercial, secured by Treaty provisions.

Satow added: "The bank is understood to demand further modifications. The last paragraph was inserted by Prince Ch'ing to meet the objections of other Powers."[127]

Lansdowne replied:

The Agreement which the Russo-Chinese Bank propose is apparently a mere subterfuge for cloaking infractions of China's Treaty engagements towards this country and other Powers. The last paragraph seems to be valueless.

We shall have to consider in what form we are to seek compensatory advantages for Great Britain if the Chinese Government accept this Agreement.

You should make the Chinese Government and Yang-tsze Viceroys acquainted with the above.[128]

On January 29, Hart called on Satow.

Sir Robert came to say that Nat'ung had brought him the only copy of the draft agreement between Pokotiloff etc., about industrial enterprises, which he repeated to me verbatim (in accordance with what Campbell had given me) with the further addition that the agreement of March with the Tartar-general of Kirin ratified in July was to be construed in accordance with the terms of this agreement, and that all agreements in the three provinces should be made by the Tartar generals with the concurrence of the Superintendent of Northern trade. As Prince Ch'ing and Nat'ung are dining with me tonight, they wished me to know it beforehand, as Uchida had been to Prince Ch'ing on the 27th and pressed him so hard that he almost lost his temper; Conger also went and spoke in the same tone as Uchida. Now the Chinese are getting reports from Manchuria about the treatment which the population experiences at the hands of the Russians, and it is necessary to finish the business, or the Russians will remain there permanently. Pokotiloff has telegraphed to de Witte, and will expect to get a reply in a day or two. Prince hopes that our objections will be made as light as possible.

I said I could not give an answer off the reel, to which he said that he did not ask for it.

On January 30, Satow received a telegram from the Foreign Office about the draft agreement between the Russo-Chinese Bank and the Chinese, refusing to sanction it. "I sent off telegram to Fraser and Sundius, and then went to tell Hart. He said it was quite true, what Foreign Office said, but Chinese felt that Russia being in possession they must give something to get her out." Satow then called on Conger and told him his instructions and that he had acted on them.

Prince Ch'ing and Hart had said to him things were getting daily worse in Manchuria, and if they made no concession, the Russians would not go out, and China was not strong enough to turn them out. He had advised them to make some concession, if they could do it without giving away the rights they had by treaty accorded to other Powers. He had acted on his previous instructions, which were to that effect. As I was going away he said that the Japanese would easily turn the Russians out of Manchuria by force, and he wondered they did not take advantage of the opportunity to come to some arrangement by which they could take Corea for themselves. Last year when he went home through Japan the trains were crowded with officers, all agog for war. Of course Russia would rally, and beat the Japanese in the end, but they could give a great deal of trouble.

I said Ito had held them back, as he was by no means disposed to go to war. (1/30)

On February 1 Satow went to Uchida and told him what he had done about Manchuria through Hart and the two Viceroys. Two days later he conferred with the American Minister.

Conger has got instructions in reply to his last telegram that any such agreement giving to a foreign company exclusive rights in mining, railways or industrial enterprises as is contemplated by the Russo-Chinese Bank agreement would be contrary to Treaties and to the policy of equal rights which Russia had assured she would adhere to, and the United States Government intended to put this before China and Russia. He has shown it to Uchida and also to Lessar, who replied that it was not more than Germany had got in Shantung. Conger said that there was no published Treaty, but Lessar replied [Chancellor Prince Bernhard] von Bülow had declared it was not expedient to publish it. He at any rate had nothing to do with the matter, which only concerned the bank. Conger then asked whether it was not possible to sign the agreement for the evacuation of Manchuria independently, to which Lessar replied that he would like to do so, but had no instructions. (2/3)

On February 5, Satow called on Prince Ch'ing. "Prince Ch'ing said it was his idea to sign the Manchurian agreement, leaving the Pokotiloff thing to fizzle out. I suggested he should leave out the words 'in perpetuity' in Article 1 [?] which has the effect of preventing the Chinese from ever getting back the Manchurian railway."

In a dispatch Satow added that he had informed Prince Ch'ing of Lansdowne's views. "He fully understands the consequences of the Agreement proposed by the Bank, and said he was trying to get the main Convention signed without it." Satow reported that Japan and the United States also pressed China not to sanction the Agreement with the Bank. "The Assurances given by the Russian Minister of Foreign Affairs as to their intention of following the open-door policy are certainly not consistent with the attempt of one Power

171

to acquire exclusive privileges, and these considerations are submitted by the United States' Government to the Governments of Russia and China."[129]

Lansdowne replied that Great Britain could not press the Chinese Government to sign the Convention without danger,[130] and on February 9 Satow went to Uchida and told him not to press the Chinese to sign the Manchurian convention, as the British Government thought it still contained some objectionable features. "He had received no instructions yet to press them, and before doing so would let me know," Satow recorded in his diary. "I said there was something up between our governments which I expected to hear of in a day or two. He knew Hayashi [Tadasu, the Japanese Minister to Great Britain] had be[en] told to urge His Majesty's Government to talk direct to Russia, as the United States have done."

On February 11, Uchida brought Satow the English text of the agreement between England and Japan, "a sort of mutual aid alliance, like the triple alliance treaty." The following day Conger had lunch with Satow.

Uchida has given him a copy of the agreement, which he is very desirous to show to Reuter's agent and the correspondent of the *Sun.* I rather discountenanced the idea. He thinks it the most important political event that has occurred for a long time, and that the Japanese could if they were so minded turn out the Russians from Manchuria. He thinks it a good thing that we have managed to prevent the Chinese signing the Manchurian convention and the agreement with Russo-Chinese Bank, and hopes the United States will be able to come into line with us. I said I felt certain it had been communicated at Washington, and that even if the United States took no active part, they would show us a benevolent sympathy.

Satow went to Prince Ch'ing intending to give him a translation of the Anglo-Japanese Agreement, Uchida having done so in the morning. "Asked if Uchida had shown it. Prince said it was very satisfactory, and a proof of the regard of

England and Japan for China," Satow noted in his diary. In a dispatch he added, "and he [Prince Ch'ing] is of opinion that his negotiations for the evacuation of Manchuria will be considerably facilitated by it."[131]

I drew his attention to the language I had used in my speech to the Emperor about independence and territorial integrity of China, which this agreement was declared to be intended to secure [Satow continued in his diary]. Then I suggested that under the circumstances he might give me text of the Manchurian agreement of which I had obtained copies that were perhaps not authentic. So he went and fetched his own most recent draft, and we went through it together. Afterwards he said we might take it away and return it to him. I told him I could not express an opinion until I had submitted it to His Majesty's Government, that we might at any rate safely wait a few days to see what effect the announcement of the Anglo-Japanese agreement made. He replied that he had seen signs quite recently of a desire to sign on the part of Russia. Pokotilof had called the preceding day, but he had excused himself, and sent out Lien-fang to say that he could not discuss the Bank agreement.

The next day Satow telegraphed the text of the draft of the Manchurian Convention to Lansdowne.

His Majesty the Emperor of Russia and His Majesty the Emperor of China, being desirous of re-establishing the relations of amity which were injured by the disturbances in China of the year 1900, have appointed Plenipotentiaries to negotiate on matters relating to Manchuria.

Article 1. His Majesty the Emperor of Russia, desirous of manifesting anew to His Majesty the Emperor of China proofs of amity and friendship, and of ignoring the hostile attacks on peaceful Russian subjects which took place along the Russo-Manchurian frontier, agrees that Chinese authority shall be restored in Manchuria, and that the country shall return to Chinese dominion and administration such as existed before its occupation by the Russian troops.

Article 2. The Government of China declares that from the date of the return of Manchuria to Chinese administration, the terms of the Agreement of the 27th August, 1896 (Russian

173

Calendar), with the Russo-Chinese Bank shall be faithfully observed for ever; and recognizes the obligation to afford the fullest protection to the railway and railway employés in accordance with Article 5 of that Agreement, and to all Russian subjects and their affairs in Manchuria.

The Government of China, having recognized the above obligations, the Government of Russia, if no further disturbances arise and no obstacles are caused by the proceedings of other Powers, agrees to withdraw the Russian forces from Manchuria gradually. The mode of withdrawal shall be as follows:

Within four months from the signature of the present Agreement the Russian troops quartered in the south-west part of Sheng-ching Province up to the Liao River shall be withdrawn, and the railways shall be restored to China.

Within a further period of four months the Russian troops shall evacuate the remainder of Shen-ching and the Province of Kirin.

Within four months after the above period the Russian troops shall evacuate the Province of Hei-lung-chiang.

Article 3. The disturbances of last year having been caused by Chinese Government troops stationed on the Russian frontier, the Governments of China and of Russia, in order to avoid a recurrence of these disturbances, agree as follows:

The Military Governors of the Manchurian provinces shall be instructed to concert with the Russian military authorities in deciding on the numbers of the Chinese troops to garrison Manchuria and their stations until the Russian troops are withdrawn; and China agrees that over and above the arrangements concluded by the Military Governors with the Russian military authorities, which shall contemplate a sufficient number of troops for the maintenance of order and the suppression of brigandage, there shall be no additions to the garrison of trained soldiers. After the complete evacuation of Manchuria by the Russian forces, however, the numbers of the Chinese troops shall be arranged by the Chinese Government, who will inform the Russian Government of their movements. For if China maintains a large military force in Manchuria, Russia cannot but strengthen her frontier garrisons, and the result will be increased military expenditure in both countries, without advantage to either. With regard to the organization of a police force in Manchuria and the restoration of tranquillity, the Military Governors of each province shall train Chinese foot and mounted men exclusively to fulfil police functions. The land assigned to the Manchurian Railway alone shall be policed by other than Chinese police.

Article 4. The Government of Russia agrees to restore the Shanhaikwan-Newchwang-Hsinminting Railways, which have been occupied and protected by Russian troops since the end of September 1900, to their owners; and the Government of China agrees:

1. In case protective measures are required that the duty of protecting these railways shall be undertaken by China alone; that it will not be necessary to invite other Powers (or another Power) to protect, repair, or maintain them, and that no other Power shall be allowed to occupy territory from which Russian troops are withdrawn.

2. The completion and maintenance of the aforesaid railways shall be conducted in strict accordance with the terms of the Anglo-Russian Agreement of the 16th August, 1899, and of the Loan Agreement concluded with the (British and Chinese) Corporation on the 28th September, 1898, for the construction of those railways. The Corporation shall abide by all other engagements which have been entered into, and shall not take possession of or on any pretext administer the Shanhaikwan-Newchwang-Hsinminting Railways.

3. Extensions of railways in South Manchuria, or branch lines, or the construction of a bridge, or the moving of the terminus at Newchwang, or such like matters shall form the subject of mutual discussion hereafter.

4. If it appears on examination that the expenses incurred by the Russian Government in the repair and maintenance of the Shanhaikwan-Newchwang-Hsinminting Railways were not included in the general indemnity, the Chinese Government shall arrange the necessary compensation with the Russian Government.[132]

On February 16 Satow telegraphed some changes in the Manchurian Convention demanded by Russia:

. . . objections raised by Russians to Article 2 are:

Instead of two years originally offered by them they propose to spread evacuation over three years.

To Article 3 Russia wishes to have power to limit the number of troops maintained after complete evacuation, instead of being merely informed by China of their movements.

175

To Article 4, paragraph 4, Russia insists that expenses of repair were not included in general indemnity and objects to the hypothetical form.

Satow added the following observations:

Article 2, intention of words 'for ever' appears to prevent China entering into possession of Manchurian Railway after lapse of eighty years (see Foreign Office despatch No. 1, of the 6th January, 1897, Article 30 of the Agreement).

There are too many loopholes in the words, "if no further disturbances arise, and no obstacles are caused by the proceedings of other Powers." As each portion of Manchuria is evacuated full liberty ought to be left to the Chinese Government to station troops in it.

No provision seems to have been made for this.

In Article 4, paragraph 2, "The Corporation shall abide by all other engagements which have been entered into" is a stipulation which the Chinese ought not to make as they cannot enforce it.

Paragraph 4. We shall have to return to China the 300,000 l. included in our private claims, should the expenditure by the Russians on the repairs have sufficed to put the line in the *status quo ante.*

The General Officer Commanding informs me that the Japanese, Germans, Russians, and ourselves, were repaid the value of material used in repairs of intra-mural line out of railway revenue, which will be charged to reconstruction in the accounts, to be provided from the 500,000 l. claimed by the British and Chinese Corporation. No charge was made for labour. I do not think, under the circumstances, that it can be held that the Russians are not entitled to similar payment for work done on the extra-mural line, and it would be more convenient that the Chinese should make the payment, and that we should afterwards repay them.[133]

That day Satow conferred with Uchida.

He says when he saw Prince Ch'ing on the 12, the latter said the Russian Minister had informed him Russia insisted upon the prohibition of cannon, the fixing of number of troops and their stations by agreement and evacuation being spread over three years. That he had so informed his Government. They were

176

acquainted with Prince Ch'ing's counterdraft, and were quite satisfied with it, but Bertie told Hayashi that Article III of the Russian draft was objectionable, and he (Uchida) had telegraphed that I objected to *yung-yüan* [in perpetuity] in Article I. So he had suggested that it would be better not to say anything more to Prince Ch'ing until Great Britain and Japan have agreed to the objections they will make. Told him I had telegraphed the text of Prince Ch'ing's counterdraft on the 14th, and my observations today. We agreed to come together and discuss the whole subject as soon as we got our instructions. . . . Japanese Minister gave Count Lamsdorff copy of the agreement on 12th, who expressed great surprise, and so the idea of the Japanese Government that the Russians hearing of it beforehand had abandoned the Russo-Chinese bank agreement and showed readiness to come to an understanding with China on other points was not justified. He had instructions to try and find out. (2/16)

On February 19 Satow went to Hart. "He says he had a visit from a Chinese a few days ago (?Nat'ung) who said the Anglo-Japanese agreement put China in the disagreeable position of having to take a part and perhaps quarrel with the power from whom she had most to fear, namely Russia; and also, did not the agreement leave it in the power of Japan to herself take possession of Manchuria if she succeeded in driving out the Russians."

On February 20, Satow showed Uchida a memorandum of observations he had been instructed to make to Prince Ch'ing regarding the counter-draft Manchurian convention. Uchida quite agreed. That day Satow gave Prince Ch'ing the criticisms of the British Government.

Told him if he had an opportunity in the course of negotiations that he should try to whittle the conditions down still more. Lessar says he can discuss all the points at issue except period over which evacuation is to be spread, which he insists on keeping at three years.[j] Ch'ing protested that this was an ad-

---

[j] In a telegram Satow reflected: "Prince Ching always speaks of "three years" in conversation with me. If, however, thirty-six months be intended, it is possible that two whole years and parts of two others are covered by this, and this might be spoken of as four.[134]

vance upon the two years originally proposed, to which Lessar's only reply was that his Government so wished it. I asked what explanation was given of the necessity of spreading the evacuation over so long a period. Prince replied that Lessar had said, Between you and me the real reason is that the military party want to retain Manchuria, while the Government, Count Lamsdorff and de Witte wish to give it up, and they had hoped that obtaining a few concessions for the Russo-Chinese Bank would enable them to influence the others. But the Prince was not quite sure that Lamsdorff was sincere in wishing to give up Manchuria, and at any rate the military men were servants of the Russian Government, and he did not see why their wishes should be consulted. I urged him to stick to his guns, and if he had an opportunity to whittle down Lessar's original draft a little more. We discussed the counter draft very carefully, the Prince first relying on his memory, but at last he ran out and brought in his own copy, after which we made more progress.

"He wanted to know what would happen if Russia still refused to sign," Satow recalled. "I told him that the Anglo-Japanese agreement was not a mere *brutum fulmen* [insensible thunderbolt, i.e. futile threat of force] but meant business."

On returning home Satow wrote to Uchida an account of what had passed, and suggested that he might possibly be able to give Prince Ch'ing some encouragement. The next day Uchida came to Satow, and said that before the Agreement had been published the Japanese Government had telegraphed that in case Russia rejected the proposal of China to dissociate the convention from the agreement and to conclude the former without the latter, and delay evacuation, the Japanese Government would take steps to approach Russia on the subject of fulfilment of his assurances regarding evacuation of Manchuria.

As Japan is now in a stronger position, he will send his interpreter to Prince Ch'ing to tell him this, and also to find out whether there is a meeting between Ch'ing and Lessar today. He says the Anglo-Japanese understanding was first mentioned in March of last year, and he thinks [Sir Claude] MacDonald [formerly British Minister to China and now to Japan] was consulted when he was at home last year. The negotiations were managed through Baron Hayashi, and kept very secret so that no one knew anything about it. He sent a copy to Yüan Shih-kai, who did not seem very pleased. Yüan in reality cares little about Manchuria, and is only anxious to get back Tientsin, which he thinks will be delayed in consequence of the Agreement. Asked him about Junglu's connexion with the Russians: he says there was a story of the Russo-Chinese bank having given him 100,000 taels, which he returned. In any case, he is not so much in their hands as Li was. Prince Ch'ing and Junglu are rivals, the former having foreign affairs the latter home; the Prince is not allowed to get into the Grand Council, because he would become too powerful. (2/20)

On February 24 Lansdowne telegraphed Satow regarding the Manchurian Agreement:

I have received from Baron Hayashi the text of M. Lessar's draft Convention, which Prince Ching communicated to the Japanese Minister at Peking on the 9th December.

The Japanese Government object to Article 3 and to clause 3 of Article 4 of the Russian draft, in addition to the objections which Prince Ching embodied in his counter-draft.

We have to make the following additional observations:

1. In the text of the Russian draft communicated by Baron Hayashi, "permanently" takes the place of "for ever" in Article 2, as given in your telegram No. 44 of the 14th. It should, however, be made clear that the provision of the Agreement of 1896, stipulating that the Railway is to revert to China in eighty years, is not cancelled by the wording.

2. Assuming that the evacuation of Manchuria is to take place gradually, Newchwang, and, if possible, the whole Province of Shengking, should be included in the first section to be evacuated. You should support the Chinese Government in pressing for a shorter term for the complete evacuation than three years.

3. The Chinese should be free, after evacuation, to settle the numbers and distribution of their troops, including artillery, without which they would not be able to suppress insurrection or prevent a "coup de main." The stipulation respecting the

179

communication of such number and distribution should be reciprocal, and should not be made by the Chinese authorities only.

4. You should support the Japanese objection to clause 3 of Article 4, although our Agreement with Russia precludes us from applying for or supporting railway undertakings in Manchuria. It interferes with the legitimate rights of China and the equality of opportunity, stipulated by her Treaty engagements to foreigners.

5. With reference to your telegram No. 49 of the 21st, you should not encourage Prince Ching to persist in his intention of inviting the Russian Minister to appoint a date for the signature of the Chinese counter-draft until the provisions are eliminated to which His Majesty's Government and the Japanese Government object.

M. Lessar's confidential statements should not persuade China to purchase a shortening of the occupation of Manchuria by granting Concessions contrary to the spirit of her international obligations and detrimental to her own interests, as Russia would welcome an early evacuation for financial reasons.

It would be most desirable that the language of your American and Japanese colleagues to Chinese Government should accord with yours, and you should confer with them to this end.

Keep me fully informed as to their action and intentions, and Yang-tsze Viceroys, of course, of negotiations.

Repeat above to Sir C. MacDonald.[135]

On February 26 Uchida came to see Satow, and Satow read him his latest instructions about the counter draft of Prince Ch'ing. "He promised to ask at Tokio for further instructions. We both thought Prince Ch'ing could not well introduce further changes in his counter draft, until it had first been rejected by the Russians," Satow jotted down in his diary.

On February 27 Satow discussed the Manchurian Agreement with Conger on the basis of the version published in the *Times* of November 9.

I told him Prince Ch'ing's counter draft of which Hart had acquainted him with the contents could only be obtained from the Prince [Satow recorded]. His general instructions are to object to the long period for evacuation stipulated for by the Russians, the limitation of troops and their stations to what Russia approves of, and the retention of Newchwang. He will see Prince Ch'ing on Saturday, and talk to him about the last of these three points. The Russian reply to the United States note he considers "no good at all."

On February 28, Mumm asked Satow how things were going on in Manchuria. "Told him I believed they were much in the same state," Satow replied, adding: "Thought that Ito's return would make the Japanese to act prudently."

On March 2 Uchida lent Satow a copy of the Russian draft given to him on December 9 by Prince Ch'ing, and stated that as some of the instructions sent to him from To- kio required further explanation he had telegraphed again. "He said Chou-fu came to sound him about what would hap- pen if Russia declined to move out of Manchuria. He had re- plied that matters had not advanced far enough to form an opinion, and that Russia had over and over again declared her intention of going out."

Satow also conferred with Conger.

As to Manchuria Prince Ch'ing has promised him a copy of the counter draft, and said it was quite understood that New- chwang is included in the area to be first evacuated up to the Liao river. As Prince asserted this and he was not strong on the geography he thought it must be all right, and merely sug- gested to Prince that it would be well to include Newchwang by name; similarly as to an understanding the Prince said ex- isted that China should be allowed to bridge the Liao river at Newchwang. Conger told me the Russians had built a railway line from Newchwang along river bank of the Liao to a point nearly opposite Moukden, their object being to divert the trade of Newchwang to Dalny and Shanhaikwan. (3/2)

On March 4, Prince Ch'ing wined and dined the diplomatic body. Uchida, who sat on Satow's left, drank a good deal and towards the end of the dinner talked in Japanese about the shabbiness of their colleagues.

181

He remarked that the Chinese and Russian officials only cared for the squeezes they could get out of the Manchurian agreement, and the latter were indifferent to the cost of occupation inflicted on their government. I said the report went about that the Russians were furious with Ito for listening to them about an arrangement respecting Corea and Manchuria while all the time he had the Anglo-Japanese agreement in his pocket. He replied that Ito was always ready to come to an understanding with Russia on those subjects, and being a good deal of an opportunist did listen to their proposals. But the negotiations between Japan and England had already gone too far, so that the Japanese Government would not support him, and when he came to London he found out that it was so. Hayashi being a sharp fellow thought it would be well to commit Ito, whom he recommended for the Grand Cross of the Bath, and now on his return to Japan he (Ito) will get a great deal of credit for having suggested the alliance, which he will turn to account to strengthen his own political position.

The next day Uchida brought Satow a paraphrase of his latest instructions, which were not to ask for alterations in the counterdraft of Prince Ch'ing, unless the Russians refused it or there were fresh developments. "He said that acting on his instructions he had told Prince Ch'ing that if the Russians unduly delayed reply Japan would make representations at Petersburg." (3/5)

On March 11 Satow graphically presented to the Foreign office translations of Lessar's original draft proposal of the Russo-Chinese Convention regarding Manchuria side by side with such parts of Prince Ch'ing's counter-proposals as differed from the Russian Minister's draft.

The following day Uchida came to tell Satow his most recent instructions were to press Prince Ch'ing to get his counterdraft signed as soon as possible. As Satow noted in his diary: "Japanese Government fear Russia may refuse, and merely repeat over again her vague assurances about Manchuria. He told Yüan Shih-k'ai that the Prince must stick to his twelve months, and the Russians would certainly go." (3/12)

The Manchurian Convention between Russia and Japan

M. Lessar's Draft of Russo-Chinese Convention.	Prince Ch'ing's Counter-Draft.
His Majesty the Emperor of Russia and His Majesty the Emperor of China, being desirous of re-establishing the relations of amity which were injured by the disturbances in China in the year 1900, have appointed Plenipotentiaries to negotiate on matters relating to Manchuria.	Same.

ARTICLE I

His Majesty the Emperor of Russia, desirous of manifesting anew to His Majesty the Emperor of China proofs of amity and friendship, and of ignoring the hostile attacks on peaceful Russian subjects which took place along the Russo-Manchurian frontier, agrees that Chinese authority shall be restored in Manchuria, and that the country shall return to Chinese dominion and administration such as existed before its occupation by the Russian troops.	Same.

ARTICLE II

The Government of China declares that from the date of the return of Manchuria to Chinese Administration the terms of the Agreement of the 27th August, 1896 (Russian Calendar), with the Russo-Chinese Bank shall be faithfully observed for ever; and recog-	Same.

M. Lessar's Draft of Russo-Chinese Convention.	*Prince Ch'ing's Counter-Draft.*

nizes the obligations to afford the fullest protection to the Railway and Railway employés in accordance with Article 5 of that Agreement, and to all Russian subjects and their affairs in Manchuria.

The Government of China, having recognized the above obligations, the Government of Russia, if no further disturbances arise and no obstacles are caused by the proceedings of other Powers, agrees to withdraw the Russian forces from Manchuria gradually. The mode of withdrawal shall be as follows:

(a.) *In the year* 1901 (*Russian Calendar*) the Russian troops quartered in the southwest part of Sheng-ching Province up to the Liao River shall be withdrawn, and the railways shall be restored to China.

Within four months from the signature of the present Agreement the Russian troops, etc.

(b.) In the following year, that is, 1902 (Russian Calendar), the Russian troops shall evacuate the remainder of Sheng-ching.

Within a further period of four months the Russian troops shall evacuate the remainder of Sheng-ching *and the Province of Kirin.*

(c.) *In the year* 1903 (*Russian Calendar*) *the possibility of withdrawing the remainder of the Russian forces quartered in the two provinces of Kirin and Heilung-chiang will be considered.*

Within four months after the above period the Russian troops shall evacuate the Province of Heilung-chiang.

The Manchurian Convention between Russia and Japan

M. Lessar's Draft of
Russo-Chinese
Convention.

Prince Ch'ing's
Counter-Draft.

ARTICLE III

The disturbances of last year having been caused by Chinese Government troops stationed on the Russian frontier, the Government of China and Russia, in order to avoid a recurrence of those disturbances, agree as follows:

Same.

The military Governors of the Manchurian provinces shall be instructed to concert with the Russian military authorities in deciding on the numbers of the Chinese troops to garrison Manchuria and their stations; and China agrees that, over and above the *numbers fixed by the military Governors in consultation with the Russian military authorities,* there shall be no additions to the garrison of trained soldiers, *and that no other troops shall be sent to Manchuria.* For if China maintains a large military force in Manchuria, Russia cannot but strengthen her frontier garrisons, and the result will be increased military expenditure in both countries without advantage to either.

The military Governors of the Manchurian provinces shall be instructed to act in concert with the Russian military authorities in deciding on the numbers of the Chinese troops to garrison Manchuria and their stations *until the Russian troops are withdrawn;* and China agrees that over and above *the arrangements concluded by the military Governors with the Russian military authorities which shall contemplate a sufficient number of troops for the maintenance of order and the suppression of brigandage,* there shall be no additions to the garrison of trained soldiers. *After the complete evacuation of Manchuria by the Russian forces, however, the numbers of the Chinese troops shall be arranged by the Chinese Government, who will inform the Russian Government of their movements.* For if China maintains, etc.

185

M. Lessar's Draft of Russo-Chinese Convention.	*Prince Ch'ing's Counter-Draft.*
With regard to the organization of police force in Manchuria and the restoration of tranquillity, the military Governors of each province shall train Chinese foot and mounted men exclusively to fulfil police functions. The land assigned to the Manchurian Railway alone shall be policed by other than Chinese police. *In the armament of this police force cannon shall be forbidden.*	Same. This last sentence is excluded.

ARTICLE IV The Government of Russia agrees to restore the Shanhai-kuan - Newchwang - Hsinming-ting Railways, which have been occupied and protected by Russian troops since the end of September 1900, to their owners; and the Government of China agrees:	Same.
1. That the troops of other Powers (or another Power) shall *not be allowed to* protect, repair, or maintain the railways so restored, or to occupy territory from which the Russian troops are withdrawn. In case protective measures are required, the duty of protecting these railways shall be undertaken by Chinese troops only.	1. In case protective measures are required, that the duty of protecting these railways shall be undertaken by China alone; that it will *not be necessary to invite other Powers* (or another Power) to protect, repair, or maintain them; and that no other Power shall be allowed to occupy territory from which Russian troops are withdrawn.
2. The completion and maintenance of the aforesaid rail-	Same.

The Manchurian Convention between Russia and Japan

M. Lessar's Draft of Russo-Chinese Convention.	*Prince Ch'ing's Counter-Draft.*

ways shall be conducted in strict accordance with the terms of the Anglo-Russian Agreement of the 16th April, 1899, and of the loan Agreement concluded with the (British and Chinese) Corporation on the 28th September, 1898, for the construction of those railways. The Corporation shall abide by all other engagements which have been entered into, and shall not take possession of or on any pretext administer the Shanhaikuan-Newchwang-Hsinmingting Railways.

3. *Without the previous consent of the Russian Government, no* extension of railways or branch lines in South Manchuria shall be permitted, *no* bridge shall be built over the *Liao River* at Newchwang, and *no* terminus of the Chinese railways in this territory shall be moved.

3. Extension of railways in South Manchuria, or branch lines, or the construction of a new bridge, or the moving of a terminus at Newchwang, or such like matters, *shall form the subject of mutual discussion hereafter.*

4. The expenses incurred by the Russian Government in the repair and maintenance of the Shanhaikuan - Newchwang-Hsinmingting Railways *thus restored shall be repaid.*

If it appears on examination that the expenses incurred by the Russian Government in the repair and maintenance of the Shanhaikuan - Newchwang-Hsinmingting Railways *were not included in the general indemnity, the Chinese shall arrange the necessary compensation with the Russian Government.*[136]

The next day Satow discussed Manchuria with Prince Ch'ing. "He sent Lien-fang to Lessar a few days ago to press for a reply but the latter said he had telegraphed, and no instructions had come. Asked if it were true that Russia had offered evacuation in 18 months; he said 'yes,' but he wanted to get still more out of them. He would be willing to give them a couple of months or so, but would not give way on any other point. I went over our principal objections again, so as to let him understand that we don't approve of it as it stands, without however dissuading him from signing." (3/13)

Satow went on to Prince Kung, who "spoke very frankly about the advantages of the Anglo-Japanese agreement, and against Russia."

On March 15 Satow called on the American Minister and told him of his talks with Uchida and Prince Ch'ing about Manchuria. "He seems to be in the same position as I am, he cannot approve of the counter-draft, nor yet press for its amendment."

On March 17 Lien-fang brought Satow the draft Manchurian agreement with Russian amendments. As Satow reported in a confidential dispatch:

In Article II, paragraph 1, Prince Ch'ing had inserted the words "of years" after "terms," so as to make the phrase run as follows: "the terms of years of the Agreement of the 27th August, 1896 (Russian calendar), with the Russo-Chinese Bank shall be observed for ever."

M. Lessar struck out the words which had been inserted, observing that the clause, if so framed, would seem to imply that the rest of the conditions of that Agreement were not to be observed. On the other hand, the words "for ever" might easily be interpreted as cancelling the Article in that Agreement by which China obtains the right of purchasing the Manchurian Railway after the lapse of thirty-six years, or of entering into possession without payment after the expiration of eighty years. If both phrases were omitted, the rights accorded to Russia under the Agreement would still remain undiminished.

In paragraphs (a), (b), and (c) of Article II, M. Lessar substitutes six months for Prince Ch'ing's four months.

It must be obvious, however, that it would be desirable, in the general interest, to curtail the period allowed for evacuation as much as possible in view of the political tension and unrest which has been caused by the prolonged occupation of Manchuria by Russia, and the known desire of the military party in that country to retain permanent possession of the three provinces.

After "withdrawn," in paragraph (a), the following substitution is made:

"If by that date the administration of Tien-tsin has been transferred by the Provisional Government to the Viceroy of Chihli, the railways and the administration of Newchwang shall be restored to China."

It is necessary to point out that, whereas five out of the six Powers represented on the Tien-tsin Provisional Government have already expressed their willingness to hand over the administration of that city, the only Power which still hesitates is precisely the Power that has declared itself indifferent to the future of Manchuria, and whose commercial and shipping interests in Manchuria are practically non-existent. Moreover, as Russia is one of the Powers represented on the Tien-tsin Provisional Government, she can by relying on this condition delay indefinitely the surrender of the railway, in which British capital alone is involved, and that of Newchwang, where the preponderant commercial and shipping interests are British, American, and Japanese. As I reported in my despatch No. 65 of the 13th March, the Russian Minister declared at the meeting held to discuss the question of abolishing the Tien-tsin Provisional Government, that he had no instructions, though he supposed his Government would not object to the course that might be adopted by the other Powers. In any case it seems an unusual arrangement to make the performance of a stipulation depend, not on the action of the other party to it, but on an event which cannot happen without the consent of the stipulator. Moreover, it would be just as reasonable for us to declare the date of transfer of the Peking-Shanhaikuan Railway to Chinese administration and the abolition of the Tien-tsin Provisional Government should depend upon the evacuation of Newchwang and the surrender of the Shanhaikuan-Hsinmingting-Newchwang Railways to China.

In paragraph (c), before "within", the words "if it is ascertained that the country is tranquil" are inserted by M. Lessar.

189

Your Lordship will remember that in M. Lessar's first draft the wording was "in the year 1903 the possibility of withdrawing the remainder of the Russian forces quartered in the Provinces of Kirin and Hei Luang Chiang will be considered." Previous experience, and notably that of the allies in Chihli, shows that foreign armies in Chinese territory are not able to maintain order beyond the districts actually occupied by them. The tranquillity of the province is not likely to be restored as long as the Russian troops remain there, hence this stipulation is clearly disadvantageous to China. I am informed that in the expressed opinion of M. Lessar, so long as Newchwang is evacuated, the interested Powers would not object to Russian occupation of the rest of Manchuria, even though it should last another century.

In Article IV, paragraph 3, the words of M. Lessar's original draft: "The Corporation shall abide by all other engagements which have been entered into" are altered to "The Corporation shall abide by these engagements."

It is evidently out of the power of Russia and China to enter into a mutual agreement as to what a British Corporation shall or shall not do. It is, however, satisfactory to see in this clause a reaffirmation by Russia of the validity of the existing contract between the Chinese Railway Administration and the British and Chinese Corporation, the conclusion of which was made a ground of complaint against the Chinese Government in the draft Convention presented in March of last year by the Russian Government (reported in my telegram No. 82 of the 19th March, 1901).

Paragraph 3 of Prince Ch'ing's counter-draft regarding the extension of railways in South Manchuria, the bridging of the Liao River, and the future position of the Newchwang terminus of the line from Shanhaikuan is left as it stands. In point of effect it limits the sovereign rights of China as much as M. Lessar's original draft did.

Paragraph 4 of the same Article IV now stands as follows: "The repayment of the expenses incurred by the Russian Government in the repair and maintenance of the Shanhaikuan-Newchwang-Hsinmingting Railways shall be arranged by the Chinese Government, these expenses not having been included in the general indemnity." It would be advisable that the Chinese Government should ask for an account of expenditure and receipts, distinguishing under the former heading between repairs and new construction.

At the end of Article IV the following stipulations have been added by M. Lessar: "The existing Treaties between the two countries, in so far as they are not modified by the present Convention, remain in force.

"This Convention comes into operation from the date on which the ratifications are exchanged at St. Petersburgh, which shall be soon after the signature.

"In witness whereof the Plenipotentiaries of the two countries have prepared Russian and Chinese versions of this Convention, and have signed two copies of each. The Russian and Chinese versions have been compared and are found to correspond, but in case of dispute the Russian text shall rule."

The clause confirmatory of other Treaties seems scarcely necessary in a Convention providing for the evacuation of a Chinese province. No such stipulation was inserted in the Final Protocol of the 7th September, 1901. It is even thought possible that there are secret Treaties in existence, which are known to but a few persons. It would be prudent, therefore, if this clause is insisted upon by Russia, to enumerate the Treaties referred to, but still better would be its complete excision.

There is a contradiction between Article II which makes evacuation begin within a certain period, dating from the signature of the Convention, and the clause by which the Convention comes into operation on the exchange of ratifications. No time is named for the exchange of ratifications, which may be indefinitely delayed. It would be better, therefore, to adopt a wording by which the Convention comes into operation on signature, and the ratifications are exchanged within three months.

The negotiations have hitherto been carried on by means of a Chinese version of a Russian text which has never been communicated, and it has been found impossible to avoid some ambiguity. Prince Ch'ing proposed, therefore, that there should be a French text, the Chinese officials being fairly familiar with that language, which should be the authoritative one, Russian and Chinese versions being, however, signed at the same time. M. Lessar, however, proposes that there should be no French text, and that the Russian should be authoritative. This would be to the disadvantage of China, as there are very few Chinese who know Russian.[137,k]

In his diary Satow recorded the gist of his remarks to Lienfang.

---

[k] Satow telegraphed a brief listing of the amendments on March 18 (Satow to Lansdowne, telegraphic).

I told him these were all unsatisfactory and ought not to be agreed to. His Majesty's Government thought Prince Ch'ing's proposal to evacuate in twelve months quite reasonable, and urged insistence, as Russia was hard up and could not but leave. Personally I thought that if Prince split the difference and offer 15 months it would be wise, if thereby a settlement could be obtained. But it would not do to make evacuation of Newchwang and surrender of the railway depend on dissolution of Tientsin Provisional Government, for I feared Lessar, who was lukewarm about the latter would help to delay it, in order to keep hold of Newchwang. He must insist on putting *nien-shien* [limit of years] in Article II about Eastern Chinese railway, or else striking out *yung-yüan* [in perpetuity]; also on having a French text as the authoritative one; also on evacuation without reference to tranquillity, as the provinces could be at once reduced to order as soon as the Russian troops retired. (3/17)

Satow added in his diary: "Uchida agrees with me about the objectionable character of Russian amendments, but thinks to save time they had better accept 18 months.

On March 18 Lien-fang came to Satow again about the Russian amendments. "Repeated all I had said yesterday, and that I had telegraphed. 'Scolded' the Chinese for weakly giving in on every occasion to Russian demands uttered in a loud voice. Li's idea . . . to obtain good treatment by making concessions was a false one. It only increased appetite." The following day Satow saw Conger.

Told him that Russia wishes to make the surrender of the Tientsin Provisional Government precede the surrender of Newchwang and of the extra-mural railway. He replied that this threw light upon a voluntary utterance of Lessar's the night we dined at Nat'ung's, to the effect that he hoped very shortly to arrange for Newchwang being returned to the Chinese . . . .

Told him also that Lessar had proposed other amendments to the Counter draft, and what they were. (3/19)

Uchida brought Satow a paraphrase of the instructions he had received about Lessar's amendments, which Satow telegraphed to the Foreign Office.[138] As he summed up in his diary: "Japan makes only two objections, viz. that the words 'if the country is found to be tranquil' would give excuse for further delay, and that the ratification clause was ambiguous. It should be made clear that the first period of evacuation began from the signature, as stated in Article II. He is going to Prince Ch'ing this afternoon, but will take care not to say anything that might interfere with what His Majesty's Government wishes to say."

On March 21, Lien-fang came to ask Satow whether he had any reply about the Manchurian convention.

I said no [Satow recorded]. He then began to tell me that Lessar had said there was a treaty, of which neither Prince Ch'ing nor the Empress-Dowager nor the Grand Council knew anything, concluded by Li at Moscow at the time of the Czar's coronation, that they were much perturbed. It would be better to enumerate all the Treaties which Lessar wants to have referred to in the ratification clause as not being affected by Manchurian Convention. Then I talked to him about the efforts made by Great Britain in 1894 to bring about an intervention of the Great Powers so as to prevent war between China and Japan, which had been bluntly refused by the others, who preferred to see Japan and China exhaust themselves, in order to come in afterwards and pick up things; and we now see as a result Russia in Manchuria, Germany in Shantung and France laying claim to all sorts of exclusive privileges in Kwangtung, Kwangsi and Hainan. . . .

Lessar by the way told Lien-fang that the other Powers did not care at all about the two northern provinces of Manchuria, and if Russia only evacuated Newchwang they would not object to Russia remaining for century in the rest of the country. I said to him that if Russia made evacuation of Newchwang depend on abolition of Tientsin Provisional Government other Powers might perhaps refuse to give up Tientsin Provisional Government till Newchwang was evacuated.

Satow went to Uchida. "As to the secret treaty, Prince Ch'ing evidently believed it to exist, but said he was ignorant of its terms. He had suggested to Prince that the safest thing for them was to strike out the reference to Treaties in the ratification clause."

On March 21 Lansdowne telegraphed Satow that in view of the fact that Japan and the United States attached less im-

193

portance to some of the points raised by Great Britain in objection to the Convention, the British Government was willing to modify its stand, but there were some points which it continued to regard as "material:"

(1.) The terms of Article II should not be held to abrogate the right of the Chinese Government to resume possession of the railway after eighty years.

(2.) The police force stipulations in Article III should not be interpreted as precluding China from maintaining, pending and after evacuation by Russia, whatever force of regular troops she may require, and no restriction in regard to employment of artillery with her regular troops should be placed on China.

(3.) Russian consent, under Clause 3 of Article IV, should not be necessary to any action by China with regard to railways within her own territory, and bridge construction and the terminus at Newchwang.

Lansdowne added:

The Russians have an equitable claim to repayment of their expenditure on the Shanhaikwan Railway, as they did not include it in their Protocol demand, and they sould be asked by the Chinese Government for an account of expenditure and receipts. I authorize you to inform Prince Ch'ing, confidentially, that any balance found due and paid to the Russian Government, up to 100,000 l., will be made good to the Chinese Government by His Majesty's Government.

You should consult your Japanese and United States' colleagues freely and endeavour to make their action run parallel with yours.[139]

On March 23 Lien-fang came to Satow in response to a summons that he might tell him Lord Lansdowne's views on Lessar's amendments to the counter draft. "After he had taken notes and thoroughly understood all I told him, he made some notes for Prince Ch'ing. I made some myself, and after lunch took a copy to Uchida and sent one to Conger, both of whom expressed their entire agreement."

On April 1 Lien-fang brought Satow the draft agreed to by Lessar, who refused the wording the English had proposed about the number of troops to be kept in Manchuria after the evacuation. "I told him the two objections of His Majesty's Government, but that under the circumstances I should advise him to sign." Uchida to whom Satow talked the following day said his government wished for his alteration beginning "*aura pleine liberté*," but under the circumstances did not insist on pressing.

On April 4 Satow went to Conger and showed him the agreement between the Military Governor of Kirin and one Luba [Viktor Liuba?] by which none but Russians or Chinese were to mine for gold, silver etc., in that province, and promised to give him copies.

Satow also talked to Uchida. "We agreed to watch closely the Manchurian agreement, lest modifications should be introduced by Russians at the last moment. Signature seems to be imminent. . . ." (4/4)

On April 8, Satow telegraphed:

I have received a message from Prince Ch'ing stating that the Manchurian Convention was signed this afternoon at 4 o'clock, and that the Emperor will ratify it to-morrow.

The Chinese Government express their gratitude to His Majesty's Government for the support they have received. It has enabled them to obtain much better terms than they could otherwise have hoped for. [140]

On April 15, Prince Ch'ing called on Satow to express the gratitude of the Chinese Government for assistance in the recent negotiations.

I impressed on him the importance of sending some one to Manchuria to organize police etc., and generally to be ready to take over as the Russians evacuated. He seemed to be quite alive to the importance of this, and said that the protection of the Manchurian railway was incumbent on China. I dwelt on the importance of preserving order in all the frontier provinces. He said they proposed to reform the administrative system of Manchuria, to have a Viceroy at Kirin with subordinate governors at Tsitsihar and Moukden. . . . Lessar at time of signing the Treaty delivered a verbal note stating that Newchwang would be restored as soon as the Tientsin Provisional Government came to an end, if within first period of six months, if not, then in the first or second month of the second period. I showed him the agreement made by Luba with the Tartar Governor of Kirin for mining to be allowed to Russians and Chinese to the exclusion of all other nations, which he reluctantly admitted had been ratified, but the [he] vehemently asserted that the recent proposals of the Russo-Chinese bank with regard to Shêngking had been definitely rejected.

Reporting this conversation in a dispatch Satow added: "I remarked to the Prince that His Majesty's Government had not, like others, taken advantage of China's difficulties to extort concessions from her during the progress of the negotiations last year, and that I looked to him to assist me now to obtain a satisfactory solution to one or two pending questions."[141]

On April 19, Satow conversed with the Russian Minister.

Lessar talked about the Manchurian convention: the sole difference between it and the original draft was that the Chinese had gained the difference between October and December 1903. They had made a great many absurd verbal alterations in the French draft, so that he was more than inclined to send a telegram advising his Government to sign no convention at all. He was very glad to have a French text, and we must try to get the Chinese always to do anything of importance in French. What they had desired was to resume normal relations with China, so important to them because of their long common frontier, and this had been accomplished by the convention. But the relations with China would never return to a normal condition, by which he meant that Peking had now become a post like Constantinople and Persia, full of rivalries and intrigues. The international position of China was now much stronger than before the troubles, as she could always get the support of one Power against another.

"Our conversation was fortunately interrupted at this point," Satow reported to Lansdowne, "or I might have been tempted to inquire to what Power's proceedings such a development was to be attributed."[142]

196

Partial Evacuation of Manchuria by Russia

DURING THE SUPPRESSION of the Boxer Rebellion the Powers had taken hold of various railroads. Once in possession, they were reluctant to give them up without retaining some sort of control or, at least, receiving certain assurances as to the future disposition of the railways. Furthermore, no power wanted to return "its" railroad before the others did so.

On August 29, 1902, Satow talked with Uchida about the Russian railway from Khailar. "He has sent a party to explore secretly. He thinks Russians intend to clear out by 8 October. Yüan up to the present had not seemed to take much interest in Manchuria, but now he is established at Tientsin, he will naturally become more active to its importance." On September 11, Hu Yü-fen, who was connected with the administration of the northern railways, told Satow that the Chinese had been informed by the Russians that the railway would be handed over on October 8.

On September 15 Satow went to Hart. "He says Lessar has demanded from the Chinese that they shall not extend their postal system in Manchuria, and withdraw what they have already established, under pain of the evacuation not being carried out. He is disposed to tell the Waiwupu [Chinese Foreign Office] to yield rather than run any risk, but it perhaps is only bluff. Lessar has said it would be all right if Hart would place a Russian at the head of the Post Office. Some time ago great efforts were made to get him appoint a Russian Commissioner of Customs at Newchwang, but he has avoided that by keeping [C.A.V.] Bowra there."

On September 22 Hu came to Satow.

Showed various telegrams from Yüan about Russians having urged the Governor General of Moukden to take over the railway on 21. Yüan had sent officials to Shanhaikwan and was proceeding there himself, as he was the proper person to take over. He said Lessar was to sign agreement in 7 articles about transfer of the railways this afternoon, and they were preparing a note to inform me of this immediately on receipt of a telegram from Yang stating that Shanhaikwan had been taken over. I reminded him that the consent of the French General had not yet been obtained by the Waiwupu. If they wrote to me that this consent had been given, and that the Russians had fixed a date for handing over the railway, I would telegraph to General [Sir Garrett O'Moore] Creagh [Commander of the British forces] to do the same, subject to clause 9 of our agreement of 29 April.

On September 23, Satow wrote in his diary: "Note came last night, and I received translation this morning. It says nothing about French general and merely asks me to fix a date for transfer, enclosing copy of the agreement. Hu yesterday said Prince Ch'ing was anxious that I should have the credit of handing over first. Telegraphed to Foreign Office also to General to ask whether it was true the Russians were handing over today at Shanhaikwan."

Two days later Satow recorded: "Last night general telegraphed recommending that we hand over Shanhaikwan at same time as the Russians, also a telegram from Yüan to same effect and a visit from Hu, who insisted that I was bound by my promise of the day before yesterday to hand over railway, as soon as Russians. Told him the Waiwupu note had greatly altered matters, as it obliged me to telegraph again to Foreign Office, nor had the Waiwupu obtained the French general's consent in writing. He got very excited. I said I had again telegraphed this morning to Foreign Office to urge for an answer. It was true that I had promised to hand over, but a certain amount of notice was required. Finally I agreed to tell General Creagh to hand over Shanhaikwan, but as to the rest to await instructions, and he said he would be contented with that."

On September 26 Satow called on Yüan. "Talked a great deal about the railway with no result, as he expected me to give it back without waiting for instructions."

On the 28th Yüan returned Satow's call.

We were talking about the handing over of Shanhaikwan station, which he said had not been done on our part, when Hu arrived, and began arguing with me that I was bound to hand it over. We were getting rather warm when a telegram arrived from Foreign Office authorizing my proceeding as I had proposed. I brought it down from my room where I had gone to decipher it, and said to Hu: "You may cut short your arguments, and have the railway in five minutes." So that restored tranquility and we agreed to hand over tomorrow. After they had departed I sent off a telegram to the Waiwupu to inform them, and that I would send official reply on my return to Peking.

On October 3, Hu came to see Satow about a telegram from Yüan that the Chinese were being told by the Russians that unless they agreed to employ no English on the line outside the wall, they would not restore the whole line, and he wanted Satow's advice. "I told him this was contrary to the Scott convention, and that he had better obtain the draft proposed by the Russians which would enable me to make a row (I did not say where, but I should write to the Chinese Government and telegraph to Foreign Office.)"

On October 13, Satow went to Prince Ch'ing and asked about Manchuria. "He said that as far as Chinchou had been handed over, but not all the territory they had expected to receive. They had written to Lessar and sent Lien-fang to him, but he said he was too ill to attend to business and referred them to Mirsky [Mikhail Sviatopolk-Mirskii, the Second Secretary of the Russian Legation]. They had not yet telegraphed to their Chargé d'Affaires at Petersburg. Asked about Newchwang, he said the Russians had promised to surrender it at the same time as Tientsin, but when recently applied to again, replied that the plague must be stamped out first. Evidently the military did not pull with Lessar."

Satow went to Uchida and told him what Prince Ch'ing had said about the evacuation and Manchuria. "On the latter he said the Prince had given him a different account."

On October 22, Satow told Morrison that he had learned from Hillier that Yüan and Hu wanted to send 200 men to put down brigands at Kupantze, and the Manchurian agreement forced them to apply to Lessar for permission, which had been delayed. Satow felt "it was the fault of the Chinese for giving way in negotiating the convention, and afterwards for not arranging number of soldiers and police in anticipation of the evacuation."

On November 5 Hu came to Satow.

Said he had been all the way to Yingkow and 70 li beyond Chinchou on the extramural railway and found the track in as good order as before the troubles, but the workshops at Chinchou and Yingkow had been almost denuded of machinery, whether by Boxers or Russians he could not say. I admitted that these losses should be made good out of the extramural indemnity. The Russians have not yet fixed the amount they are to receive for restoring and maintaining the line, but they now talk of 2,000,-000 rubles. They have an accumulation of customs duties at Newchwang, and will pay themselves out of that. As to giving up Newchwang, he thought a suggestion of mine that they would stick to it at least till they got all the money they require very likely to turn out true.

On November 6, Satow forwarded to Lansdowne a note from Prince Ch'ing reporting Russian evacuation of the south-west portion of the Province of Moukden and the restitution of the railways to China.[143] On the 14th, Satow transmitted a dispatch from Consul Hosie at Newchwang testifying that "with the exception of the country bordering on the Ya-lu, where Russian troops occupy certain places in the sub-prefecture of Feng-huang T'ing and the district of An-

200

tung Hsien, the east of this province has been evacuated by the Russians, who have withdrawn to the railway line, leaving the Chinese in absolute control," and that "the Governor-General at Moukden has been permitted to add to the number of his military police, to enable him to keep order in the evacuated districts, and a missionary who has visited the country since the Russian withdrawal assures me that far better order is now maintained than during the Russian occupation, and that the numerous heads exposed on trees along the highways indicate the vigorous measures that are being taken to suppress brigandage."[144]

But on November 13, Charles Hardinge had sent a very confidential dispatch from St. Petersburg on Russian reluctance to withdraw from Manchuria.

The telegram from the *Times* correspondent at Peking, which appeared in the newspapers two or three weeks ago, describing the manner in which the Russians, although adhering to the letter, had succeeded in stultifying the conditions of the Agreement between the Russian and Chinese Governments for the evacuation of Manchuria, has attracted a good deal of attention in official circles, and I have been very confidentially informed from a Russian official source that Dr. Morrison has in no way exaggerated the actual state of affairs in that province.

From information obtained confidentially from the same source, it appears that whatever may have been the former divergence of views amongst the Ministers as to the retention of Manchuria, they are now unanimous in their opinion as to the necessity of strengthening the hold of Russia on that province by every means in their power. It is recognized that owing to the sparse population of Eastern Siberia and the absence of any strong natural frontier to prevent the immigration of Chinese into Russian territory, the danger of a large influx of Chinese would become in time a very real one, and that the only way to counteract such a development is to push back the yellow race by forming large Russian colonies throughout Manchuria, who would introduce Russian civilization, and by giving employment to large numbers of Chinese would increase their prosperity, and form a natural barrier to the migration of Chinese natives into Siberia.

M. Witte is of opinion that the opening of the Chinese Eastern Railway in Manchuria will cause serious injury to the trade and prospective industries of the Amur territory, and during his recent visit to Vladivostock . . . . he has taken the necessary steps to obviate this danger. He, moreover, recognizes the fact that the existence of Dalny as a free port at the terminus of the Manchurian Railway will offer great facilities for the development of British, Japanese, and American trade and industry in Manchuria, which might in time supply the entire needs of the population, and of which the surplus might eventually be imported into Siberia.

This, however, is not the state of affairs which M. Witte intends should exist, and I am informed that he is determined to make every effort in his power by preferential railway rates and other restrictions to impede and restrain the development of Manchuria, which he intends should become a market for Russian products, and not a manufacturing country, which, by the aid of foreign skill and Chinese labour, would be able to flood Russian territory with manufactures produced at so cheap a cost that no Russian industry would be able to compete.

From a military point of view, General Kouropatkine is of opinion that the protection of the Russian frontier and the Manchurian Railway entails too great and permanent a strain upon the forces at his disposal, and he is strongly in favour of planting colonies of Cossacks in different spots, as was done in the Caucasus, who would receive a military training, and be available to augment the Russian forces in case of need.

M. [Viacheslav] Plehve, the Minister of the Interior, is also in favour of a scheme of colonization of Manchuria, but he wishes to plant there the Dukhobors, Menonites, and other sects which he finds troublesome in Russia.

There is apparently a consensus of opinion amongst the Ministers upon the necessity of consolidating the hold of Russia on Manchuria, and althought the information contained in Dr. Morrison's telegram respecting the Russification of Manchuria caused surprise to many of the readers of the *Times*, it seems likely, according to my informant, that the process will be still more diligently applied in the future.[145]

On November 20 Satow departed on home leave. On the 22nd he stopped at Nanking and drove to see Chang Chitung. He warned Chang, as he had Prince Ch'ing and Na, that China must not fail to pay in gold the indemnity imposed by the victorious powers.

To speak to them of the bad effect in trade was useless; they cared much more for something else, territory. If China declined to pay in gold, they would simply credit her with the gold value of the silver received every six months. From time to time they would present the bill for arrears, and demand something as a consideration for granting a delay. It would not be merely railway or mining concessions, but something far more disastrous for China. As a friend, about to absent myself from China for six months, I gave him this warning exactly as if I were on my death bed. . . .

I then passed to the subject of Russian territorial ambitions and expressed the opinion that she would hold on to the other two-thirds of Manchuria if the indemnity was not paid. I said that Junglu was said to have made an agreement with the Russo-Chinese Bank that he should be maintained in power when the Empress-Dowager dies, in return for their getting a free hand in Mongolia, Chinese Turkestan and Thibet. Had he heard any news with regard to these questions. I could not find out whether he had recently been telegraphing for information, and he would not admit knowing anything. (11/22)

On November 30, while at Shanghai, Satow received F. Anderson and Dudgeon who came about certain mining concessions in Manchuria in which they were interested along with the Russo-Chinese Bank. "The latter have more than half the shares, and are unwilling to part. Japanese have offered to buy 800 shares which would reduce the Russians to one half. I said I could not say whether His Majesty's Government would strongly support them in case of difficulty, and rather hinted that they had better try to get out of it."

On December 1, Sir Robert E. Bredon, Deputy Inspector General of the Chinese Customs Service came to Satow. "Says the Chinese will not pay indemnity in gold. I told him that the Russians will then keep Manchuria," Satow noted in his diary.

On April 23, 1903, while in London, Satow visited Hayashi, the Japanese Minister to Great Britain. "He regards Manchuria as gone; to turn Russia out would be no good, for China could not govern it properly, and no one else could afford the expense," Satow recorded.

On April 29, Satow went to Lord Lansdowne to talk about Manchuria.

It appears that the versions do not agree as to the exact nature of the Russian demands. He asked what our real interest were. I said British imports into Manchuria were estimated at about £2,000,000 and there was a considerable export of beancake which benefited the British shipping trade. Moukden and Kirin were valuable, but Hei-lung-chiang sparsely inhabited that might go. I suggested that an additional gunboat at Newchwang might be useful as a warning, especially if the Japanese did the same, and of course a joint naval demonstration would have a powerful effect. Naturally the possession of the railways gave Russia practical dominion. I cited German action as to post offices along their line in Shantung, which they would eventually prolong to Chêngting, and the Franco-Belgian refusal to allow likin-stations on the Luhan line. I said in reply to a question that we had better wait till our railway concessions were ratified by the Chinese Government before we claimed similar rights and powers. Suggested that some day we might have to fight Russia, and that she was not so strong as she looked. To the former he replied "Perhaps" with a smile, to the latter nothing. But added that judging by their attitude in other parts of the world they had no desire for war.

On May 7 Satow dined with Sir Edward Seymour. They discussed the situation in Manchuria.

I told him I thought it not worth while for either England or Japan to try to turn out the Russians, but that my advice to His Majesty's Government was to maintain gunboats at New-chwang, and that if we made a joint naval demonstration with Japan it would cause the Russians to withdraw their demands.
[Sir A.] Buller [who was among the guests] says that when he had sent ships to Port Arthur in 1898 he got instructions from home to withdraw them. When the Reuter telegram came out stating that they had been withdrawn at the request of Russia he sent others. Lord Salisbury foreseeing the trouble with France over Fashoda and with the Boers became alarmed, and

insisted that the Admiralty should instruct him to withdraw. The Foreign Office sent almost daily to the Admiralty for a whole week to urge despatch of these instructions, and yet Lord Salisbury stated in the house that the ships were taken away by him (Buller) because the exigencies of the service required their presence elsewhere. The Russian Admiral in fact received instructions almost simultaneously to remove *his* ships, so if Lord Salisbury had held firm, the Russians would not have got Manchuria. I replied that Lord Salisbury should have taken his stand on the Treaty, and have sent orders to him to remain.

On May 12 Satow went to Lord Lansdowne and discussed the Manchuria question further. "He said Lessar according to [Count Alexander] Benckendorf is not Anglo-phobe, but I said I had never found him ready to come to an understanding with us in Peking."

On May 13, while lunching with Ignatius Valentine Chirol, Foreign Editor of the London *Times*, Satow sat next to John St. Loe Strachey, editor of the *Spectator*, who asked a lot of questions about China, and discussed Germany and Russia. "Said I thought we were bound to oppose Russia tooth and nail in Afghanistan, Thibet, Persian Gulf and Manchuria. He is against me and others on the Persian Gulf, and I said tooth and nail meant war. I said that a challenge would not be accepted by Russia."

On May 15 Satow went up to Chirol and had a chat. "As to Manchuria, I did not think either Japan or England would appeal to force, but it would not do to say so. The Americans had fluttered the Russians by putting forward a demand for the opening of Mukden and Taku-shan."

On May 21 Satow saw Sir Thomas Sanderson.

As to Manchuria he does not think the Russians at present will annex, or try to keep out our trade, but later on will do so when they have strengthened their hold on the three provinces. They probably will manage to get the appointment of a Russian as Commissioner of Customs made permanent, but we must insist that next time someone of a different nationality must be appointed. Also they will do their best to get the sanitary matters of the port into their hands. I said that we had hitherto said nothing about Manchuria in meetings of the Diplomatic Body, but I thought it would be advisable to take, not *make*, opportunities of doing so, as we must maintain the right of our people to import into Manchuria under Chinese tariff. He approved of this idea (I should get the United States and Japanese colleagues to combine with me). Churchill [the British Military Attaché in Tokyo] tells him that the Japanese think nothing can be done to save Manchuria, but if Corea is touched Japan will fight.

On June 10, Satow lunched with the Japanese Minister. "Hayashi says the Chinese like Li Hung-chang did not care a bit about Manchuria, which they thought was an incumbrance. They had in the T'ang period got rid of it, and been strong."

On June 13, Satow went to take leave of King Edward VII.

He talked a good deal about Russian duplicity in connexion with Manchuria, and hoped we should in conjunction with America and Japan insist upon the maintenance of the "open door." Of course we had known all along that they would not evacuate, but why did they promise to do so? He told me to give Lessar a friendly message, to remind him of their conversation when Lessar came to take leave of him on leaving London in 1901, and to add that His Majesty had followed his career with interest. His Majesty says Lessar has not yet reached Peking. (If so he must be dawdling some where in Manchuria). I explained that in my view the question of Manchuria was done for when they got Port Arthur and the right to construct the railway. Told him of the £200,000 expended to get it. The Empress-Dowager not likely to run the risk of being turned out of her capital a second time. Li Hung-chang missed by no one but the Russians. . . . Finally he told me to write now and then to Lord Knollys [his private secretary] anything of special interest, and it would be kept quite private. He sees my letters to Lord Lansdowne. Went in to say goodbye to Knollys, and to tell him this. The sort of topics anything about the Empress-Dowager or the colleagues, or the designs of Russia.

On June 16 Satow saw Sanderson. "Said goodbye to Sanderson, who àpropos of Germany said we *ought* to work with them, but they were very tricky. He had told Metter-

nich that some day the ill feeling would blow over. Of course
we should be glad to come to an understanding with Russia,
but it seems impossible, though there are indications that they
desire it; but they want us to take them on trust, which will
not do."

On June 19 Satow started back for the Far East. Sailing
by way of the Suez Canal, Satow reached Bombay, from
where he went by train to Kalka and thence in a landau to
Simla. On July 10 he talked with Baron George Curzon,
Viceroy and Governor General of India.

Viceroy thinks Russians are destined to possess Kashgaria sooner
or later and it might be inconvenient if British people from
Hunza were found to be residing in a portion of the territory so
annexed. It might therefore be desirable to compensate the Mir
in some other way, only for the loss of prestige involved in our
not getting the Raskam leases through, it is only [Nikolai] Pe-
trovski the Russian consul at Kashgar who opposes. Question of
Miles being appointed consul. On this matter the Viceroy has a
decided opinion in favour. I suggested that he should ask Home
Government to authorize me to inform Chinese Government
that Miles is consul without asking for exequatur; if they objected then I should argue with them that they must not expect
us to accept worse treatment than Russia, and again, that our
interests in Kashgaria are equally important as being adjacent to
British territory. I also said that if the thing were feasible, an
undertaking obtained from China not to cede Kashgaria to any
other Power might be a good thing, of course with instruction
from Foreign Office. Only it might seem perhaps that we had
gone too far already in tacitly admitting Russian predominance
there, and might be accused of bad faith if we tried to get such
an undertaking. To this he replied that Russia in the first abor-
tive Manchurian convention had tried to get reversion of Mongolia and Kashgaria, and what they did we had equal right to do.

During Satow's absence from China, a fairly lively correspondence had been carried on between the Chargé d'Affaires
Walter Townley and the Foreign Office regarding the opening of a custom-house at Dalny, with branches in other parts
of Manchuria. "The Director is M. Protassieff, formerly Fi-

nance Minister at Port Arthur, and it is not yet decided whether he should be under Sir R. Hart or independent of him; the customs would be levied for China. As the Inspector-General realizes that he would be a figure-head only, the result would be the same," Townley reported in the first of many dispatches. In connection with the custom-house a postal service was to be established over the Manchurian Railway, with post-offices in Manchuria at places where the Chinese Imperial Post was not represented. "If Russian designs succeed," Townley warned, "they will have a firmer hold on Manchuria than before the Manchurian Convention was signed."[146]

Talk of a compromise by which China would appoint at Dalny a Chinese Commissioner of Customs with a staff half Chinese and half Russian, did not satisfy Townley. "I pointed out [to the Foreign Board, he telegraphed] that it would be better to delay and lose some months customs revenue rather than the entire civil control of the province, and I strongly warned the Board against any such compromise, which, I said, must eventually end in a purely Russian control."[147] Sir Robert Hart agreed with Townley. As he pointed out to him, "with the railway, the post, and the Customs in the hands of Russia, there would be but little of China left in Manchuria but the name, and that the Russian flag, which would be all that was wanting, even after the military evacuation had been carried out, could easily be hoisted at any moment."[148] Townley advised Prince Ch'ing, if the Russians persisted in their plans, to frustrate their designs by establishing custom-house stations on the Chinese side of the leased territory, as well as on the trunk line.[149]

On March 7, Townley wrote that Prince Ch'ing "had reason to believe that the custom-house [at Dalny] would not be established, for the present at all events, since he understood that the scheme had originated with the Russo-Chinese Bank, and was not supported by the Russian Government," and added: "I have, since my conversation with the Prince, learned that the custom-house was actually opened for two days last month under Messrs. Protassiew and Stipanow that no business was done, and that it was then closed by order from St. Petersburgh pending further instructions."[150]

Meanwhile Russian evacuation of Manchuria had ground to a halt. In a series of dispatches Townley and others reported that the Russians demanded of China seven, then six, conditions before resuming their evacuation. The texts differed, but the gist of the demands was reduced to the following:

1. For every foreigner employed in the Administration a Russian colleague shall be appointed.
2. Same status as regards Administration as during occupation.
3. Newchwang customs to be paid into Russo-Chinese Bank.
4. Newchwang sanitary Regulations to be managed by Russians.
5. Russia to have right to use Chinese telegraph poles in Manchuria for Russian wires.
6. No portion of the three provinces to be ever alienated to any foreign Power.[151]

Townley at once informed the American Minister of the conditions demanded by Russia.

Mr. Conger expressed his opinion that China would have to yield to the Russian demands unless the friendly Powers interested were disposed to come to her assistance in such a manner as to let Russia see that they were prepared to support her by force, if need be, in her just rights. Russian predominance in Manchuria would be all very well, and, indeed, likely to do more for the development of the country than a Chinese Administration, if some reliable assurances could be secured from the Russian Government that the trade of the country should be open to all on equal terms. Such assurance could, however, only be obtained, he added, if the Powers interested were prepared to go to war upon the question.

Mr. Conger became quite bellicose in some of his expressions, and rather reminded me of the American eagle in the *Punch* cartoon, who was ready to flap his wings for all he was worth if the lion and the bear would do the fighting.[152]

Great Britain, the United States and Japan individually voiced their opposition to the Russian conditions, both in St. Petersburg and Peking. On April 28, Townley reported yet another Russian demand, namely that navigation on the Liao River be reserved exclusively to vessels flying the Russian or Chinese flag.[153] The intimation by the Russian Ambassador in Washington that the condition that for every foreigner employed in the administration a Russian colleague shall be appointed "is aimed entirely against Great Britain, as without it the country would be flooded by Sir R. Hart with his employés"[154] satisfied no one. Nor did the assertion of Count Lamsdorff that no such demands had been made at all.[155] Foreign Minister Komura Jutaro, summed up the problem neatly. As MacDonald reported from Tokyo:

His Excellency specially drew my attention to the remarkable variations noticeable in Russian utterances. There is the undoubted fact that the Russian Chargé d'Affaires at Peking has presented demands. Secondly, there is Count Lamsdorff's solemn denial that any demands have been made. Thirdly, there is an explanation by the Russian Ambassador in Washington to the United States' Government of a portion of these demands, that they are merely directed against His Majesty's Government. And, finally, there is an official notification published by General Alexeieff that Shing-king having been completely evacuated, it is now free of foreigners. Baron Komura is of opinion that these discrepancies must be the outcome of serious diversity of opinion in the counsels of Russia.[156]

The contradictions that seemed to multiply with every dispatch and newspaper report were as puzzling as they were frustrating. Discussing the unusual situation, Sir Charles S. Scott, the British Minister at St. Petersburg, and his Japanese colleague, Kurino Shin-ichiro, arrived at the following possible explanation:

A Russian Chargé d'Affaires furnished with instructions of a general character from his Government, and urged on by military and other Russian influences on the spot to try and secure a clever diplomatic success before the return of his Chief by giving them a concrete form and liberal interpretation.

The Chinese Government, on their side, anxious to test how far they could count on the effective support of other Powers in resisting Russian demands, contriving to get them conveyed secretly and in an exaggerated form to the foreign Legations, and then declaring to the Russian Legation that the opposition of the foreign Governments obliged them to refuse them.[157]

Impressed by the sincerity of Count Lamsdorff's denials, Robert Sanderson McCormick, the American Minister in St. Petersburg, agreed with Scott and Kurino "that the whole question might have originated in the extra-officiousness and zeal of a young Russian diplomatist [during the absence of the Russian Minister on sick leave], and in the diplomacy peculiar to Chinese officials when desirous to test the amount of foreign support on which they might count in any case of emergency."[158]

If, as we must, in simple justice to Count Lamsdorff, infer, the Russian Government had not authorized the Russian Chargé d'Affaires at Peking to prefer any demands such as Prince Ch'ing said he did in an official note, M. [Grigorii] Plançon [the Russian Chargé d'Affaires] has rendered a very bad service to his official chief [Scott concluded].

Owing to the publicity given to these alleged demands, and the scathing comments and charges of perfidy heaped upon the Russian Foreign Office in the American and English press, on the assumption of the perfect authenticity of their information, it seems safe to conclude that the public will still be encouraged to believe that the Russian Government really made the demands and only withdrew them under foreign pressure.

This impression is calculated, as on a previous occasion, to seriously compromise his Excellency's position and influence in this country.[159]

After further deliberation with the Japanese Minister, Scott gave a more detailed interpretation of the contradictions underlying Russian policy and pronouncements:

The most probable explanation in my opinion, and I believe also in those of my Japanese and American colleagues, is to be found first in the fact that Count Lamsdorff's policy, as approved by the Emperor, in regard to the final evacuation of Manchuria in strict accordance with the terms of the Manchurian Convention and the public Declarations of the Russian Foreign Office, has been adopted in opposition, not only to the Russian military party, to which any withdrawal from a territory once occupied is always extremely distasteful, but also to the aspirations of the Russo-Chinese Bank, and that it is not even heartily approved of by many of Count Lamsdorff's own subordinates in the Foreign Office and Russian Diplomatic Service.

These influences have, no doubt, been very active in giving as wide an interpretation as possible to the reservations and conditions contained in the Manchurian Convention and Imperial assurances, the stated object of which was to secure the necessary guarantees from China for the adequate protection of Russia's special interests in Manchuria on the retirement of her troops, viz., the security of the frontier, the line of railway, and the Russian lease.

The military authorities have, ever since the decision to evacuate was taken, been contending that they alone can properly decide what constitutes an adequate guarantee for the military protection of these interests.

The Russo-Chinese Bank has, no doubt, been insisting on adequate guarantees of the observance of the obligations imposed on China by the Convention to execute strictly the provisions of the Contract signed with the Russo-Chinese Bank in 1896 at St. Petersburgh, and it must be remembered that, as was pointed out by one of the Chinese Viceroys to Sir E. Satow, when the Manchurian Convention was under negotiation, we are still in the dark as to the exact extent of the obligations incurred by China under that Contract.

These influences greatly embarrassed Count Lamsdorff when he was negotiating the terms of the Manchurian Convention at St. Petersburgh, and as they have Representatives at Peking, they have no doubt been equally embarrassing the Russian Representative there. . . .

If we are to conclude that general instructions were sent to the Russian Legation to obtain from the Chinese Government the required guarantees, in strict accordance with the terms of the Convention and of the official declarations and assurances, but in consultation with the military authorities and the Russo-Chinese Bank, it may be well that M. Plançon, who was, previously to his present appointment, attached as Diplomatic Secretary to Admiral Alexeieff, has not felt himself strong enough to decline submitting for discussion some conditions proposed by his late Chief, which were not contemplated by Count Lamsdorff, and that the Chinese Government has interpreted these as finally approved demands of the Russian Government.

I have, since commencing this despatch, learnt from the Japanese Minister that Ho-Wei-Teh tells him that he received a few days ago a telegram from his Government, instructing him to tell Count Lamsdorff that the Chinese Government were unable to give the assurances which the Russian Legation was asking for, but that no information was given in this telegram as to what the assurances referred to were.

On the Chinese Minister communicating this message to Count Lamsdorff, his Excellency replied that he also did not know what assurances M. Plançon had asked the Chinese Government to give, and he thought that it would only lead to confusion if they attempted to discuss the matter in hand at two places at the same time.

I cannot help thinking that the theory of a confusion of authority and of a disagreement of views between different Departments of the Russian Government offers a safer explanation of the contradictions which have mystified everyone concerned during the past week than any explanation tending to affix a charge of deliberate deceit and breach of faith on the Emperor and Count Lamsdorff—a suspicion which would be deeply felt and resented by His Imperial Majesty, and would seriously impair Count Lamsdorff's authority and position.[160]

On May 2, Townley telegraphed from Peking that he had been "allowed in strictest confidence by the Chinese Foreign Office to take copy of the Russian text of note containing demands, dated the 5th April, old style [April 18, new style][161] and on May 4 transmitted what he himself called a "very clumsy" translation of the Russian note and the reply of the Wai-Wu-Pu or Chinese Foreign Office.

By command of the Imperial Government, I have the honour to make to you, honoured Prince and Ministers, the following communication:
Russia and China have for more than 200 years had with each other relations that have been always distinguished by their very

friendly character, and this very naturally—two neighbouring people, having a common frontier more than 5,000 versts in length, and many common affairs and interests, may easily come to an understanding about everything. The interference of strangers in these mutual relations only spoils them and impedes the settlement of affairs. It is for this reason that Russia, highly prizing friendly relations with China, considers it her duty to guard them from alien interference.

This applies particularly to Manchuria. Russia has sacrificed thousands of lives and millions of treasure for the pacification of this country and for the restoration in it of lawful Chinese authority, quite apart from the millions that have been expended in the construction of a great railway for the common benefit of all nations. Other Powers have not expended on the pacification of Manchuria a single rouble or a single soldier. It would seem, therefore, full just that Russia should have the right to safeguard her interests, bought at so high a price, in that country, without evoking the jealousy of other Powers. All foreigners have profited by the tranquillity established in the country and by the roads opened up in it, and with this they ought in justice to be satisfied, remembering that only a few years ago access into Manchuria was entirely closed to them.

Many states, after the expenditure of treasure and military force in the pacification of some country or island, habitually unite it to their own dominions for ever, by right of conquest. Russia does not wish to profit by that right, and precisely as in 1881 she returned Ili to China, and last year the south-western portion of the Moukden Province, so now she is ready to fulfil her engagement and to return to China not only the remaining portion of the Moukden Province and Kirin, but also the Port Newchwang, provided she receives full assurance that after the departure of the troops the lawful interests of Russia in these adjacent territories will be disturbed neither by China nor by other States.

In order that she may be thus assured, the Chinese Government must give to Russia the following pledges:

1. That the restored territories, in particular Newchwang and localities on the Liao Ho, shall not be transferred to another Power, whether by way of cession, lease, concession, or in any other form. An attempt at such a transfer Russia would regard as a threat, and for the protection of her interests would have recourse to the most decisive measures.

2. That the organization at present existing in Mongolia shall not be disturbed, seeing that such disturbance will inevitably produce commotions amongst the people, and that an unquiet state of affairs along our frontier will entail very serious and undesirable complications.

3. That the Chinese Government will not take a decision with regard to the opening to foreign trade of any new places (lit. points) in Manchuria and of the admission to them of Consuls, without previous communication with the Imperial Administration.

4. That if China should have recourse to inviting foreigners for the management of any branch of her Administration, the authority of such foreigners shall not extend to the affairs of North China, where Russian interests predominate. In such an event these affairs shall be allotted to entirely separate departments, and their direction shall be entrusted to Russians; thus, for instance, if a foreign Adviser is engaged for mining matters, his advice will not extend to the mining affairs of Mongolia and Manchuria, for which there will in such case be appointed a Russian Adviser.

5. Russia will retain in her own control the existing telegraph line between Port Arthur, Ying K'ou, and Moukden for the whole term of the existence of the Peking-Ying K'ou line, of which the above-mentioned line serves as an indispensable prolongation.

6. After the transfer of Newchwang to the Chinese Administration the Russo-Chinese Bank will continue, as at present, to fulfil the functions of the Customs Bank at the port named.

Finally, 7, it is understood that all rights obtained in Manchuria by Russian subjects or establishments during the occupation shall remain in full force after the departure of the troops.

Further, Russia is charged with the protection of the health and lives of the numerous inhabitants of the places traversed by the railway. Opening free access for the movement of travellers and of merchandise, the railway may with equal ease facilitate the penetration into the north of infectious diseases, if there is not established at its starting point, that is at Ying-kou, a sound sanitary organization and a strict watch for the appearance of epidemic diseases. Last year the greed of a captain and the carelessness of the Customs Commissioner and doctor caused the carrying into Manchuria and Siberia of an epidemic of cholera, from which there died many thousand people, both Russians and Chinese.

In transferring the administration of Newchwang to China, the Russian Government asks that the model sanitary organization established there by the Russian administration shall be preserved, and that the local authorities shall always be prepared for the struggle with epidemics. To this end it is indispensable that the Commissioner of Customs and the Customs doctor should be Russian subjects, subordinate to the Chinese Customs Administration. This subordination fully secures the proper discharge of their direct obligations and the maintenance of Chinese Customs interests; but, as Russians they will have an interest in the work of protecting the Russian dominions from the introduction of epidemics which cannot be expected from foreigners of another nationality.

For the management of sanitary affairs there will be established a permanent Commission, the President of which will be the Taotai, and the members of it: all the Consuls stationed at Ying-kou, the before-mentioned Commissioner of Customs, the Customs doctor, and medical bacteriological expert, and the representative of the Chinese Eastern Railway.

For the settlement of the details of the organization and the functions of the Commission, the Taotai will consult with the Russian Consul, who has great experience in these matters.

The means for the sanitary work, and for the struggle with epidemics, shall be found by the Taotai. This will present no difficulty if the existing assessment of the local merchants is retained, permission for which shall be given to the Taotai from Peking.

Such, Honoured Prince and Ministers, are the conditions in presence of which the Russian Government will be convinced that its political interests, and also the interests of the health and lives of a large population, will be safeguarded in a fitting manner.

As soon as your Highness and your Excellencies reply with an official note, in which, in the name of His Majesty, the Bogdo Khan (Emperor of China) is expressed assent to the requests of Russia that have been set forth, the Russian troops will be withdrawn from the Moukden Province and from Kirin, and the civil administration of Newchwang will be transferred to the Governor of the town, the Chinese Taotai.

In the event of there being any doubts as to the interpretation of the present note, the Russian text of it shall be considered authoritative.[162]

The Chinese Foreign Office had replied to Plançon:

On the 18th April we had the honour to receive your note, stating that you had received a telegram from your Government, in which they refer to the friendly relations which have prevailed between Russia and China, and which should be for ever preserved in order to guard against alien interference. They consider that this applies particularly to Manchuria, and Russia is now ready to fulfil her engagements and return to China not only the remainder of Moukden province and Kirin, but also the Port of Newchwang, provided she receives full assurance from China that after the withdrawal of the Russian troops the legitimate interests of Russia in adjacent territories will not be disturbed either by China or by other States. In order that she may be thus assured, the Chinese Government should give seven pledges, which you proceed to enumerate, and when these have been given in the form of an official note from this Board, the Russian troops will be withdrawn from the Moukden province and from Kirin, while Newchwang will be restored to the Chinese Administration.

After giving your note due consideration, we have the honour to observe that the Convention between Russia and China for the handing back of the Manchurian provinces was signed by the Plenipotentiaries of the High Contracting Parties, and ratified by the Imperial assent on both sides. This Convention provides that upon the signature thereof, the Russian troops occupying Manchuria shall be withdrawn in three instalments, and China's sovereignty restored, by the country relapsing under Chinese rule and Administration, as was the case before the Russian occupation.

This provision clearly demonstrated Russia's friendly feeling and good faith towards China, and attracted the admiration of all nations. Russia has evacuated the south-west portion of the Moukden province as far as the Liao River, and restored the railways to China. We have now come to the second period when the evacuation of the rest of the Moukden province and of Kirin is due. This Board addressed you on the subject, with the request that you would move your Government to hand over on the due date, and we informed you that Tseng Chi and Chang Shun had been Imperially appointed to take over from your authorities. To this communication you have made reply in the note now under acknowledgement. Russia having thus not yet restored the country according to the Treaty stipulations, further imposes conditions outside the scope of the Convention, which are prejudicial to China's sovereign rights. It is impossible that we should consent to these conditions. China and Russia have enjoyed friendly relations for many years, but if on this occasion the Treaty stipulations are not observed, it would appear as if Russia were disregarding the general situation and the principle of preserving friendly relations between our Empires.

We trust, therefore, that you will inform your Government of our views, and move them to comply with clauses 2 and 3 of the Convention by handing back and evacuating the territory of Manchuria and the Port of Newchwang, in accordance with the stipulated terms. By so doing, all questions affecting the Peace Protocol will be carried out in their entirety, and the good relations between our two countries will be clearly manifested; while, hereafter, whenever matters arise involving advantage to both Powers, they can be arranged and discussed in an amicable manner. Our desire, then, is that the handing back of Manchuria should be proceeded with according to the terms of the Convention, and that no complications beyond the scope of the Convention should be imported into the matter at issue. Such would be the fair course of action, and the one dictated by good faith. We earnestly desire that it may be pursued.[163]

With the return of the Russian Minister to the Far East, it seemed likely that the question of the evacuation of Manchuria would be resumed. Townley consequently addressed a note to Prince Ch'ing, warning him to be careful in his language, "lest M. Lessar should construe some polite phrase into an acceptance of one or other of the supplementary conditions."

I have found in recent conversations with the United States' and Japanese Ministers that they agree with me in thinking that there is some danger that in the course of interviews with M. Lessar something may be said by your Highness that will subsequently be interpreted as an admission or assurance binding on the Chinese Government [Townley wrote]. The interest taken by His Majesty's Government in the maintenance of the integrity of the Chinese dominions, and the preservation there of China's sovereign rights, justifies me in offering to your Highness what would in other circumstances seem intrusive advice, to observe more than ordinary caution in answering Russian requests for explanations and assurances.

I venture to add that while His Majesty's Government is most anxious to help China in finding a satisfactory solution of the Manchurian question, it is impossible for them to judge the situation correctly if they are not kept informed of the course of negotiations on the subject. Judging from past experiences, it is probable that the Russian Minister will invite the Chinese Government to observe secrecy with regard to his proposals. Such a requirement is justifiable in ordinary cases, but hardly in connection with a question the solution of which affects the interests and Treaty rights of other Powers. Were China to grant without the knowledge of other Powers Russian demands of the same character as those already put forward she would alienate the sympathy and goodwill of those who have shown the greatest anxiety for the maintenance of her integrity and she would create among all Powers the conviction that there was no security that their Treaty rights in other parts of the Empire would not be infringed by arrangements made in secrecy with other States, and they would be compelled to consider what independent steps they should take to safeguard their interests by similar action.[164]

On July 21 Townley himself talked to Lessar, who said that Russia "must do all she can to encourage foreign capital to undertake enterprises such as mines and branch railways in Manchuria in order to develop the country, Russian capital not being forthcoming."

He spoke as if the development of a Russian province were under discussion [Townley reported]. To my inquiry as to whether he could say when the evacuation negotiations were likely to be concluded, he returned an evasive answer, but said that it was foolish of China not to have accepted the conditions at once, as considerable additional expense had been put on Russia by her refusal to do so, so that China must not be surprised if she find the final terms harder than those originally offered. He wished, doubtless, to impress me.

In the course of our conversation, M. Lessar spoke with much heat of the interference of others in the Russo-Chinese negotiations, saying that it would never be tolerated by Russia.[165]

219

The Approaching Confrontation between Russia and Japan

D URING SATOW'S ABSENCE the Manchurian questian had become complicated by a clash of Russian and Japanese interests in Korea, precipitated by the granting of a Russian timber concession on the Yalu River. The Japanese were perturbed, regarding Russian activity as "political designs marked in an economic guise." As J. N. Jordan reported from Seoul:

The banks of the Yalu and Tumen, which form the northern and western frontiers of Corea, like most border lands in loosely governed countries, are, it is pointed out, practically under no administrative control, and in a country like this where, even in settled districts, missionary propaganda finds no difficulty in creating its *imperium in imperio*, the prospect of a Russian Concession assuming territorial privileges in its weakest outskirts, and of Russian rangers becoming permanent settlers is regarded by the Japanese as one of the contingencies which require to be guarded against.

But apart from this perhaps somewhat remote danger, there is the risk of actual collision between Japanese and Russian interests should full scope be given to the present Concession. That there is room for all in Asia may be true as a general maxim, but cases frequently occur in which it is not applicable to Corea. Dagelet Island, which possesses a very valuable timber of which whole temples are built in Kyoto and other parts of Japan, is practically in the hands of Japanese wood-cutters who number 400 or 500 and are policed, and in a measure, controlled by their own authorities from Fusan. Any attempt to oust them in favour of Russians is certain to provoke strong opposition.

Japan's absorption of Corea has been carried on so successfully during the last few years by the simple process of pacific penetration, that her Agents naturally view with much uneasiness any attempt on the part of her great Northern rival to imitate her example in this direction.[166]

In June, 1903, MacDonald telegraphed from Tokyo that Baron Komura and the heads of the Naval and Military Departments shared his belief that the Russians would "effect a permanent settlement" on the Yalu "unless they are prevented."[167]

The conflict of Russian and Japanese ambitions in Manchuria and Korea gave rise to rumors of troop movements and preparations for war. Hence the Japanese Government decided that the time was ripe "for concluding a definite arrangement directly with the Russian Government with regard to the maintenance of the 'open door' policy in Manchuria and the securing of equal advantages and opportunities for all nations both in China and Corea." As MacDonald wrote in a "most secret" telegram:

The Japanese Government fear that, if the present unsatisfactory condition of affairs be allowed to continue, the feelings of the Russian and Japanese peoples will become excited, and so render the task of preserving the peace a very difficult one. Consequently they are strongly of opinion that a satisfactory arrangement should be made with Russia as soon as possible which would terminate a state of affairs which is, in their opinion, rapidly becoming dangerous to the peace of the two countries.[168]

On July 3, Lansdowne relayed to MacDonald the views of the Japanese Government, conveyed to him by the Japanese Minister in London:

The Imperial Government had been observing with close attention the development of affairs in Manchuria, and they now viewed with great concern the present situation there.

So long as there were some grounds for the hope that Russia would in good faith fulfil her engagements with China and carry out her assurances to other Powers in regard to the ques-

221

tion of the evacuation of Manchuria, the Imperial Government maintained an attitude of watchful reserve; but the recent action of Russia in demanding from China new conditions in connection with the evacuation and in consolidating rather than relaxing her hold upon Manchuria compelled them to believe that she had abandoned the intention, if she ever seriously entertained it, of retiring from that province.

Unrestrained permanent occupation of Manchuria by Russia would create a condition of things very prejudicial to those interests, the defence of which was the object of the conclusion of the Anglo-Japanese alliance. Such occupation would be destructive of the principle of equal opportunity. It would also manifestly impair the territorial integrity of China. Moreover, it would be a continual menace to the independence of Corea, which Japan was bound to maintain at all hazards for the sake of her own tranquillity and safety.

The Imperial Government believed that the policy of forbearance which they had hitherto pursued was a wise one, but they could not but come to the conclusion that the time had arrived for a change in that policy.

In these circumstances, they found it absolutely necessary to ask themselves what course they should now take in order to safeguard their imperilled interests. In studying this question, the Imperial Government had not failed to keep constantly in mind their special relations with the British Government.

That Russia had certain legally-acquired and well-established special interests in Manchuria was a fact which it would be as unwise to ignore as it was impossible to deny. Starting from that point of view, the Imperial Government, for their part, were disposed in the first place to offer to Russia a solution of the present situation based on the clear definition of those interests, as well as of Japan's interests in Corea, mutual recognition of the right of the two Powers to take certain defined measures for the protection of those interests, when and so long as they were menaced, and a mutual engagement to respect the independence and the territorial integrity of China and Corea, and to maintain the principle of equal opportunity for the commerce and industry of all nations in those two countries. A settlement embodying these principles would, it was believed, be entirely fair to all parties.

It was not necessary at this time to attempt to say what the result of Russia's rejection of such proposals would be, but the responsibility for whatever consequences might ensue would lie solely upon her.[169]

The contradictions inherent in the Russian system made the negotiation of differences difficult. As the Russian press wrote:

The vacillations, inconsistencies, and obscurities so often observed in our policy are to be explained by circumstances sufficiently known to us all, but with which foreign Cabinets are unfamiliar.

Manchuria occupies the attention of three different Departments, each of which has its own views, each of which considers the question of Russian policy from a different standpoint. The Foreign Office is naturally chiefly occupied with the question of avoiding conflicts or misunderstandings with foreign Powers, and is inclined to make pacific assurances even in the cases where it is not in the power of that Department to carry them into effect and in matters wholly outside the diplomatic sphere. The War Office, on the other hand, does not see its way to withdraw its troops from a territory which is still in need of military protection, and is therefore very often compelled by the force of circumstances to resort to measures inconsistent with the assurances given by the Foreign Office. The Ministry of Finance has its attention fixed on the immense material interests involved in the Eastern Railway, and is compelled to insist on the greatest circumspection in the manner of evacuation and on the very gradual withdrawal of our forces. Where three Departments are involved, it is in the highest degree unlikely that unity of purpose or consistency in word and act should mark our policy. . . .[170]

Taking issue with reports that Russia "intended to force a war on Japan in the late autumn or early winter"[171] Major General Sir Garrett Creagh and the Japanese Commander in Tientsin agreed "that the Russians, while making ready for any eventuality, wish at the same time to impress the Powers with the preparedness for war, and their intention to fight rather than withdraw from Manchuria, but that they do not intend to force hostilities."[172]

The British Minister in St. Petersburg favored the view

that "the Russian Government would be glad to see its way
to arrive at a peaceful arrangement with Japan if that country seriously desired it, and made practical proposals." He
reported:

There can be little doubt that the military party in Russia
has been urging on the attention of the Russian Government
the probability of Japan desiring to take advantage of its present
naval superiority to attack the Russian position before the situation is reversed at the end of the present year, when, I understand, the Russian fleet will be of considerably superior
strength in those seas, and Russia's mistrust of the intentions of
Japan probably at present equals, or even surpasses, Japan's mistrust of Russia.

I am therefore of opinion that the Japanese Government is
right in regarding the situation as a very delicate one, requiring
very careful handling, and that the prospects of conducting
successful negotiations for an understanding with Russia depend
on the way in which the latter Government is approached.[173]

As Satow was on his way back to Peking the confusion of
Russian policy making was compounded by the creation of a
Viceroyalty in the Far East and was rendered "most serious,
and pregnant with the seed of fresh complications and dan-
gers to the peace of the Far East." Noting that the Tsar had
decided to attach greater weight to the views of the military
authorities in the Far East than to the diplomatic and financial considerations of Count Lamsdorff and Sergei Witte, the
British Minister in St. Petersburg briefed his Government on
the administrative changes entailed, then explained why he
regarded the situation as "serious":

The Foreign Minister will have only one voice in the Con-
trolling Council, which will no doubt include the very persons
whose influence he is believed to have been combating ineffec-
tually before the creation of the Council.

Admiral and General Alexeieff is understood all along to have
offered an energetic opposition to the decision to eventually
withdraw the troops of occupation from Manchuria, and has
chafed under the restrictions hitherto placed on his actions in
deference to diplomatic considerations and to the public decla-

224

rations, engagements, and assurances which Count Lamsdorff had with the Emperor's sanction given to foreign countries, as he regarded them as incompatible with military requirements and interests.

He is understood further to have formulated without reference to Count Lamsdorff the recent further conditions and guarantees to be obtained from China before effect is given to the evacuation Convention.

He is understood to have strongly encouraged, if not initiated, himself the acquisition of the Concessions on the Yalu River and on the Corean frontier, which have so justly alarmed the Japanese Government, and to have been opposed not only by Count Lamsdorff, but also by M. Witte and General Kouropatkin.

And yet, in spite of these considerations, he is selected by the independent act of the Emperor to fill the new post of Viceroy, equipped with supreme power of disposal over the Russian naval forces in the Pacific and all military forces of Russia east of Irkutsk, charged with the protection of all the Russian interests in the districts of his Government and in the adjoining countries, and with the whole service of diplomatic relations with neighbouring States in regard to those interests, in short, powers of unprecedented extent, and only limited by the condition of the Emperor's ratification, and this at a moment when the Japanese Government is understood to be making an attempt to come to an understanding with the Russian Foreign Office in regard to evacuation, and judging from the reports of His Majesty's Representatives at Peking and Tokio, the question of peace and war in the Far East is already trembling in the balance.[174]

The same day Scott summarized the strengthening of Russian naval and military forces in the Far East.

Unless ships in commission in the East are sent home on the arrival of those sent out from Russia, the Imperial Government, in the course of a little more than a year, will have doubled the number of battle-ships and cruisers of over 5,900 tons in Eastern waters.

Two new first-class battle-ships, two first-class cruisers, seven new torpedo-boat destroyers, and four first-class torpedo-boats are under orders for the Far East, or are already on their way.

In the last two months, in addition to the dispatch of about 8,000 men from Russia to the Trans-Baikal, a railway battalion has been dispatched from Askabad, which, in the opinion of the Military Attaché to this Embassy, is probably part of an additional force of 8,000 men which will be dispatched to the Far East.[175]

Returning to China, Satow stopped at Wei-hai-wei on August 14.

The Admiral came on board in the forenoon and we had some talk [Satow recorded in his diary]. He says the Japanese sent for Trowbridge to the Naval Department, and remarked on the paucity of first-class cruisers in the British squadron. This he believes Hayashi also must have mentioned in London. The Admiral himself wrote home to the same effect, also pointing out that the Russians now for the first time in history outnumber us in battleships and cruisers. We have always and everywhere been hitherto superior in numbers to any single power. . . . I told him that Lord Lansdowne had remarked to me that the Japanese seemed to think we were not supporting them sufficiently, and he thought they were probably right. . . . [The next day] we had some further talk. He considers that our people at home have not played the game as regards the Japanese alliance, and ought to have done much more. Claude MacDonald does not get on well with the Japanese, rather to the contrary, and seems to give the tone to some of his subordinates. Bonar particularly anti-Japanese. Barclay very nice fellow. Churchill rather rubbed the Japanese up the wrong way, by going to the War Department in dittoes and a straw hat when other military attachés went in frock-coat and tall hat. We both agree that it would be very bad policy to allow Russia to crush Japan, and that we should favour her trying to resuscitate China, also that Japan would [not] attack Russia about Manchuria, but would fight for Corea.

On August 20, at Tientsin, Satow called on the Viceroy. There had been rumors of an offensive and defensive alliance concluded between Russia and China,[176] but the Viceroy "declared there was no secret agreement between Prince Ch'ing and the Russians, and showed some curiosity to know what England would do."

The next day Satow returned to Peking. On August 23 he called on Uchida.

He says Kurino on 12 August presented proposals to the Russian Government for mutual definition of their interests in Manchuria and Corea, which would lead to evacuation of the former (exactly what Hayashi told Lord Lansdowne on 13 July).

Chinese Government being asked by Japan to suggest opening of Wiju instructed their Minister at Söul that China would neither propose nor oppose opening, but being unable to open ports as desired by themselves in Manchuria, did not see their way to recommending Corea to take steps with regard to Wiju which were opposed by Russia.

Satow then went to Monsieur Dubail, the French Minister, who said Lessar had informed him Russia would evacuate on October 8. "Russia having made declaration to the Powers that she does not oppose opening of ports in Manchuria all difficulties have disappeared!" Satow also saw Conger. "Told him briefly what Uchida had confided to me, and begged him to keep it secret." On August 29 Satow called on Uchida again. "He says he was instructed to tell me only of the presentation of the Japanese proposals at Petersburg, and not to say anything to Conger. From his tone I drew the conclusion that he expects war."

On August 31, Satow went to Chang Chih-tung, who talked about Manchuria. "I told him that any cooperation of England, America and Japan to drive Russia out of Manchuria was not to be thought of," Satow noted in his diary. "If China could not fight her own battles she must not expect us to do it for her."

On September 1, Satow called on Hu.

He says the Tientsin report of the intended issue of bonds to construct a railway from Kalgan to Peking with Chinese capital is not true. The railway cannot be built with English money for the Russians would object, nor with Russian for England would oppose, nor with Belgian, for both Russia and England would protest, nor with Chinese for they have it not. . . . He

227

displayed curiosity to know what I thought about Manchuria, and whether we were going to do anything. Prince Ch'ing sent Lien-fang to Lessar a couple of days ago, but he (Hu) did not know what had taken place. Lien-fang seemed to have lost his former confidence in the value of Russian assurances.

On September 7 Satow saw Uchida. "Says he rather thinks it would be difficult to avoid war, and that Japan will not allow the Russian concession at Yongampho to be ratified." Later Mumm came to Satow. "Tried to pump me about Japanese negotiations with Russia: referred him to telegrams from Kobe in North China Daily News."

On September 9 Satow conversed with Prince Ch'ing about the new Russian proposals for Manchuria, telegraphing the result of his conversation to the Foreign Office.

I am informed by Prince Ch'ing that fresh proposals have been made by the Russian Minister. These include:

1. Appointment to the Newchwang Sanitary Board of a Russian doctor.

2. Duties on goods imported by the Chinese Eastern Railway to be no higher than those on goods imported by road.

3. That at the two ports to be opened in Manchuria, no foreign Concessions or Settlements should be created.

4. That the Russians should establish post stations between Kirin and Tsitsihar (Prince has probably made a mistake here, and means Kirin and Blagovestchensk).

5. Permission to be given to the Russians to construct wharves on the Sungari River, and station troops for their protection.

If the Chinese Government accept these proposals, the rest of Moukden to be evacuated on the 8th October, Heilung Chiang in twelve months, and Kirin in four.

Prince thinks that the negotiations will be lengthy; but he has made a counter-proposal that these periods should be reduced to four and two months respectively.

He says that he is quite alive to the desire of Russia to retain Manchuria, and feels that China, since she cannot use force, must make the best terms she can.

He explains that the acceptance of condition 1 would not prevent the appointment of doctors of other nationalities as well as the Russian, and that condition 3, which is in accordance with the wishes of the Chinese Government, would not hinder the acquisition of land for building purposes by foreigners.

With regard to condition 4, his Highness' reply to Russian Minister is that China has no objection to the construction of the wharves, but that her own troops would protect them, and with regard to 5, that post stations will be re-established by China herself.

I warned Prince Ch'ing that he must exercise care and not concede any conditions by which the Treaty rights of other Powers might be interfered with.

(Secret).

Japanese Minister says that he has advised Prince Ch'ing not to be in a hurry to conclude with Russian Minister, and has informed him that negotiations are proceeding at St. Petersburgh.[177,1]

Somewhat later Satow transmitted the text of the various draft notes. "As the Chinese Government did not accept these proposals, it is to be presumed that the notes were never definitely presented," he remarked. He summarized the Russian demands as follows:

The first condition is that China undertakes never to alienate to any Power any portion of the territory of the provinces of Manchuria, whether by way of lease or mortgage, or in any other manner.

Russia, on her side, restores Manchuria to China, abolishes the existing state of siege, delivers over the government of the three provinces to the Chinese Administration and carries out the final evacuation in the following order:

1. In the Province of Moukden, she withdraws at once the garrisons of Newchwang, with the restoration of the civil government of Fen-huang, Shahotsu (i.e., Antung), and Liaoyang.

2. In the Province of Kirin, withdraws the troops within four months from the town of Kirin, from Yi-tung-chou, Kuang-cheng-tzu, Lo-sha-tzu, and T'olai-chao.

3. At the expiration of a year she withdraws the remainder

---

[1] A more detailed account may be found in Satow to Lansdowne, No. 319, Very Confidential, Sept. 10, 1903, F.O. 405-139, pp. 31-32. The text of various draft notes is given in Satow to Lansdowne, No. 344, Oct. 6, 1903, F.O. 405-139, pp. 80-82.

of the troops in the Province of Kirin, that is to say, from Ninguta and Ashiho and in the Province of Hei-lung-chiang, that is to say, from Tsitsihar and from Hailar.

The draft goes on to say that as the Chinese Eastern Railway is far enough completed to start regular working, it becomes necessary, in the interests of China, to whom the railway will belong, as well as in that of Russia, to facilitate the line being fed from distant points. The Sungari River and the high road from Tsitsihar to Blagovestchensk are of prime importance for this purpose. Hence, in order to insure the safety of navigation and telegraphic communication on the Sungari, Russia is to be allowed to have the requisite number of landing-stations with the necessary guards, and in order to insure the communications between the railway and Blagovestchensk, she is to be allowed to have temporarily a few stations on the high road.

A second note states that it is necessary to establish that China will not levy exclusive (?prohibitive) duties on goods transported by the railway, and secondly, will not levy higher duties on goods transported by rail than on those conveyed by road or river.

A further note or Memorandum provides for the protection of the branches of the Russo-Chinese Bank, which is the common property of the two Powers, by Chinese troops after the evacuation is carried out.

Lastly, in order to prevent the spread of epidemic disease introduced through the port of Newchwang, and in order not to delay the restoration of Newchwang to the Chinese authorities, it is necessary that there shall always be a Russian doctor on the Sanitary service to be organized by the Taotai.[178]

On September 11 Hohler of the Tokio Legation came up and stopped with Satow. "He tells me that the Japanese as a whole want to go to war with Russia, but Ito is trying to stave it off. It was not at first intended to let even Uchida know that negotiations would be attempted at Petersburg." The Uchidas and Congers dined at Satow's that night. "Uchida says he yesterday by instructions from his government saw Prince Ch'ing and urged him strongly not to accede to the Russian terms, and the Prince promised to delay."

On September 21 Satow saw Hillier.

Hillier came to tell me that Lessar was reported, on authority which he believed, to have within the last few days written again to the Chinese that they must give to Russia the same advantages that they granted to Great Britain in any part of China, which they interpreted to mean a reference to our agreement about the Inspector-generalate of Customs, and also that they must accept the terms offered for the evacuation of Manchuria speedily, as it was their last chance. I sent a short red note to Prince Ch'ing warning him not to give anything to Russia that conflicted with our interests, if they wished to preserve the friendship of England, and telegraphed to Foreign Office that I had done so.[179,m]

Satow then went to Uchida.

He had not heard of this, but at the outset a fortnight ago had heard of Lessar's attack on our interests, but was told afterwards that it was conceived in more general terms. He did go to the Summer Palace on the 10th to present the protest of his government. He has seen the first Russian demands of a fortnight ago, which were written on separate sheets of paper, and cannot be sure that he has seen all. He thinks Lien-fang saw Lessar and received verbal communication for Prince Ch'ing, and that to some of the five he agreed as far as he was concerned. Apparently he wrote down in Chinese copies of something shown him at the Russian Legation. In reply to an observation of mine that we cannot hope for peace in the far east so long as Russia does not give Japan satisfaction in regard to Manchuria, he agreed, and his face assumed an expression of strong hostility. He thinks Ito is for peace, but that Yamagata [Aritomo] supports the view of the Cabinet, which is his protégé. He has heard that Prince Ch'ing, alarmed at finding himself between Japan and Russia, is going to Conger tomorrow to ask his advice and assistance.

The next day Uchida came to Satow. "He says Prince Ch'ing is going to see Conger this afternoon, presumably to ask him to mediate between Russia and Japan." Hu called.

Says I ought to go to see Prince Ch'ing and advise him to follow the counsels of Uchida and refuse to accept the Russian

[m] The text of the note and Prince Ch'ing's reply are inclosed in Satow to Lansdowne, No. 336, Sept. 28, 1903, F.O. 405-139, p. 78.

demands, especially those for military posts along the Sungari river and along the road from Tsitsihar to Blagovestchensk. . . . Hu also said that Lessar had written privately to Lienfang saying that Sir Robert Hart had been very harmful to Chinese interests as Inspector-General and that now China and Russia were on such friendly terms, they should agree to have a Russian Inspector-General for Manchuria, and appoint Russians to be Commissioners at Moukden and Antung hsien.

On September 24 Satow went to see Conger and got from him the account of his conversation with Prince Ch'ing.

Prince Ch'ing called the day before yesterday on my United States' colleague to ask his advice respecting the demands made by Russia in connection with the evacuation in Manchuria. He detailed the conditions exactly as we now have them, and said that the Chinese Government feared that if they refused to agree, Russia would permanently occupy the three provinces.

Mr. Conger pointed out that the conditions in question would practically confer upon Russia the sovereignty of Manchuria, as they included the military control of all the main thoroughfares of communication, both by land and water. Even supposing Russia declared her intention of remaining permanently in possession, China would be in no worse position than she would be if she signed a written agreement accepting those conditions. In either case Russia would be mistress of Manchuria. China should therefore, refuse categorically, and call upon Russia to carry out the original Convention, in accordance with which the whole territory was to be evacuated by the 8th October next.

Mr. Conger observed that China had no reason to suppose Russia would, in case of her present demands being accepted, carry out her proposed new engagement for completing the evacuation in another twelve months, any more than she had fulfilled the previous one. She would simply utilize the interval to consolidate her position, and frame fresh demands to be presented later on. If, in consequence of China's refusal, Russia declared her intention of remaining, the former could appeal to the public opinion of the civilized world, whereas her consent would render it impossible for her best friends to help her, and would, moreover, alienate their goodwill on account of the Treaty rights of other Powers which she would have sacrificed to Russia.

Prince Ch'ing replied that China would act on this advice and oppose a resolute negative to Russian insistence.

I understand that this step of consulting Mr. Conger was taken by Prince Ch'ing on his own initiative, possibly in consequence of his having seen the Reuter's telegram stating that the United States was indifferent to the fate of Manchuria, and my United States' colleague, who for some time past has not spoken to His Highness of this question, was no doubt pleased to have the opportunity of clearing up any doubts that might have existed in his mind as to the attitude of the United States' Government.[180]

The next day Satow called on Prince Ch'ing. He embodied his talk in a dispatch.

In the course of conversation with Prince Ch'ing to-day, I asked him whether he could tell me anything with respect to the Manchurian negotiations.

His Highness promptly replied that he had yesterday addressed a note to M. Lessar, refusing to accede to the demands which had been made by Russia as conditions precedent of the evacuation. He pointed out that by a Convention regularly negotiated by Plenipotentiaries appointed by the two Governments and afterwards ratified by the respective Sovereigns, Russia undertook to withdraw from Mukden and Kirin on the 8th of April last, and from Heilungchiang (Tsitsihar) on the 8th proximo. He called upon the Russian Government accordingly to redeem their pledges, and to proceed to carry out the evacuation in accordance with the terms of the Convention. After that was done, the Chinese Government would be prepared to consider the settlement of various questions outstanding between the two countries.

Prince Ch'ing said that Russia had acted in a most unjustifiable manner in putting forward fresh demands. To allow Russia to post soldiers to guard the landing stages on the banks of the Sungari River, and to establish military posting stations on the road between Tsitsihar and Blagovestchensk, coupled with the construction of Russian railways through the three provinces already conceded, would give her complete control of all the arteries of communication, and he was determined not to give way on these points. If, in consequence of the Chinese refusal, the Russians remained in Manchuria, it would come to the same thing as their ostensible evacuation on her compliance with the new conditions. The withdrawal would be only nominal, while she would remain in *de facto* possession.

I replied that I thought the Prince had taken the correct course in refusing, as China was thus shown to be in the right, and the Russians were put in the wrong. It seemed, indeed, that the latter were conscious of this, as they had been so careful to refuse all information to Powers who had addressed to them inquiries as to the nature of their demands.

The Prince added that he had made a further observation to M. Lessar, namely, that whereas the Concession for the construction of the "Eastern Chinese Railways" accorded only the right of stationing railway police along them, Russia had now claimed the right of protecting them with troops. China herself was quite ready to assume that duty, as soon as the evacuation was completed.

He remarked, incidentally, that the original Convention for the lease of the Liaotung Peninsula made with Li Hung-chang stipulated for a period of twenty-five years only, but for aught he could see, Russia had no intention of surrendering her lease at the expiration of that time. All that China could do was to wait for the 8th of October, when he believed that she would receive the support of other Powers against Russia.

It is probable that besides the support of Japan, he expects to derive assistance of some kind from the United States. . . .

I was much struck with the confident air of the Prince today. At the end of the conversation he alluded to newspaper reports of a secret understanding between himself and M. Lessar, to which he professed entire indifference, saying that his conscience was perfectly clear in the matter. I assured him that I felt convinced myself that there was no foundation for such accusations and they might safely be disregarded.[181,n]

The following day Satow went back to Conger and communicated to him the conversation with Prince Ch'ing about Manchuria, "which was in accordance with advice he had given to Prince, and he beamed all over." (9/26) Satow then saw Uchida and told him the same. "He had received Chü

---

[n] For a telegraphic resumé see Satow to Lansdowne, No. 224, telegraphic, Sept. 25, 1903, F.O. 405-138, p. 108.

Hung-chi yesterday and found out from him about the Manchurian Note." Finally Satow went to Sir Robert Hart to ask about the Russian demand for separate Russian organization in Manchuria.

He declared he had not heard a word of it, which was absolutely false, as he had some days ago told the whole story of Lessar's note on the subject to Morrison. He mentioned [N. A.] Konovaloff [who had been named Commissioner at Newchwang] with praise, on which I remarked that the appointment had given great offence to senior men in the Customs service, who had been passed over. He defended himself rather feebly I thought. Then he said he had signed an agreement with Alexeieff that the Newchwang customs revenue should be paid into the Russo-Chinese bank 'to the credit of China' . . . but could not tell me whether the Chinese government could draw or had drawn any part of the balance remaining after payment of the Russian claim for repairs to the extra-mural railway, which he said had been paid by China with an order on that fund. Altogether he produced on me the impression of quite Chinese shiftiness and evasion.

He is no doubt unfriendly to us. 1°. It was not the British Government nor Sir. F[rederick] Bruce [one-time British envoy at Peking] which put him where he is, but the Chinese, and the rest is his own creation. 2°. The choice of the British Government of Bredon to be his successor some years ago, and the stipulation that after him the Inspector-General should always be an Englishman offended him, as being unnecessary interference. 3°. The most recent intervention of the Foreign Office in the spring of this year, by which they told Bredon he was no longer their candidate, and they put Hippisley forward as favorite has again vexed him. He does not want anyone to be Inspector-General after him, but a committee of different nationalities, for in his opinion no single man is up to the weight of responsibility but Robert Hart. In past times he has been so flattered and rewarded by His Majesty's Government and the world in general that his head has been turned, and his chief characteristic now is senile vanity. (9/26)

The following day Satow recorded in his diary: "Sir Robert having apparently repented of his prevarication about the

Russian proposal for a separate Inspector-General in Manchuria has now written and told the truth." (9/27)

On September 30 Mumm came to Satow.

He said that we were credited with an intention of claiming compensation as a set off to the Russian possession of Manchuria [Satow noted]. I told him that if he would believe me, there was nothing in the story, that I had absolutely no instructions of the kind from His Majesty's Government. He said he believed me, and that it would be a great pity if any other Powers began to take bits of China, as that would probably not be allowed. Russia could of course do as she liked. No one interfered, because even the boys in the street regarded Manchuria as somehow hers.

On October 19 Lienfang, then Senior Vice President of the Foreign Board, and Ku Chao-hsin, its secretary, brought Satow the Chinese versions of the correspondence between Lessar and the Chinese Government about the new conditions precedent for the evacuation of Manchuria.

The only explanation obtained from the Russians for the presentation of fresh demands was that it is usual when evacuation is carried out to stipulate for safeguards. He hoped that His Majesty's Government would speak the 'word of justice' to Russia. I replied that I had done my best to put the state of the case before His Majesty's Government and that it was for them to decide what line they would adopt. Supposing His Majesty's Government made observations to Russia, and they met with an unsatisfactory reception, then the discussion might proceed and finally become so heated that the two parties would stand ready to come to blows, and therefore much consideration was necessary. I said I thought China was entirely in the right. Some of the proposals, as that the branches of the Russo-Chinese Bank should be protected by Chinese soldiers were innocent enough, but to proposals about landing stages on the Sungari River and posting stations on the road from Tsitsihar to Blagoveschensk amounted to giving up control of all the arteries of communication. China ought never to give up the control of her railways to any foreign government. Only to companies could she safely entrust them.

On October 27 Mumm came to Satow. "He asked whether I could give him any information about Manchuria, but I had none, except that from the way in which the negotiations were prolonged I anticipated a peaceful solution," Satow recorded.

On October 29 Viceroy Yüan Shih-k'ai sent Tang Shao-yi to Satow.

The Russians have resumed control of the telegraph office at Mukden and another place between it and Tieh ling, and had also sent parties of soldiers across the Liao river to intimate to the telegraphists at certain stations that they must not forward telegrams [Satow noted in his diary].[182] This last news he had this morning from the Viceroy, and he did not know the names of the places, but was going to Lessar to ask what it meant.

He then said that the Viceroy was much concerned about the negotiations between Japan and Russia; if war was the result what attitude should China take. She could hardly remain neutral if there was fighting in her territory.

I said I should hesitate before advising China to adopt a course that would land her in greater disasters than she had yet experienced. Had she troops and officers capable of leading them, that would be of any use to an ally?

He said no, but she could furnish provisions and transport. If Japan had allies, would that affect the operation of the Anglo-Japanese agreement?

I replied that it would not.

He said that if there were war, the Japanese ground of action would be a desire to force Russia to fulfil her obligations to China, and what *casus belli* could Russia put forward which would give her as good, or a better title to a Chinese alliance. But there was a fear that if Japan were victorious, she would become very domineering.

I replied that as far as I could gauge Japanese feeling in the matter, it was a sincere desire to help China in every way against foreign encroachment. Nearly all Asia was dominated by Europe, and Japan felt that if China fell under their control, her own independence would be endangered. It was unlikely therefore that she would feel inclined to herself domineer over China, but rather to afford her assistance.

He acknowledged that this was the view of all sensible Chinese. But the Viceroy fears that in case of war one or the other party may occupy Peking, in order to put pressure on China to take sides. Suppose Japan sent 5,000 or 6,000 men here with that object. I thought it unlikely that Japan would do that as long as the Russian fleet was afloat, but possibly Russia might.

He asked whether Russia or Japan might not land a large force at Shanhaikwan.

The answer to this I said was the same as in the other case.

He observed that the protocol limited the number of foreign troops, and could not the other Powers appeal to that to prevent any increase being made.

I told him that the protocol did not fix the number of troops at Peking or anywhere else, and that it was arranged between the generals, but when 300 each was fixed as the limit at Shanhaikwan the Russians declared they would not be bound by the agreement, and would station there 1500. I told him the recent incident about the Russian offer to hand over part of the site of Fort No. 1 on condition that they might have it back whenever they gave notice of a desire to return.

What was to be feared he said was that the Russians would seize the railway and rolling stock, and bring troops up to Tientsin and Peking.

I tried to comfort him by observing that if war came, the Japanese strategists might possibly not fight in Manchuria, as the public expected them to do, but go for Vladivostok. This I begged him not to repeat to anyone, but to regard it as confidential.

The following day Satow discussed the Manchurian situation with Conger.

His opinion in the Manchurian question is that the Powers ought to have long ago insisted on Russia giving up Newchwang, a Treaty Port, where they are assuming powers that infringe upon the authority of the Foreign Consuls. But as far as he can see their interest in whole question has much abated. Germany and France never took much, as their object is to do in Shantung and in the South what Russia is doing in Manchuria. He doubts whether Japan will take any steps against Russia there, it is only if her interests in Corea are affected that she will take up arms. I did not contest this view, and said that considering the long time expended in negotiation it was probable that peace would not be disturbed. If war did unfortunately break out

China would be in an uncomfortable and abnormal position. He asked whether if China went to pieces, Japan was likely to assert her claims to Fuhkien. I replied that in my opinion no Power would follow the Russian example.

On November 1 Chang Chih-tung sent Liang to Satow to say that he was going to the Summer Palace and would like to know his opinion on the Manchurian question, as he expected that he would be consulted on that.

I said that I thought China should stick to her refusal. That I was certain Japan had not agreed as the newspapers reputed, to let Russia do as she likes in Manchuria in return for a free hand in Corea. That Russia intends to stay in Manchuria unless turned out by force. Whether there will be war or not I could not say, but that peace is by no means certain.

He asked whether China might not appeal to the Powers to express their opinion that Russia ought to clear out.

I said no, because Russia would regard that as an unfriendly act and the Powers would either refuse or give no answer. Her best plan is to remain still, and not to listen to Chinese newspapers who argue that China should ally herself with Japan. That would provoke Russia to do something still worse than merely remaining in Manchuria.

(Conger told me a day or two ago that Lessar says Russia will either continue the occupation by a friendly understanding with China, or failing that take over the country for herself and disregard an unfriendly China.

My conjecture is that if war breaks out, it will take first the form of an endeavour to destroy or neutralize the Russian fleet, and be followed by an attack on Vladivostok, thus avoiding war in either Chinese or Corean territory.)

On November 6 Morrison told Satow that the Russians had again made a demand that China should accept a Resident at Mukden, "returning thus to one of the demands in their early convention of January, 1901 about Manchuria."°

On November 9, Satow received the French Minister.

° On October 20, the Russians had reoccupied Moukden under the pretext (false in the opinion of Satow) that the Chinese authorities could not maintain order.[183]

I chaffingly asked Dubail whether there was any truth in the Reuter that Russia, France and Germany were combining together to make war on England and Japan [Satow noted in his diary]. He replied that he had reason to believe that it was quite the other way, France having been asked by England and Japan to mediate between them and Russia with the object of preserving the peace, and that he was confidentially informed that matters were proceeding hopefully. He remarked that Germany was now particularly detested in Japan, and I told him the history of Gutschmid and his doings there, the sudden German volte-face in 1895 after having flattered and congratulated the Japanese on their successes.

On November 11, Chang Chih-tung sent Liang to Satow with a picture scroll of bamboo of the beginning of the Ming dynasty. "He asked about the negotiations, I said they were apparently proceeding smoothly, and that there would not be war," Satow entered in his diary. "He asked whether it would not be well to appeal to the Great Powers. I said no. Well to England alone. I replied that Lord Lansdowne would probably answer that IIis Majesty's Government were using their influence to bring about a satisfactory result, and would refuse to undertake to make special representation at St. Petersburg."

On November 12, V. H. Caesar Hawkins called on Satow and told him as a great secret that Lessar had been to the Waiwupu the day before to advise the Chinese to telegraph to Petersburg about Moukden. That day Satow also spoke with the Japanese Minister. "Uchida says that his government must conclude something before 5 December, for which date the Diet is summoned, for if they don't the Cabinet must fall under impeachment, and if they try to quiet things by dissolving the Diet and so preventing the impeachment, [Premier] Katsura [Taro] or [Foreign Minister] Komura will certainly be assassinated!"

On November 17 Conger visited Satow.

He says that the United States seems indifferent to the fate of Manchuria, and he does not believe that the Russian reoccupation of Moukden is in any way connected with the American Treaty by which it is stipulated that this city shall be made an open port.ᵖ Germany is only waiting for an example in order that she may do the same thing in Shantung that Russia is doing in Manchuria. The Chinese Government is more effete than ever, and it is not worth while fighting to help them. He hears that there is a good deal of unrest in Central China and along the Yangtze. The people attribute the heavy burdens imposed on them in consequence of the events of 1900 to the Tartar dynasty, and feel that the only hope for China lies in getting rid of them.

On November 21, Satow conversed with Wu Ting-fang about the international policy that China should follow.

I advised her keeping quiet until the negotiations between Japan and Russia were decided [Satow noted in his diary]. We must not invite Russian hostility, which was looking for an opportunity to seize Peking. He said the Foreign Ministers ought to prevent that. I said that speaking confidentially I did not think Japan would attack Russia in Chinese or Corean territory. He guessed Vladivostok. He also alluded to the reports that other Powers would take advantage of the occasion to seize territory, and he particularly feared Germany. I said I thought not; at any rate they must be on their guard against Russian suggestions that Japan would come to an agreement to leave Russia in Manchuria and seek compensation in Fukien. He might banish that idea from his mind altogether.

Satow dined at Uchida's. "He says the Chinese are not giving way about Manchuria, and reiterated his view that the Japanese cabinet must arrange something to satisfy public opinion before 5 December. There had been a great meeting of business men and journalists at the Teikoku Hotel, where Shibusawa [Eiichi?] had made a fiery speech, and a resolution was carried, calling on the government to take decided steps without delay."

ᵖ The Port Arthur newspaper *Novyi Krai* gave out that the reoccupation of Moukden "was intended as a retort to the United States' demand for the opening of Moukden to American trade."[184]

241

On December 7 Conger came to Satow. "We discussed the Manchurian situation and I told him that I had advised the Chinese to be very careful not to enter upon hostilities with the Russians. If they did, I felt sure that the position of the foreigners in Peking would be very precarious," Satow recorded.

On December 13, Satow and Conger talked about the dissolution of the Japanese Diet. Afterwards Conger went to Uchida and, as Mumm told Satow, learned what had happened. "That the Diet in its address in reply to the speech from the Throne had touched upon Manchurian affairs, which proceeding had brought about the dissolution. As the new Diet cannot meet till March, the Japanese Government has time before it. He thinks this event looks peaceful. I said it had that appearance, though I did not feel sure. Certainly if the Diet had not been dissolved it would have looked much worse, as the whole nation and the Diet were for war."

On December 14 General Yamane came to say good-bye to Satow.

We discussed the situation [Satow recorded]. He finally asked me whether Japan ought to fight now or delay, not as minister, but as a private person acquainted with Japan and the general situation. I pondered, and then said yes, for if Russia is left undisturbed in Manchuria out of which she will never retire willingly, she will end by taking Corea, and the position of Japan would then be imperilled. China I thought ought to be very careful not to join in too soon, as the Russians would come down on Peking.

On December 17, Satow noted in his diary: "Reuter telegrams from Tokio that the Japanese Government are made gloomy by the Russian answer. Morrison came to ask about the negotiations. I told him that Reuter's telegrams from Tokio were much more reliable than those from Petersburg, but avoided giving him anything confidential."

Mumm came before dinner, and we talked about the situation, but guardedly. He says, evidently from Russian inspiration that no concession will be made to Japan about Manchuria. Gave him the *Japan Times* of 11 and 12 December to read, showing the real meaning of the dissolution of the Japanese Diet. He thinks the chances of a peaceable solution are less than they were, or looked some time ago. It certainly looks as if the future of Japan depended on her resolution now.

On December 21, Satow called on Uchida.

I gathered from him that he knows more than he has hitherto admitted [Satow recalled]. I observed that the press were beginning to be told what is passing. He admitted that the Tokio Reuters were in the main correct, e.g. in saying that the Russians ignored the basis of negotiations, and that Japan would make one more effort, but as to fixing the date by which an answer would be expected, he did not think that would come next. He observed that if Corea alone were concerned Japan would have sufficient in the agreement of 1896 and 1898. He admitted that Japan having started this negotiation for the sake of Manchuria, would not and could not be satisfied with the subject being ignored. I went on to discuss what would happen if war broke out in the way of others taking part, and remarked that China would no doubt join in if she saw that Japan was having some successes. He nodded his head most emphatically. We discussed whether France was obliged to join Russia, but not knowing the conditions of that alliance, could not decide the point. He thinks Dubail's intervention was not very urgent, and that he merely spoke to Lien-fang, suggesting that it would be well to come to an understanding with Russia before Alexeieff went to Petersburg. So Prince Ch'ing sent Lien Fang to Lessar to ask what they wanted, and he replied that the matter was in Alexeieff's hands and he had nothing to do with it. He saw Prince Ch'ing on the 10th, who evidently thought Dubail's suggestion came from himself, and not from the French Government. As to Dubail's story to me that Japan and England had asked France to mediate with Russia, he had asked his government who told him it was a fable. I suggested that possibly Germany might join in, and so revive the 'triplice' of 1895. It was true there were no signs of this as Hohler had written to me from Tokio, but in 1895, also there was no warning, Germany up to the last moment having manifested the greatest friendship to Japan. Uchida said that Mumm had been to see him, and on two occasions lately had gone out of his way to assure him that Germany would observe the strictest neutrality in the coming struggle, which meant that they certainly would not back up Russia. I observed that for Germany it was a question whether Kiaochou and the rest of Shantung were more valuable than Asia Minor and the relief of her Eastern frontier from the pressure of large bodies of Russian troops. It certainly did seem that the distance of Kiaochou from Germany must greatly diminish its value.

Going away I said that if war broke out, it might have far reaching consequences, and China might in consequence become able to retain her independence, to which he heartily assented.

On December 24, Satow talked with Dubail, who, he had heard, offered his good offices to the Chinese Government in facilitating an arrangement with the Russians. "His language appears, however, to have been tantamount to advising China to accept the demands of Russia," Satow had reported.[185] Satow described the meeting of the 24th in his diary:

He asked me what news I had from Tokio. I replied that it was not pacific, and it seemed to me that the Russians made a mistake as to the temper of the Japanese people. They thought that their preparations would frighten them, but various incidents made me think they were wrong. The dissolution of the Diet in consequence of the address to the Emperor did not mean much [i.e. had not the conciliatory meaning that had been attributed to it]. The address was the result of a political intrigue against the cabinet; as soon as the leaders saw the result of their action, they wanted to reverse it, but Kone the President of the lower house interfered.

He said that what Japan wanted was a free hand in Corea, in exchange for giving Russia freedom of action in Manchuria.[q] In fact Ito last year went to Petersburg with such an offer. I rejoined that as soon as the Japanese Government knew what he was up to, they recalled him. It was true that Ito was pacific,

[q] "M. Dubail seems not to appreciate sufficiently the temper of the Japanese, and to be under the impression that all Japan wants is a free hand in Corea, in return for letting Russia do what she likes in Manchuria," Satow commented in a telegram to London.[186]

but it seemed to me that his influence had diminished. It was remarkable that Saionji who was Ito's henchman, and had been put in by him to head the Seiyukai, had uttered warlike sentiments and the party had allied itself with the Shimpoto.

I said that the Russians appeared to me to have been too grasping in regard to Manchuria, which they aimed at acquiring as a consequence of 1900. They went even to Yongampho [in Korea]. Dubail agreed that for Japan Corea was a vital question, but said that Yongampho was merely a commercial speculation in timber. I said not so, for the President of the company was [A. M.] Bezobrazoff [the Russian Secretary of State], and the manager Ginsburg, the *âme damnée* [damned soul, i.e. tool] of [Col. Konstantin] Wogack [the Russian Military Attaché for China and Japan]. As to Japan not being willing to fight about Manchuria, it must be remembered that people had said to them that their China campaign of 1894-95 was a mere military promenade, and that they would never get their position as a nation recognized until they crossed swords with an European power. That was a strong motive with them ["a warlike people," as Satow added in his dispatch].

Yes, he replied, that old samurai spirit. But war would ruin Japan. At the outside she had only £ 16,000,000 of gold, and the first result of a declaration of war would be the return to forced currency. The resources of Russia were so enormous.

I agreed with him that in the long run the result must be disastrous for Japan.

He went on to say that he hoped the Chinese would observe neutrality. They had neither officers nor men, and in three weeks Russia would be at the gates of Peking. He had advised them on no account to join the Japanese, as Russia would then leave Japan alone and hurl her forces upon them; they would have to pay the piper, and Russia would probably take Chihli as well as Manchuria. He had been asked for his advice by the Empress Dowager and Prince Ch'ing and had as a friend counselled them to keep aloof. Could I not do the same.

I said I had not seen Prince Ch'ing for some time, but when my opinion had been asked I had given the same advice as himself. I was afraid that if China joined in the whole country would be in flames. But suppose an European country were in the same position, could she without sacrificing her self-respect refrain from taking part. I asked what were the obligations of France in such an event, would she be obliged to join Russia.

He smiled and said he was not able to tell me exactly, but he thought not. When the [Franco-Russian] counter-declaration of last year which followed upon the Anglo-Japanese treaty was being discussed he advised against it [on the ground that it was unnecessary]. What France had gained by her alliance with Russia was the certainty of not being attacked by Germany, but Russia could not help France in the Far East.

I said that in England there was not the slightest feeling of unfriendliness towards France, and we should regret it very much if we found ourselves in the opposite camp to her. Yet we were under obligations to Japan.

He replied that the relations between London and Paris were such that he thought their efforts would be rather directed towards the maintenance of peace, or to restricting the area of disturbance. He knew that England had given strong advice to the Japanese not to break the peace.

I observed that Russia was an absorbing Power. She aimed at universal domination, being the youngest of the nations, full of sap; Eastern Europe and the whole of Asia was what she aimed at. Just as a century ago Napoleon was able to conquer Europe because of the jealousies of the Powers, so now Russia was enabled to acquire a predominant position by reason of our existing jealousies.

He attributed the continued occupation of Manchuria to the military party in Russia, and said that Lessar was quite opposed to it. I responded that I believed that too. Lessar who had negotiated the convention would certainly have desired to see it carried out.

We talked about the absurd reports in the newspapers about an English Viceroy of the Yangtze, and he said that Chang Chih-tung had sent Liang to him to ask if it was true! I again affirmed my opposition to a partition of China and so did he. How could we possibly find the men to carry it out, and then just think of the difficulties among ourselves.

Reporting this conversation to the Foreign Secretary, Satow added:

Your Lordship is probably aware that the question whether China should make common cause with Japan in the event of war, has been much debated by the leading members of the Chinese Government as well as urged by the native press. It is

246

believed by my Japanese colleague that she will certainly take this step if the course of events should appear to hold out any hope of its turning to her advantage. I have learnt also from a confidential source that the newly-arrived Japanese military Attaché, who has conferred with the Viceroy, Yüan Shih-kai, talks as if he counted on it. The warlike tone of Peking has rather abated in the last three or four weeks, and the prevailing feeling on the part of the Chinese is one of despair at the impotence of which they are conscious. I doubt, however, whether its continuance can be relied on. The occurrences of 1900 have sufficiently shown that the Chinese are people capable of suddenly taking fire, and in that condition of performing acts of the rashest desperation.[187]

On December 26 Satow confidentially related to Conger his talk with Dubail. "He thinks perhaps the Russians may avoid a quarrel with China, in order not to bring France in and so necessitate our joining Japan. He thinks also that even if the Japanese and Russians fight it out, that will by no means settle Far Eastern affairs."

That day Satow noted in his diary: "MacDonald is active in telegraphing 1° privately to me that Dubail is not to be trusted 2° to Foreign Office that his object in trying to persuade the Chinese to remain neutral is to avoid having to take up the cudgels on behalf of Russia 3° that Scott's opinion that the Emperor of Russia animated by peaceful intentions is all wrong and 4° that Japan has not seriously considered the question of an alliance with China in the event of war. He seems to be in a critical mood, and to think we are blind to things he sees."

On December 28, Satow conversed with Joostens. "Talking of the probability of war he said that [the Commander of the American Asiatic Fleet] Fighting Bob Evans' opinion was that the war, if there was one, would be quickly over, as the Russians would finish off the Japanese fleet in one battle. The ships were good, but the men and officers inefficient. I said that rather surprised me, as I had heard quite a different estimate from English naval officers."

247

On December 30, Hu Yü-fen, who had recently made a visit of inspection to the newly completed extension of the Tientsin-Shanhaikwan railway line to Hsin-ming-ting and had extended his tour to Port Arthur, where he had had an interview with the Russian Viceroy, called on Satow.

He said that while at Hsin-ming-ting he received a telegram from the Russian railway authorities at Harbin, suggesting that he should visit Port Arthur, and placing a special car at his disposal [Satow reported]. He accepted the offer, and arrived at Port Arthur on the 18th December.

M. Plançon, lately Russian Chargé d'Affaires at Peking, called on him and asked whether he wished to have an interview with Admiral Alexeieff, to which he cautiously answered that he had not come on any official mission, but that he would be glad to call if Admiral Alexeieff desired to see him. An interview was accordingly arranged for 3:30 P.M., and a carriage was sent for Hu an hour in advance with a military officer, who took him for a drive through the town, with the flourishing appearance of which he was much impressed, as also with the number of forts.

Admiral Alexeieff received him with much cordiality, the only other persons present being M. Plançon and an interpreter. After preliminary greetings the Viceroy asked how many English engineers were employed at Hsin-ming-ting, to which Hu answered that there were none; there were three Chinese, whose names he gave, and an English engineer at Newchwang, which was in strict accordance with the Anglo-Russian Agreement.

The relations between the Chinese and Russian Railway Administration were, he added, of the most cordial character. The Viceroy expressed satisfaction, and went on to say that it was his own earnest wish that the same might become true of the political relations between Russia and China, which had been to some extent disturbed by the interference of Japan, which China ought not to allow. Hu "tajên" turned to M. Plançon, and suggested that the demands put forward by him last spring had much to do with the creation of the present position by varying the terms on which Russia had agreed to evacuate Manchuria. The Viceroy said that he personally was most anxious to see the evacuation carried out, but that the intervention of Japan had complicated matters. If China would but deal directly with Russia alone, he felt sure that a satisfactory solution would be reached, and he inquired of Hu what were the real opinions of the Chinese Court and Government.

Hu said that he had left Peking merely with instructions to inspect the railway, and had no knowledge of his Government's views on the Manchurian question. After further assurances of his friendly sentiments to China, the Viceroy suggested that Hu should inspect the Russian fleet. A launch was in readiness, and he was taken just on board a battleship and shown the guns and torpedoes and other objects of interest, and was taken up and down the harbour and invited to count the Russian vessels, to the number of fifty-two. His guide, a Russian officer, told him that there were yet twenty more outside, and offered to take him to see them, but Hu excused himself on the ground of the lateness of the hour, adding, for my information, that the launch was small and the weather outside uncertain.

Next day being the name day of the Emperor of Russia, Hu called by arrangement to offer his congratulations, and made a short speech, proposing the Emperor's health, closing with the usual hope that the relations of the two countries might become more and more cordial. On this the Viceroy slapped himself vigorously on the chest, and loudly declared that Hu had exactly expressed his own sentiments. M. Plançon accompanied Hu out of the house, and took the opportunity of again inquiring what were the real views of the Chinese Government on the Manchurian question. Hu repeated that he had no authority to be their spokesman, but that, so far as he knew, they were determined to agree to nothing that would impair the sovereign rights of China, or infringe the Treaty rights of other Powers. With that reservation he thought that they would have no objection to discussing the other proposals of Russia; but he again reproached M. Plançon with the demands he had put forward in the spring, and also asked how Russia reconciled the progressive withdrawal of her troops, to which she was pledged, with the reoccupation of Mukden. M. Plançon said that the Tartar General has shown ill-will to Russia, and referred also to her demand for the dismissal of Yuan Taotai (who, as Hu pointed out, had now been removed), but laid most stress on the fact that the reoccupation of Mukden consisted merely in sending a couple of hundred more troops there; there had been no interference with the Administration, and the troops would, he believed, soon be withdrawn again. He then proceeded to

press on Hu the desirability of the Chinese Government sending a special Commissioner of high rank to Port Arthur to negotiate with the Viceroy, on whose anxiety to meet the wishes
of China he again enlarged. Direct negotiation at Port Arthur
would, he felt sure, lead to a satisfactory solution, but he warned
Hu that the Viceroy Yuan would not be a suitable representative of the Chinese Government because he was known to be
wholly under the influence of Japan.

On his way back by train from Port Arthur, Hu travelled
in the company of a Russian official, who pressed on him the desirability of extending the line from Hsin-ming-ting to Mukden, and stated that the Russo-Chinese Bank would readily advance the necessary funds.

On his return to Peking Hu ta-jên learnt that the Chinese
Government had written to the Russian Minister to ask when
Russia proposed to carry out her pledge to evacuate Manchuria,
but had received no reply. At Prince Ch'ing's suggestion, Hu
called on the 29th instant on M. Lessar, who told him that it was
with the Viceroy Alexeieff that the Chinese Government must
negotiate, as Manchurian affairs were entirely in his hands, and
who repeated the recommendation to send a high official to
Port Arthur.

I have reported Hu ta-jên's account of his interviews at some
length, because I think they show what is Russia's present line
of policy towards China. There is evidently a desire to impress
her with Russia's strength, and also with her good-will towards
China if the latter will only not be misled into trusting to the
support of other Powers. Evidently, also, the Russians consider
that from a special Chinese delegate to Port Arthur they could
easily obtain some assurances, written or verbal, that could be
construed as legalizing their occupation of Manchuria.

I did not gather from Hu ta-jên that the Chinese Government were inclinded to take any such step as long as the Japanese negotiations with Russia continue.[188]

On January 3, 1904, Kuei-chun, nominally governor of
Tungchow called on Satow "to make a new Year's call, but
really to talk politics."

Knew all about the Russian striving toward an ice-free port, and
that Ambassadors were supposed to be entitled to have audi-
ences of sovereigns. I told him Russia was not contented with

Port Arthur and Talien-wan Bay, but now wanted Masampho, and that she talks of annexing Mongolia and Kashgaria. He thought that these annexations would do her no good, but cost her a great deal of money, as they are not self supporting territories, and would distract her attention from getting to the sea, besides Port Arthur and other places of the kind made her very vulnerable. Manchuria was regarded as of vital importance by the Court, because Kirin was the cradle of the dynasty and Mukden is where their tombs are. . . . Kuei-chun also asked whether it was true that England and France had given urgent advice to Japan not to go to war. I replied that war was always an inconvenience to neutrals, as it interfered with their commerce, and so of course they always expressed a sort of platonic hope that war would be avoided, but we had not gone further than that.

On January 4, Conger came to Satow.

He told me very confidentially that [Lloyd C.] Griscom [the American Minister to Japan] telegraphed that he had it on excellent authority that Japan would send an ultimatum shortly after the 4th and asked if I had the same news. I said no, but Kurino was to see Lamsdorf the day before yesterday and Bezobrazoff had given it out that whether Russia retired or remained in Manchuria, other Powers would not be allowed to have equal rights with her there, which I said was a denial of our most favoured nation clause which he had always maintained. According to Uchida, said Conger, neither China nor Corea would be regarded as a 'third power' in the sense that their participation would oblige France to join Russia. And he felt certain that considering the recent exchange of friendly visits between the King and Monsieur Roubet, the French would be very loath to fall out with England. I reminded him of what I had told him of Dubail's language, and said that no doubt France felt less dependent on Russia since she had now a friendly understanding with England and Italy; and I told him what was reported from Paris as to Lamsdorf's visit there.

That day Satow talked about Manchuria with Dubail.

He said the Chinese could not turn the Russians out by force, and therefore they must save all they can by giving way on some points. He had told them it was no use relying on Japan, which would be satisfied if she had a free hand in Corea. No-

251

body was going to fight the Russians for Manchuria. I objected that 1°. the Chinese said they could not trust the Russians to carry out any new convention as they had broken the first, 2°. the Russians now say they will not admit other nations to equal participation there, whilst the Powers went on telling China that they insisted on the most favoured nation clause. For example, the Russians would not allow any other nations to carry on mining enterprises, and it was possible they might interfere with missionaries. They had annoyed ours a good deal, and probably disliked the Catholics as much. He replied that the Greeks were hostile to the Catholics no doubt. In his view Russia had made a mistake in spending such vast sums in Manchuria. Possibly they might therefore consent to let the Chinese continue the administration, if they gave way on other points. They should send some one on a special embassy to Russia. When one is the weaker *il faut être le plus malin* [one must be the more cunning one.] I said Lamsdorff aparently had no power in the matter, but he replied that for the past two months he had been regaining favour. The man to influence was Bezobrazoff, who has so much influence over the Emperor. I observed that the Emperor had apparently not a very strong character, and easily let himself be influenced. There was a strong party in Russia that disapproved the enormous expenditure on this Manchurian enterprise. Mongolia and Kashgaria were notoriously not self-supporting, and their acquisition would bring on profitless expenditures. Yes he said, I have told Lessar this over and over again; what the Chinese ought to do however is to get the moderates in Russia on their side, and so overcome the forward party. I did not say what I thought, namely that the Chinese are also playing a waiting game, believing that the money will not last. . . . It would be interesting to see *his* journal of our conversation, and amusing to see what he gets out of it! . . . (1/4)

On January 7 Satow talked with Hillier.

Hillier says that when the Russian 4½% loan was made, the Russians kept back 5,000,000 taels as Chinese capital in the to be established Russo-Chinese Bank, on which they undertook to pay 4% interest. But they did not pay this over, retaining for a deposit on account of the Chinese University. Recently the Chinese induced the Russo-Chinese Bank to let them have 300,000 taels, which they promptly brought round to him. They then tried to get another 200,000 taels, but meanwhile the Russo-Chinese Bank had taken the alarm, and on one pretext or another refused to shell out. He says Japanese have sent up 400,-000 Mexican dollars to the account of the Yokohama specie bank, to be retained in safe deposit, and this is to be followed by 600,-000 more. These coins are used not in Peking or Chihli; but at Newchwang. It looks as if this money was to be deposited in Tientsin to meet certain eventualities.

On January 8 Hu came to tell Satow about Russian talk of occupying Hsin-ming-ting, and Satow asked him to let him know when they came.

He told me that he had been received by the Empress-Dowager two days ago, and told her about his experiences at Port Arthur, and how Alexeieff had recommended that China should negotiate about Manchuria direct. But the Russians still stick to their six demands; of these China might agree to let the Russo-Chinese Bank's establishments being guarded by Chinese troops, and use the branch at Newchwang as the Customs bank. Apropos of this I asked whether they ever received any of the revenue of the customs. He said that after the expenses of the Russians for the extramural line had been deducted, the Hupu was able to draw on the Russo-Chinese bank in Peking for the balance. I advised China to remain still, as it was not certain that if it came to war, there would be fighting in Chinese, or even in Corean territory. It seemed unlikely that war could come for another couple of months. There were signs of Russia beginning to give way, and she would give way more, as Russians in Europe did not at all want a war. He suggested that Conger and I should advise the Japanese not to go to war and the Russians to evacuate Manchuria, but I said this was beyond my powers.

On January 11 Wu Ting-fang came to see Satow. "He says that China is resolved to remain neutral and that Japan desires it. He has been instructed to draw up a neutrality proclamation which he thought should be communicated to the Foreign Representatives that they might devise in conference means for treating the question of China's position. I said he had better also lay before us the Manchurian evacuation convention and the Russian demands which had led to delay in carrying that out, but he thought that would offend Russia."

On January 12 Satow conferred with the Japanese Minister.

Uchida came to say that on the 7th he informed Prince Ch'ing by instructions from Japan that China had better remain strictly neutral in the event of war 1°. in order to limit the area of hostilities, 2°. in order to limit the number of belligerents, 3°. in order that China might not be put to trouble in maintaining order in the provinces and open ports, where if disorder arose foreign intervention would be sure to happen. Prince Ch'ing said he was ashamed that in a matter like this where China ought to take the lead, she was obliged by her impotence to remain quiet. She would take the advice and remain neutral.[r]

I told him of my conversation yesterday with Wu Ting-fang and previous conversations with Liang, Tang and Dubail, and explained the difficulty I had been in, because I did not wish to go counter to what might be the wishes of Japan, and hold back China from giving some useful services.

Uchida seemed quite happy. He says the railway to Soul will be completed in August or September next.

On January 15 Satow went to Uchida and told him of his instructions about Chinese neutrality, and suggested that it might be well if he told Prince Ch'ing of the reference to Manchuria in the last Japanese Note. "Also, that Griscom had been shown the Note by Komura; he said that Komura had told Chinese Minister also. . . . Uchida told me that Yüan Shih-kai had sent a message to ask that the portion of Manchuria already retroceded to China should be regarded as neutral. I observed that this was a matter that would have to be decided by strategists. (But it is one of those cases where strategy and policy may not harmonize)." Satow then went on to Conger, and found that he had received a short telegram from Griscom, who said the Japanese answer to Russia was not in the nature of an ultimatum. "I disabused his

---

[r] "The reasons given to the Prince for urging China to remain neutral appear to me judicious, and I propose, with your Lordship's sanction, to offer the same advice," Satow telegraphed to Lansdowne.[189]

mind on this point, and he was much relieved, for he had been under the impression that the Japanese were still merely trying to gain time. Told him also that I was to tell Prince Ch'ing that His Majesty's Government approve of the advice given to China to remain neutral, of which Conger also entirely approves. He said Uchida had given him a careful statement of the grounds on which they recommended neutrality to China, which he had evidently got by heart."

Satow added in his diary: "The dispatches by bag that arrived yesterday show that Lord Lansdowne is not letting the grass grow under his feet in the matter of putting pressure on the Russians at the present juncture."

On January 16 Satow went to Prince Ch'ing, where he found Conger just going away.

Uchida had been there before him to communicate the contents of last Japanese note, in which the demand for an agreement to respect the integrity of China in Manchuria, in return for Japan declaring Manchuria and its littoral outside her sphere of interest is renewed. A declaration by Russia that Corea and its littoral are outside Russian sphere of interest is asked for, the Russian proposal for a neutral zone on Yalu is rejected. Prince Ch'ing radiant. Told him His Majesty's Government approved the advice to China to remain neutral, for which expression of opinion he expressed his gratitude.[s] Told him I had begged Hopkins to warn the Tientsin Viceroy to repress popular excitement, which he also said was a real act of friendship. Natung was with him. As Yüan told Hopkins a few days ago that he feared the effects of news of a Japanese victory upon the popular mind, he may perhaps have given the same idea to Prince Ch'ing. Prince evidently has been told that the first thing will be a naval battle. He said they would on no account bring the Peiyang Squadron up north; they have only three cruisers which are of a little good as being fast.

In his report of the conversation Satow wrote that Prince Ch'ing considered Russia "had acted towards China with flagrant injustice." Prince Ch'ing inquired about the obliga-

---

[s] "A Proclamation of Neutrality will be issued when war breaks out," Satow telegraphed.[190]

tions of Great Britain toward Japan under the Anglo-Japanese Alliance. "I said that under it Great Britain was not positively bound to assist Japan unless the latter was attacked by two Powers in combination, but there was nothing to prevent her coming to the assistance of Japan under any circumstances that might seem to justify such a course, and I felt persuaded that His Majesty's Government would not permit Japan to be crushed by her adversary." Satow added:

In conclusion, I told the Prince that Japan, having assumed the leading position in championing the rights of China in Manchuria, it was naturally to the Japanese Minister that the Chinese Government would look for advice and guidance, and I should consider my Japanese colleague as having a superior right to tender counsel to him on behalf of his Government. Nevertheless, my sympathies were entirely with China in her difficulties, and I should always be ready to afford him whatever assistance was in my power. He replied that he should be anxious to have the benefit of my advice on difficult occasions.[191]

The following day Satow saw the American Minister, "who said he went to Prince Ch'ing yesterday about opening of Moukden and Antung [to American Commerce] for which Prince said he would give instructions to declare open, to the Tartar General of Moukden."

Conger told him that if the Russians made any objection, the United States would take care of that.[t] According to him it is difficult for the Russians to draw back. Lessar and all the others think it would be an easy business, and that these dwarfs were quite out of their reckoning in thinking they would stand up against European troops. I said to him I did not think England could stand by and see Japan crushed, or allow Corea to pass into the possession of Russia, as Masampho directly threatens

[t] "My colleague believes that the Russian Legation had made some observation to the Chinese Government to the effect that it was not advisable at present to ratify the Treaty," Satow reported. "If so, it had fallen on deaf ears. Press telegrams stated that the President had already appointed a Consul-General to Mukden and a Consul to Antung, and he thought that this had probably been done, though he had not received any direct intimation to that effect from his Government."[192]

the Yangtze, and seeing the interests United States have in Japan, which she brought into the world and educated. I did not think they would either. He replied that the present President is a man of courage and determination, who has always carried the country and Congress with him in whatever he has undertaken, and possibly he might think action to pressure United States commerce in Manchuria. Finance and commerce usually carry everything before them.

On January 18 Satow met the Japanese Minister at a dinner. "Uchida had heard from Kurino of a stormy interview between Scott and Lamsdorf, in which the latter had complained of the tone of the English press and of five Russian torpedo boats being warned out of Malta. Also that Lamsdorf had hinted at mediation, and that Japanese Government had probably sent instructions to Hayashi to say that they would not agree to it at the very last moment, when all the Russians want is to gain time." The next day Satow went to talk to Uchida about Hsin-ming-ting and what the Chinese should do if the Russians seized it.

His advice, in which I concur, is that the Chinese should not resist. His Government when consulted about an undertaking not to land troops in Manchuria west of the Liao river, said that this was premature.[u] They might want to land troops there after the naval engagement which must be the first incident of the war. Yüan Shih-kai wishes to station troops at Kinchou and Shaoyang. As to the latter, there can be no objection, as it is in the Mongolian portion of Chihli, but he has recommended to Yüan to defend Shanhaikwan from Yungping. I said that it seemed to me that just as in 1894 Japan had put the extra-territorial character of foreign vessels and foreigners aside when it became necessary to arrest two hostile foreigners on board the *Gaelic* at Kobe, so here the safety of Chinese territory ought to take precedence of the Protocol. We discussed Yüan's ques-

[u] "I am informed by Japanese Minister that in the opinion of his Government, an announcement that no operations of war would take place in the portion of Manchuria restored to China on the 8th October, 1902, would be premature," Satow reported. "The Japanese Government have advised the Viceroy not to station troops at any point where a collision with the Russians might be risked by their presence."[193]

257

tion to Hopkins about the moving troops, and agreed to tell him that he could do this, but to advise their being sent by road, not rail so as to avoid notice by newspaper correspondents. He agreed with me that the allied troops could not undertake the defence of Shanhaikwan against the Russians. (1/19)ᵛ

In the afternoon Satow went to see Viceroy Chang Chih-tung, who wanted to consult him but was not well enough to come and see him.

What the Grand Council had charged him to do was to ascertain from me whether His Majesty's Government would be willing to mediate between Japan and Russia with a view to averting war [Satow reported]. China had determined to remain neutral, but in reflecting on the possible results of a war, the Grand Council had come to the conclusion that she might be dragged into the fray in spite of herself. They thought it possible, for instance, that if Russia were worsted in Manchuria, she might seek compensation by attacking China through Mongolia, where Japan could not effectually interfere, and she might also force war on China by moving troops to Shanhaikwan. Troubled with these misgivings, the Grand Council earnestly hoped that war might even now be avoided, but the only chance of this seemed to them to lie in the mediation of Powers friendly with one or other of the two contending States. The French Minister had been approached on the subject a few days before by a member of the Board of Foreign Affairs, and had intimated that France would be willing to mediate with Russia if Great Britain would mediate with Japan, and the Viceroy wished, therefore, to know what hope there was of this. France had lent large sums to Russia for the construction of the Siberian Railway, and it was obviously her interest that peace should be preserved.

I answered by giving him a number of instances of modern European wars, in which the efforts of different Powers to avert a conflict had proved vain, and showed him that all experience was against the success of attempted mediation, when it was desired by neither of the hostile Governments or by only one of them. In the present case, the Japanese Government could not

---

ᵛ "The military authorities are of opinion that the Russians would endeavour to dispose of the Japanese before attempting an advance on Peking," Lansdowne informed Satow.¹⁹⁴

but be opposed to the idea of it, for they knew that the delay it would cause would be utilized by Russia to continue the policy she had pursued during the whole of these protracted negotiations of steadily strengthening her naval and military forces in the Far East. Nor had I heard anything to make me suppose that the Russian Government had invited the mediation of France, and I imagined, therefore, that the French Minister, in his observations, had merely expressed his personal views. Generally speaking, it was only after war had resulted in the defeat of one party, or both had begun to feel exhausted, that the interposition of other Powers was asked for, or could be usefully rendered.

The Viceroy accepted, with some reluctance, my conclusion that mediation was out of the question unless genuinely desired by both parties, and then inquired whether it would not be possible to leave Japan aside, and for France and England to mediate as between China and Russia, with a view to settling the main question at issue, namely, the destiny of Manchuria; but this, I told him, seemed to me even more hopeless than the other proposal, for Russia had steadily adhered to her refusal to make Manchuria the subject of arrangements with any Power but China alone, and had declined to give the pledge to respect the territorial integrity of China for which Japan had asked at the outset of these negotiations, and for which, in her last communication, she had asked again. It would be impossible to expect Japan, after five months' fruitless negotiation on this very point, to stand aside and wait while other Powers discussed it, equally fruitlessly for many months more, during which she would see her adversary's forces continually increased.

I reminded his Excellency, moreover, of the warnings continually addressed to China by Russia, both during the negotiation of the Manchurian Convention and later, against divulging to any other Power the nature of the Russian demands, and of the refusal of the Russian Government to give any information to that of His Majesty, on the ground that it was without precedent to acquaint third parties with the nature of negotiations still in progress. . . .

On the general question of China's neutrality, I recommended great prudence, so as to give Russia no pretext for infringing it; but if, as the Viceroy and the Grand Council seemed to fear, Russia were to invade Chinese territory within the Great Wall, I could see nothing for them to do but to protect themselves as best they could, addressing at the same time a protest to all the Powers.[195]

But Satow discounted the likelihood of a Russian attack on China. "I said they would have their hands too full with the Japanese to think of such enterprises," he noted in his diary (1/19).

On January 21, Wu Ting-fang, recently appointed a Vice-President of the Foreign Board, called on Satow. "I told him that the French idea of mediation first between Japan and Russia and as an alternative between China and Russia was nonsense." On January 23 Chang Pohsi, the Chancellor of Peking University, and Hu Yu-fen talked to Satow.

Would it not be better if England for instance were to try and persuade Japan not to fight, but to let things slide, and then as Lessar says, it would be easier for Russia to withdraw, and to arrange comfortable terms with China. Lessar said Hu, entirely disapproved of Plançon's demands and earnestly desired to carry out the convention. China had refused those demands said Hu, and would go on doing so to the end of the chapter. Now the Russians said the reoccupation of Moukden was partly caused by the conduct of certain Chinese officials, partly by Japan and America insisting on China signing treaties with them about Manchuria. It was not until Japan began to interfere that the Plançon demands were renewed. Why could not England, America and France talk to Japan and get her to be moderate, so as to avoid war, with all its attendant losses to the commerce of everybody.

I replied as befitted such nonsense that His Majesty's Government would not think of making a suggestion of this kind to Japan, because they considered her to be entirely in the right [Satow recorded]. Russia had signed a solemn agreement to evacuate; it contained some hard conditions for China, but she had consented to it. The Russians carried out a part, and when the second term came produced fresh conditions. Let her abandon those and carry out the Convention. But everyone knew she meant in any case to remain in Manchuria. The Russians themselves all said so. But for what purpose had they taken Port Arthur and acquired a right to build a railway through Manchuria? In order to possess the three provinces. That Lessar who had negotiated the convention should desire to see it carried out was natural. But he was expressing only his personal opinions. The matter was not in his hands any longer, but in those of Alexeieff. It was Alexeieff's man Plançon who had put forth the conditions, and given a copy of the document, made by his own hands, to Conger. But the Russian Government said they knew nothing about it, and that Conger had sent home incorrect information. Plançon had blundered. They would send back Lessar, who would arrange the affair. And when Lessar came out, he presented the same set of demands. He did this by order of his Government, not approving of them, but he had to obey. Had the Russian government disapproved of them, they would have recalled Plançon and his chief. But far from that they had made him Viceroy, promoted him and loaded him with honours.

Chang said they had been asked by a member of the Foreign Board to take the opportunity of this visit to sound me about giving advice in the matter, and if they found me favourable, they would go on to Conger and Dubail and ask them to help.

I said I could tell them what Conger and Dubail would say. The former would use the same language as myself. The latter would say that Japan would be beaten and that China should come to an agreement with Russia now, giving way on some points.

Hu said Dubail thought Japan would win. I said that Japan's attitude had been misunderstood by Russia (Chang had previously suggested that the length to which the negotiations had gone proved that Japan did not wish to fight and would therefore be amenable to reason, to which I replied by explaining her desire to show the world that she had not hastily or unjustifiably taken up arms) and that she had thought the Japanese would be afraid to challenge her. The Russians quite misunderstood that Japan in opening the discussion meant to persevere to the end. She had at last perceived that it was a serious matter, and was beginning to climb down. China should possess her soul in patience and let Russia climb down further.

To some arguments of Chang's that the Japanese might be successful at the outset, the war would be prolonged for two or three years and then exhaustion would come. Was it not better then to do without going to war?

I answered that there were situations in which a nation *must*

261

fight, and that was when to abstain from war would mean the same thing as a complete defeat. The future result might be uncertain, but that was no reason for lying down and letting your adversary walk over you. Besides I felt convinced England would not let Japan be crushed. They said Russia as well as Japan had advised China's remaining neutral.

From all this conversation I am led to think that the French and Russian Legations have been trying to persuade the Chinese that they have committed a serious blunder in leaning on the Japanese and that it is still not too late to come to terms independently of her; and that the Chinese are thoroughly frightened. Perhaps there may also being [be] at the bottom of their minds an uneasy feeling that if Japan wins they will be under her tutelage.

In his report of the conversation Satow remarked that "a revulsion of feeling" seemed to have occured since Prince Ch'ing, a week earlier, had expressed much gratification that the Japanese Government had asked Russia for an undertaking to respect the integrity of China in Manchuria.

It is evident that the Chinese Government are now beginning to be seriously alarmed at the prospect of a war, in which they fear to become involved against their will, since they are not strong enough to defend their neutrality [Satow wrote]. They apprehend that the consequence will, in any case, be greatly to their disadvantage. It has been impressed upon them by a least one of my colleagues that a victorious Russia will probably impose on them terms still more onerous in comparison with the conditions on which she professed herself prepared to evacuate Manchuria six months ago. . . .

Mistrust of Japanese aims has also been a factor in the Chinese change of attitude. Though it has not been said to me directly, I know that they suspect the Japanese Government of an intention to acquire Manchuria for themselves, and this idea I find to be entertained by some foreign observers. At the same time the Chinese are afraid that Russia will eventually get the better of her adversary, and they feel that their own position would be more precarious than ever. Underlying all this there is probably a feeling of pride, which makes them unwilling to rely on a lesser nation, that they have been accustomed to despise, for help and protection in difficulties out of which they ought to extricate themselves unaided. Hence their only wish is for the maintenance of peace, even accompanied by the permanence of the existing situation in Manchuria.[196]

Later in the day Satow had a longish talk with General Allen. "He says that if his countrymen could look ahead a couple of generations they would take a much more serious view of the Far Eastern question. Has compiled a list of Russian declarations and undertaking which she has later on departed from. Seems disposed to think the general result of war will be the partition of China, as she is quite unable to make any stand. Is going on into Manchuria and then to Corea and Japan."

On January 25, Satow saw Conger and told him his conversation with Chang Pohsi and Hu Yü-fen. "They had not been to see him. But Liang had come from Chang Chih-tung on a similar errand, and he had replied that mediation was out of the question. Then Liang inquired which was worse for China, a Russian or a Japanese victory. He answered the former, because she would take Manchuria, and Japan by way of compensation would perhaps fall back on Fuhkien [?]; this would be followed by Germany and France, so that Russia victorious meant the partition of China. While Japan victorious meant the restoration of Manchuria to China."

Satow then went to Uchida and told him all that had happened in the last few days.

I thought Dubail and Lienfang were at the bottom of it. He said most distinctly that Motono [Ichiro, the Japanese Minister to Paris] had been instructed to tell [Tésphile] Delcassé [the Minister of Foreign Affairs of France] that Japan did not accept mediation, to which Delcassé replied that he did not propose it, but on his own account he was advising Russia to give way about the neutral zone!

Conger also said that about the beginning of this month Komura and Rosen had come to an agreement ad referendum, but when it went home through Alexeieff, the latter put such a colour on it that it was refused. However on getting out his papers he found that what Griscom had written to him on January 2 was that Russia had refused all Japan's demands, even those points on which Rosen and Komura had come to an agreement. On Saturday he was dining with Dubail who said his news was that things would be arranged. Conger retorted that he did not believe it; the telegrams from Shanghai gave us to understand that Russia was ready to make some concessions, but the Reuters were so contradictory that they could not be true.

Hu came along in great triumph to say that Japan accepts mediation, in reply to a telegram sent by him from here on the 18th.[w] Also that the Russians came from Tashihchiao [?] by land and went on to Yichow, apparently for purposes of reconnoitering to see whether any were about. There was no need for alarm, and he advised that Yüan's troops should not be withdrawn.

I begin to think Hu is under Russian influences. Uchida says Tsai Taotai, who acts as interpreter for Yüan is probably unfaithful, and perhaps through him may have got to the Russians an inkling of Yüan's inquiry about neutrality of Manchuria west of the Liao river and Japan's cautious reply. I had suggested that a knowledge of this question having been put was the cause of this Russian reconnaissance.

Later Mumm came to Satow. "He had been to see Conger, who knew nothing. I said I had no official news since the despatch of the Japanese note on the 13th. The Chinese I said were apprehensive. Mumm thinks the dénoument must be close at hand."

The next day, Kamei, correspondent of the Japanese newspaper *Jiji* called. "He says that letters from Fukuzawa the editor in chief tell him that Japan does not expect any further answer from Russia, and is simply completing her prepa-

---

[w] "The Japanese Minister declares, however, that instructions were sent to the Minister in Paris that mediation was to be declined," Satow added in his report of the conversation. "Nothing which we have hitherto heard leads us to suppose that the views of the Japanese Government with reference to mediation have changed," Lansdowne replied. "As far as we know, there has been no indication that Russia is prepared to modify the conditions which she demanded in September, and which were rejected by the Chinese Government."[197]

rations," Satow recorded. "He does not expect anything to happen until the two new cruisers reach Japan. All the women and children in Japan are contributing to the war fund." After church Morrison visited Satow. "Told him what Kamei had said to me, and also what had really happened to me about mediation and my reply as to the attitude of his Majesty's Government and the United States. He thinks Lessar first put the idea into Prince Ch'ing's head. Hu yesterday gave him a different account of what Dubail had said to that which we received from Hu. It was merely to the effect that his government would propose to Great Britain and United States to join in offering mediation and if it came off, China would benefit thereby."

Satow went to return Wu Ting-fang's call.

He told me a curious story about the Russians refusing to allow the new Lieutenant Governor of Tsitsihar to proceed to his post, because Alexeieff had not been officially informed. The Empress Dowager had approved of the proclamation of neutrality being communicated to the Foreign Representatives with a request to confer together for the purpose of taking measures to have China's neutrality respected. . . .

On January 29 Satow recorded:

Morrison says it was he who telegraphed Lessar's remark about twisting the Chinese pigtails till they bite to the *Times* after taking the advice of two other men. It had made a sensation it seems, having been reprinted in French papers.
Told him no answer had yet been delivered by Russia to the last Japanese note. They had no intention of giving a pledge as to non-annexation of Manchuria, and I did not think the Japanese would be contented till they saw them out of that. He has received a letter from Moberly-Bell, who says Chirol saw Hayashi before he went to join Curzon, and that Hayashi said war would not take place before March.

On February 1, Satow talked with another journalist, T. Koizumi of the *Kokumin Shimbun.*

He says when he left Tokio everyone was clamouring for war. Bankers had been summoned by the Government to confer about raising a domestic loan of ten million sterling. The Government feeling that as this is the first time they have found themselves face to face with a war with an European Power it is needful to have everything in good order are making very thorough and careful preparations. As Bower says they are like a man who has to undergo a stiff examination, and prepares himself accordingly. Koizumi, who speaks excellent English, says the feeling is that the Government has allowed the Russians to interpose delays. I suggested that the military authorities probably knew what they were about and perhaps had not been in a hurry to begin before the spring.

The day before Conger had produced a telegram from Collins to John Gardner Coolidge, the U.S. Chargé d'Affaires in Peking, that Scott had telegraphed to MacDonald that the Russian answer was satisfactory. "I said I had not heard this and did not believe answer had yet been given. A telegram that came today round by London and Tokio says it will not get to Alexeieff before the 3rd, and that the Emperor resists giving any pledge to Japan about Manchuria."

On February 3 Satow conferred with Prince Ch'ing. "As for the rumour that the Empress-Dowager had been advised to withdraw to Hsianfu if war broke out, Prince Ch'ing denied that there was any such intention, and agreed with me that it would be disastrous," Satow noted in his diary.

Lister Kayes dined with Satow, also Mumm.

The latter said Dubail had been to him with a proposal from himself that the neutral powers should impress on the belligerents the necessity of barring Chihli alone, as it is in a manner occupied by neutral troops. He had said that of course as to Manchuria we could not ask them to make any stipulations. Whether Dubail was moved by French, Russian or Chinese considerations he could not say. But evidently if the neutrals did this it would be a friendly act to China, besides helping to keep the peace. Dubail proposed also to sound me and [Count Giovanni] Gallina [the Italian Minister to China].

I said that I did not mind telling him that ten days ago I had telegraphed in the same sense to His Majesty's Government but had got no instructions on the point. Perhaps Dubail was doing it in the interest of China. If he got Mumm, me and Gallina to take the same views, he would then take credit for himself with the Chinese.

Mumm said he had replied rather cautiously, as he had no instructions, and did not know how the Japanese would take it. I replied that as far as they were concerned, I thought they would have no objection at all. The Chinese no doubt would ask us to take the very step proposed by Dubail. But I did not feel certain about the Russians. They had already sent troops into the evacuated portion of Manchuria. They might claim to send a legation guard to Peking and troops to Shanhaikwan, at least up to the figures agreed upon among the generals in 1901, and we could not say them nay.

Mumm seemed to think such a proceeding unlikely. When he saw Yüan Shih Kai the other day about railway matters, Yüan had talked to him on this subject and hinted that the Powers occupying points in Chihli ought to defend them, and I gathered that Mumm shared this idea.

Dubail had prefaced his remarks by saying that the news yesterday morning was very bad. Mumm rejoined that a couple of days earlier he had said it was pacific, and added that he too had heard the same the day before yesterday. I said that although the announcements from Paris and Petersburg had always been of that character, yet the naval and military reinforcements sent out here had showed that Russia meant to make no concession to Japan. Early in the negotiations a very small assurance with regard to Manchuria would have contented them, and now they wanted more.

Mumm said that the question of peace or war now depends on whether the Japanese were confident. I said that I gathered they were, and every day they were completing their preparations. They had been taught German methods of thoroughness by the officers attached to the general staff before 1894, with whose aid they had no doubt worked out the plan of the North China campaign.

I conceive that the Germans will not be at all sorry to see Russia engaged out here, as that will weaken them at Constantinople. (2/3)

The next day Satow saw the German Minister again.

Mumm brought me a translation of a telegram from Shanghai which reproduces one sent from here on 2nd February to the effect that Russia had induced China to offer Japan important concessions in another quarter if she would desist from her demands about Manchuria, which was favourably viewed by "some of the Foreign Representatives" at Peking as a means of averting war. Japan it said was willing to accept provided China acted quickly and the concessions were of real value. How much of this is true it is impossible to say, but something is being tried no doubt by Lessar and Dubail in the way of drawing a herring across the scent. Got Morrison to come round and talked with him about it, he thought it was without foundation, at least as regarded Japan, but that Dubail had a hand in it. Later in the evening came a telegram from Petersburg that the reply had not been despatched, but that a telegram had gone off to Rosen, thus confirming the Japan telegram of 2 February that a long telegram had come to Rosen, been translated and sent to Komura. Might not this contain the insidious proposal put forward by Russia? It would also account for Dubail not coming on to see me on Wednesday (3 February) as he told Mumm he intended doing, if he happened to look in at his Legation on the way and find a telegram informing him of this step. Wrote to Morrison and told him that the reply had not left Petersburg, but that a telegram had, which might be about this very thing. (2/4)

On February 5 Satow sent a telegram to the Foreign Office and Tokyo reporting the above. In his diary he reflected:

It seems unlikely that Japan would accept such a combination, which is entirely at variance with her previous declarations, and contrary to the spirit and terms of the Anglo-Japanese alliance, which it would at once put an end to. But that is one of the objects at which Russia was aiming when she sent Rosen back to Tokio. Also one could easily understand Dubail persuading the Chinese that it was a way of avoiding the war the results of which they dread so intensely. They would I believe rather sacrifice Manchuria even, provided it were not done openly, rather than let the Japanese have a chance of taking the place of the Russians, for Dubail would demonstrate that it is more easy in every way and more profitable to their pockets to be friends with Russia than with Japan.

268

"The *Kokumin* correspondent passing through the hall," Satow recorded, "I captured him and told him about this curious telegram, and the probable origin. I said he might inform Uchida, but without mentioning the source of his information." Meeting Conger in the street, Satow told him also. "He said Mumm had said to him that the telegram had been sent to Paris, not Shanghai." He went on to Mumm and told him what he had heard from Petersburg. "He then informed me that it came to him not from Shanghai, but from his government who asked what it all meant. As they did not tell him to consult his colleagues, he had not thought himself authorized to say where it really came from (But why tell me a fib?). He thinks it was probably concocted between the Russian and French governments."

On February 6, Satow went to Conger and told him instructions were sent the night before to Kurino to break off negotiations. The following day he learned from Uchida that the Japanese consul had been ordered away from New-chwang, and O'Brien Butler telegraphed that the Japanese Consul at Chefoo was to withdraw all Japanese subjects from Port Arthur and Dalny.

On February 9, Dubail visited Satow.

As he was going away he said Russia had made a great blunder about Manchuria in not evacuating. They would still have exercised a virtual protectorate. He said just as is our case with regard to Yünnan. We are there on the frontier. When our military people wanted last summer to pour in troops, I protested against the unnecessary and wasteful expenditure that would be involved in an occupation, pointing out that we could always exercise a preponderant influence because we have troops in our colony closeby. The Russians could have done the same. Now they will have to spend an enormous amount of money in beating Japan, as they of course eventually will, and without getting anything more than they could have acquired by peaceful means.

"Koidzumi of the *Kokumin*," Satow added, "in the course of conversation said that what preoccupied people in Japan was the question of the future of Corea. Should it be made a province of Japan or a protectorate, like that of England in Egypt. I said that we had not assumed a protectorate in name, but merely an occupation."

That day Satow telegraphed to the Foreign Office:

My colleagues of France, Germany, and Italy, and I, as Representatives of Powers whose troops occupy various points in Province of Chih-li from Peking to Shanhaikwan, are anxious to avoid possible incidents, or even occasions of conflict, which might arise if the forces of either belligerent enter province. On the other hand, in view of the fact that China had made known her intention of observing neutrality, and that occupation stipulated for by the Protocol of September 1901 compels China to keep her troops at a distance from the points so occupied, we consider that the obligation of maintaining the neutrality of those points devolves upon foreign detachments.

We have agreed to ask our respective Governments whether they do not regard it advisable, in order to obviate any difficulty, to suggest to belligerents that they should declare their intention of abstaining from sending troops into the province.

This step would have further advantage of reassuring the Imperial Court, and of providing against any sudden panic, causing the Government to take to flight—an eventuality which would be followed by most serious consequences throughout China.[198]

On February 11, Satow went to Uchida. "He had heard of the safe landing of four regiments at Chemulpho, and the sinking of a Russian man of war, the *Koreetz*. This is official. Also the British steamer *Columbia* brought news last night to Chefoo that the previous night the Japanese suddenly attacked Port Arthur and torpedoed a couple of battleships and a cruiser, but this is not confirmed officially. The Japanese fleet is blockading Port Arthur." Satow also went to Dubail. "He sent yesterday for Lien Fang and through him advised Prince Ch'ing that he should not on any account let the Court leave Peking." Afterwards Satow saw Hu.

He asked whether it would not be wise for China to ask of the two belligerents an undertaking that whatever the event

270

Manchuria should remain Chinese. I replied that Japan had already given China an undertaking to that effect. He asked could we not suggest the same to Russia. I replied hardly, since Russia had preferred going to war rather than give it to her and now there was still less chance. He replied that Posdnief [A. M. Pozdneev, the representative of the Russo-Chinese Bank in Peking?] had told him the English had been egging on the Japanese to war, when they could easily have prevented it, and Russia would listen to nothing from us. I said we had been asked by the Russians to mediate, but as Japan was justified in asking a pledge as to Manchuria, which Russia wanted to keep for herself, we could not listen to any such suggestion. Posdnief he said was not aware last night, or said so at least, that he knew nothing about war having begun. . . .

Mumm remarked today [Satow continued in his diary] that whichever comes out victorious it will be bad for us, i.e. England and Germany. For Japan would become so all powerful that she would be an inconvenient commercial rival to us both, irrespective of alliances. If Russia, then our commerce will be shut out from whatever territory she acquires.

I think this was a feeler, for it is much more for her political position in Shantung that Germany has to fear.

I told him what I had said to Uchida and Dubail this morning, and especially to the former that having themselves urged China to observe neutrality, they could not consistently be the first to violate the neutrality.

Satow also saw Tseng. "He talked a good deal of the discovery now made by China that all Russia's talk of friendship in 1900 and withdrawal of their troops from Chihli after the relief of the Legations was a mere hollow pretence to cover her design of annexing Manchuria."

On February 12, Hu told Satow to inform the Russian and Japanese generals and ministers that the extra-mural railway line would carry no more troops or munitions for either belligerent. Going to Prince Ch'ing, Satow ran into Uchida, who asserted the Chinese had made a stupid mess in their declaration of neutrality to the Powers by including Manchuria, and related that he had told them to except the portions where the Russians held sway. "When I asked the

Prince he said the declaration was all right, and gave it to me just as he had been told by Uchida, but when I asked to see a copy was not sure that he had one in the house," Satow noted. "Told him we were going to send Consular officers to Mukden and Antung, which he said was excellent from a political point of view, though commercially perhaps not much. He hoped they would be able also to open Talienwan Bay. Prince suggested that after one or two more knocks Russia might be glad to have peace. Told him the attempt of Dubail, self and Co. to get Chihli neutralized, for which he was grateful."

Mumm told Satow that Lessar was apparently not quite pleased with their suggestion to the belligerents to keep out of Chihli, upset though he was by the news of naval disasters. Uchida reported that the Japanese Government was conversing with London on the matter, "but he had got Prince Ch'ing to insert in the declaration to be given to us all a statement that China feared she would be unable to enforce neutrality on Chinese subjects in those parts of Manchuria which are in adverse occupation by foreign troops."

That day Prince Ch'ing sent Satow copies of the Proclamation of Neutrality and of a Proclamation enjoining Measures for Maintenance of Order. He also wrote the following note:

At present Russia and Japan have severed their peaceful relations and appealed to arms. China is on friendly relations with both. The Imperial Government, considering the importance of maintaining friendly relations with neighboring Powers, has already issued an Edict declaring neutrality, and commanding the various Tartar Generals, Viceroys, and Governors in all the provinces to uniformly and reverently observe the same.

Instructions have therefore been already sent throughout the Empire, directing a uniform observance of this Edict, and the issue of strict orders for the maintenance of the peace and the thorough protection of foreign commerce and religious missions.

The "Three Eastern Provinces" (Manchuria) are Chinese territory; Moukden, the capital of Shengking, and Hsingking are the sites of the graves and temples of the Imperial ancestors, and of the palaces of the secondary capital. Their importance is, therefore, very great, and it is naturally the duty of the Tartar General of Moukden to carefully and reverently guard them.

The two Powers (Russia and Japan) must not injure the cities and public buildings of these "Three Provinces," nor the lives and property of the people, and the Chinese troops which have heretofore been stationed there must not come in conflict with either of the Powers.

The territory west of the Liao River is that from which Russia has already withdrawn her troops according to Convention, and the Superintendent of Trade for the North is sending military forces to be stationed there.

In all the provinces, and along the frontiers, as well as Inner and Outer Mongolia, China will observe the laws of neutrality, and the military forces of the two Powers (Russia and Japan) must not invade these regions.

But at such places in Manchuria as troops of a foreign Power are still stationed, and from which they have not yet been withdrawn, China's strength is insufficient, and it is feared that it will be difficult to strictly observe the laws of neutrality there.

No matter which of the two Powers may be victorious, the sovereign rights of China over the territory of Manchuria will remain intact. Neither of the two Powers may usurp them. The anxious desire to safeguard the general interest which animates China at this juncture will, it is hoped, receive due recognition at the hands of all the Powers.

Besides sending despatches to the Ministers for Russia and Japan in Peking, I, as in duty bound, send this to your Excellency that you may transmit it to your honourable Government for its consideration.[199]

On February 13, Satow telegraphed home:

A note has been addressed to each of the foreign Representatives by the Chinese Government, declaring that China remains on friendly terms with each of the belligerent Powers, and intends to observe neutrality; that strict injunctions for the protection of trade and missions and the maintenance of order have been issued to the provincial authorities.

The note goes on to state that the belligerents ought not to come into collision with Chinese forces stationed in Manchuria, nor injure life or property since Manchuria is Chinese territory.

The territory west of the Liao River, which Russia, in accordance with Convention, has already evacuated, will be guarded by troops to be sent by the Tien-tsin Viceroy.

The forces of the belligerents ought not to encroach on the provinces (i.e., China proper), or on inner or outer Mongolia, since China will be guided by the Rules of neutrality in all these territories. But it is to be feared that China will not be able to fulfil completely the duties of a neutral in those districts of Manchuria still occupied by foreign troops, since she has not sufficient power of control there. In making this declaration, China is entitled to the sympathy of all the Powers.

The territory, authority, and revenues of Manchuria must remain within the sovereign control of China, whichever Power is victorious, and neither Power must appropriate them.

The note concludes with a statement that it has already been communicated to Russia and Japan, and a request that it may be transmitted to His Majesty's Government.[200]

That day Wu Ting-fang came to Satow, "as usual, to talk nonsense."

Had I heard that Russia was giving out that she would like peace? I said not, as Japan certainly would not, unless Russia gave up everything in Manchuria, evacuated the province, surrendered Port Arthur and handed over the railway to China. He laughed and said Russia was not prepared to do that. If Japan succeeded in capturing Port Arthur, would she not retain it. I said no, had not Japan given an assurance to China regarding Manchuria? Yes, she had. But how could China hold it. I replied that Japan would help her. (2/13)

Menzies came to Satow in the afternoon.

He said Yüan wanted my advice on certain points, and also that the railway authorities were handing protests to Russian officers against their travelling by it. I told him this must be stopped at once, as Russians and Japanese have the same right as any other military to use the intra-mural line; 2°. to remember that China is neutral; 3°. that we were trying to prevent belligerents entering Chihli. 4°. that they must wait to see how Japanese land forces get on.

On February 14, Mumm informed Satow he had heard from his Government that they had received the American proposal about China's neutrality and had made the same reply as Lord Lansdowne, that Manchuria could not be neutralized.

He then recurred to his previous talk about the effect of the war, and the great comparative disadvantage to European Powers of a Japanese success over a Russian victory. The latter would establish a protectorate over Manchuria and Corea, but would probably come no further south. If she did, the other Powers could unite to restrain her. Not that Germany had any particular interests in Chihli. But the Japanese, if they won, would establish a virtual protectorate over China, which would be contrary to all foreign interests.

I said that I supposed which ever way it went the Great Powers, say France, Germany, England and the United States would insist on having a voice in the settlement [Satow continued in his diary].

This he said was a capital idea. Whether we should have to invite the cooperation of Austria and Russia [Italy?] I could not forecast. If there were a conference in Europe they could not be left out, but if it were on the spot, then as their interests were so much less, perhaps we need not take them into our counsels. Anyhow we ought not to let in the Minor Powers, Belgium, Holland, Spain and Portugal. He replied that apart from the fact of Italy and Austria being members of the triple alliance, he thought they must have a voice in the final settlement.

As to the results of a Japanese victory, I did not think they would be so extensive as he feared. The Japanese had not a light hand, and their endeavours to exercise predominant influence in Corea in 1894-95 had been altogether unsuccessful. Like most people of a determined character, they failed in tact, because they could not bring themselves to humour other people's susceptibilities (I was thinking of the Germans when I said this). The Chinese were a proud people and would resent the feeling that they lay under an obligation to Japan, as we had seen during the past few weeks, during which they had made strenuous efforts to ward off war, almost at any price. I did not anticipate that Japan would be any more successful with China than she had been with Corea.

275

Mumm responded that the Japanese were certainly hated in Corea, and as for China he had observed that their instructors at various places were not much liked either. My view was a comforting one to him.

(I certainly think that a little disturbance of the balance of power in the far East in favour of Japan is better than Russia having her own way. The rise of Japan as a military and naval Power and the construction of the Siberian railway have completely altered the situation out here for us as for all other European Powers, and we cannot expect to have things entirely our own way, as in 1842. But Japan will not be able to rule China. The latter will rely on European Powers to prevent Japan having her own way entirely.)

In the afternoon Satow went to Conger, and found that he had received from Washington exactly the same communication as he had gotten from Lord Lansdowne, but without Lord Lansdowne's reply regarding Japan and Manchuria, and that he was instructed to pass it on to the Chinese.

Told him about the Russian officers and sailors on board *Talbot* and a French and an Italian man of war at Chemulpho, and the idea that if proper guarantees were given against their serving again in the war or going north, they might be landed at Shanghai and handed over to the Russian consul-general. He agreed that they would be probably a source of trouble. I was careful not to say that this was a proposal of the British Government.

On February 15, Satow went to Gallina and "found he had nothing from his government either about the American proposal to recognize Chinese neutrality and restrict the area of hostilities as much as possible, nor about the Russian officers and men who were on board the foreign men of war at Chemulpho, and the manner of disposing of them." Later he talked to Azevedo Castello-Branco, the Portuguese Minister, who came to tea.

He predicts that if the war lasts three months the Western Powers will intervene, and that the result will be to give Manchuria

276

to Russia definitively and Corea to Japan. That a defeat of Russia would be a blow to European prestige generally in Asia, and cannot be permitted. The result will be the partition of China. He thinks the Chinese declaration of neutrality is inept. She would have done better to say nothing about it, as she is now exposed to the consequences of any failure to maintain it. He has been reading the procés-verbaux of the conference of 1900-01, and is shocked to find how the colleagues were thinking of their own private interests. He says [J. B. de] Cólogan [the Spanish Minister] got an indemnity of 4,000 though not a single wine glass of his was broken. [Marquis] Salvago[-Raggi, the Italian Minister] got indemnities all round. The Belgians, whom he calls the Jews of the Latin race, made more than anyone. The Russians have a great future before them, the Latin race is perishing. Germany is playing a deep game, and before long we shall see her throwing in her lot with Russia. France is now more independent of her than she was. I told him it had been judged absolutely necessary to insist on China declaring herself neutral and sending orders to the provinces to remain quiet, for had she joined Japan there would have been a general conflagration throughout the country, missions would be attacked and perhaps other foreigners also. I thought a slight disturbance of the equilibrium in favour of Japan would not be disadvantageous. . . .

I said that though Chinese lived tranquilly under the English flag in Hongkong and Singapore having voluntarily placed themselves under it, that was a very different matter from our planting the flag in Chinese territory and trying to govern the people. We had not the men to organize and run the administration of Chinese provinces, and would have to do it through Chinese agents, all of whom would be just as corrupt as the present mandarins.

At dinner Satow conversed with the Japanese Minister.

Uchida says that as soon as the Chinese put out their declaration of neutrality, he went to them about the Russian gunboat at Shanghai, with the result that the ammunition is now being landed and deposited in the Russo-Chinese bank. What is to become of the ship itself he does not yet know. As to the Russian sailors at Chemulpho on board foreign warships, his government has consented to what Foreign Office telegraphed to me, but Uchida agrees with me that if they are landed at Shanghai, China of course will be quite unable to fulfil her duties as a neutral in regard to them. He has not yet replied to the Chinese Note about neutrality, as he must first hear what his government has to say about the neutralization of the evacuated part of Manchuria. The portion of the note referring to the occupied portion was inserted at the request of his government, and the Chinese at first worded it to mean such parts of China where she had not permitted foreign troops to be stationed, whereas the Japanese Government wished it to be 'places in the adverse occupation of foreign troops.' The Chinese wording would thus have applied to the whole of China. Mumm on the 8 at Conger's talked to him about neutrality being confined to the 18 provinces, because in Urga the Russians have several thousand troops which they keep there for the protection of their Siberian railway. He was himself however aware that the Russian detachment consisted only of one hundred men, and he protested to Mumm against the idea of excluding Mongolia on grounds entirely opposed to geographical facts.

On February 16, Satow jotted in his diary: "Kidston says Mumm was seen by Straight last night getting into a jinrikisha at midnight and going off to the Russian Legation. The Americans think he is up to some tricks, and sees that after all their position in Shantung would share the fate of the Russians in Manchuria." Later Mumm himself visited Satow. "He stayed a long time talking most amiably, as if he had no *arrière pensée* at all. But the story of his going at midnight on the 15th to the Russian Legation is getting diffused, as Menzies told me it today," Satow recorded.

On February 18, Morrison came in for a few minutes. "Says Hart thinks Mumm is up to some mischief; he sits two or three hours daily with Lessar, according to his own account." Gallina also called. "Said his Government in accepting the United States proposal about Chinese neutrality, had added a rider that Manchuria could not be included in the area where China must behave as a neutral, but in spite of that the Chinese sovereignty over Manchuria must be recognized as a fact. Which is unlike the attitude of the Germans."

On February 19, Satow reported that the Japanese Minister had informed the Chinese Government, in reply to their note on the subject of China's neutrality, that, except in territory occupied by Russian troops, this neutrality would be respected by Japan. "With regard to the retention of Chinese sovereignty in Manchuria at the conclusion of the war, which is referred to in the last part of the Chinese note, Mr. Uchida has replied that Japan has no intention of remaining in permanent occupation of Chinese territory, and has entered on this war solely to protect her interests."[201]

That day the Portuguese Minister came to Satow and sat for an hour, talking Far Eastern politics.

He predicts that however neutral Germany may appear now, she will be found on the side of Russia at the final settlement, which I told him must be made by the Powers. I said also that England and probably America would not allow Japan to be crushed. He was under a belief that we had suggested to Washington to make the proposal about neutrality of China to Petersburg, but I explained how it had really happened. Washington has invited Portugal to join, and he has advised his government to agree, as it will save her position. He also thought it was a mistake for Japan to urge neutrality on China, but I showed how necessary it was in the interest of the tranquility of everybody. Then he wanted to know with whom it had originated. I told him of my conversation with Dubail on 26 December but not of my telegram to Foreign Office repeated to Tokio, saying that Uchida evidently believed China would join, which seems to have led to the advice given by Japan 7 January. Hinted to him that it was impossible to say what China would do if Japan had success on land, which I however had an impression she would not obtain. (2/19)

On February 20, Uchida called on Satow to convey the thanks of his government to O'Brien-Butler for helping to get Japanese away from Port Arthur and Dalny.

It is true that the Russians maltreated a number of Japanese from up country and carried off a hundred or so to Port Arthur, but he hopes to get them all released. He had four men in Manchuria sending him reports up to the outbreak of hostilities, but the Russians never found out what they were doing, and they got away safely. Does not know what is going on as to movements of Japanese troops, but Conger has heard from his Söul colleague that they are moving northward from there. I suggested that when the river opens at Newchang the question of blockading the port will probably come up, and asked whether they had notified a blockade of Port Arthur and Dalny [Satow remarked]. He said he had no knowledge of it. The *Mandjour* is not landing her ammunition but taking it on board from the Russo-Chinese bank, where it was stored. Japan demands of China that she shall order the *Mandjour* to leave. (Warren telegraphs the same information from Shanghai.) Seems to think some time must yet elapse before we get any news of land operations. As to contraband of war being notified by Japanese government has no knowledge.

Satow went to Congers to tea. "He showed me the Russian reply to Washington about observing Chinese neutrality, which the United States Government have accepted as responsive," Satow noted. "He thinks the phrase about Japan observing the engagements with the Powers is obscure and I agree with him."

On February 24 Wu Ting-fang came to Satow with an idea of his to ask England, France, Germany and the United States to allow their Consuls-general at Shanghai to join with the Taotai on a Commission to decide knotty questions of International Law, like that of the *Mandjour*.

This is because Prince Ch'ing is so weak. First Uchida induced him to order the Shanghai Taotai to give the Russian ship twenty-four hours notice, or to stop throughout duration of the war. Then Lessar made him countermand these instructions. It is however nearly arranged that she shall be disarmed, her armament being placed in the charge of the Municipal Council, Lessar giving a written undertaking that she shall remain at Shanghai till the end of the war, but Uchida's instructions were to insist that some of her machinery should be removed. The proposed commission would relieve the Chinese Government of such troublesome questions. Dubail had been sounded by Lien fang and had said it was a good idea. He wanted to know my opinion. I said it was unworthy of the dignity of China, who ought not to abdicate her duties to a mixed commission of consular officers who not being professional lawyers would have to refer to their governments [Satow observed]. He said he hoped I would not oppose it even if I did not approve, and I promised that. I said my personal idea was that the Chinese Government should get hold of a sound international lawyer and be guided by his advice, like the Japanese, but he replied that when formerly the Yamen had one, he was never consulted.

On February 25, Satow spoke to Mumm. "The United States' intervention had secured more in the way of neutrality of China than we even hoped for, but we had done right in calling the attention of our governments to the question." From Mumm Satow went to Dubail, who talked about the future.

Russia must crush Japan and then Corea, Manchuria, North China all Russian. Supposing for the sake of hypothesis that Japan got the upper hand, she would turn us out of Asia. I admitted that Russia could not accept a defeat at the hands of Japan. That I had always when in Japan done my best to preserve peace, and had pointed out to Ito when they began doubling their army that it would be regarded as a menace. It was already large enough for defence; they could fairly increase their navy as they were an island nation, but such a large army could only be needed for enterprise on the continent of Asia. Dubail said the Russians could have had everything they wanted without a costly war; if Lessar had stopped here the additional proposals of Plançon would never have been presented and the evacuation would have been carried out, leaving Russia at liberty to pour in troops whenever she chose. It was *"une gaffe"* [a blunder]. I agreed that Lessar would never have done this stupid thing.

Uchida came to tell Satow about the *Mandjour* negotiations. "He insists on a part of the machinery being removed. Lessar objects and offers to give written undertaking that she will not leave port during war. I suggested that this would suffice." Uchida related the Chinese Minister at Petersburg

281

had telegraphed that the Russians said they did not wish to intrude into evacuated region, but would probably be unable to prevent the operation from extending west of the Liao river. "I gather that Uchida does not regret this Russian answer, but I told him we were particularly interested on account of railway."

Conger came to call. "Told him my talks of the morning and all the news I had gathered," Satow recorded. "Said that when the war comes to an end the United States will have to take a part with us and the other great Powers in arranging terms. He hesitated to agree to this, on account of the traditional dislike to being mixed up with the European Powers. But Judge [William Howard] Taft who is now his War Secretary sees that the United States cannot keep out of world affairs, and if [President Theodore] Roosevelt is re-elected, he will probably not take a different line."

Notes

1. The biographical data in the introduction is based on Bernard M. Allen, *The Rt. Hon. Sir Ernest Satow, G.C.M.C. A Memoir* (London: Kegan Paul, Trench, Trubner and Co., Ltd. 1933), Satow's *A Diplomat in Japan* (London, 1921), and on the unpublished diaries of Satow for the years 1861-82.
2. *The Dictionary of National Biography 1922-1930* (London: Oxford University Press, 1937), p. 748.
3. *Ibid.*, p. 749.
4. Baroness Albert d'Anethan, *Fourteen Years of Diplomatic Life in Japan, Leaves from the Diary of Baroness Albert d'Anethan* (London: Stanley Paul and Co., 1912, second edition), p. 121.
5. "Address delivered by Sir George Sansom at the Annual Ceremony of the School of Oriental and African Studies in 1956," reprinted in *The Journal of Asian Studies*, vol. XXIV, No. 4 (August 1965), p. 566.
6. Satow to the Marquess of Salisbury, No. 250, Tokyo (hereafter deleted), Aug. 25, 1895, in Great Britain, Foreign Office, *Confidential Correspondence and Papers, China (Confidential Prints* [hereafter cited as "F.O."]) 405-65, p. 5.
7. Satow to Salisbury, No. 268, Sept. 27, 1895, F.O. 405-65, pp. 29-30.
8. Satow to Salisbury, No. 279, Confidential, Oct. 16, 1895, F.O. 405-65, p. 34.
9. Satow to Salisbury, No. 284, Confidential, Oct. 16, 1895, F.O. 405-65, pp. 37-40, and No. 90 (telegraphic), Oct. 17, 1895, F.O. 405-65, p. 8.
10. Satow to Salisbury, No. 288, Oct. 18, 1895, F.O. 405-65, pp. 66-67.
11. Satow to Salisbury, No. 290, Confidential, Oct. 23, 1895, F.O. 405-65, pp. 67-69.
12. Satow to Salisbury, No. 297, Confidential, Oct. 29, 1895, F.O. 405-65, p. 99.
13. Satow to Salisbury, No. 96 (telegraphic), Oct. 28, 1895, F.O. 405-65, pp. 15-16.
14. Satow to Salisbury, No. 305, Nov. 8, 1895, F.O. 405-65, p. 100.
15. Satow to Salisbury, No. 306, Nov. 12, 1895, F.O. 405-65, pp. 102-103.
16. Satow to Salisbury, No. 307, Confidential, Nov. 15, 1895, F.O. 405-70, p. 13.
17. Satow to Salisbury, No. 311, Nov. 19, 1895, F.O. 405-70, p. 17.
18. Satow to Salisbury, No. 333, Confidential, Dec. 23, 1895, F.O. 405-70, pp. 49-50.
19. Satow to Salisbury, No. 332, Confidential, Dec. 21, 1895, F.O. 405-70, p. 49.

20. Satow to Salisbury, No. 12, Confidential, Jan. 23, 1897, F.O. 405-70, p. 93.
21. Satow to Salisbury, No. 15, Jan. 28, 1896, F.O. 405-70, pp. 93-99.
22. Appended to Satow to Salisbury, No. 34, Feb. 17, 1896, F.O. 405-70, pp. 127-28.
23. Satow to Salisbury, No. 35, Feb. 20, 1896, F.O. 405-71, p. 6.
24. Satow to Salisbury, No. 39, Feb. 24, 1896, F.O. 405-71, p. 7.
25. Satow to Salisbury, No. 41, Feb. 27, 1896, F.O. 405-71, pp. 7-8.
26. Satow to Salisbury, No. 48, Very Confidential, Mar. 12, 1896, F.O. 405-71, p. 43.
27. Satow to Salisbury, No. 51, Mar. 14, 1896, F.O. 405-71, p. 14.
28. Satow to Salisbury, No. 87, Apr. 21, 1896, Very Confidential, F.O. 405-71, pp. 74-75.
29. Satow to Salisbury, No. 59, Confidential, May 4, 1896, F.O. 405-71, pp. 75-77.
30. Satow to Salisbury, No. 96, Very Confidential, May 6, 1896, F.O. 405-71, pp. 77-78.
31. Satow to Salisbury, No. 17 (telegraphic), May 13, 1896, F.O. 405-71, p. 65.
32. Satow to Salisbury, No. 102, May 13, 1896, F.O. 405-71, pp. 82-84.
33. Satow to Salisbury, No. 109, Confidential, May 21, 1896, F.O. 405-71, p. 88.
34. Satow to Salisbury, No. 156, Confidential, Aug. 19, 1896, F.O. 405-72, pp. 48-49.
35. Satow to Salisbury, No. 157, Very Confidential, Aug. 19, 1896, F.O. 405-72, p. 49.
36. Satow to Salisbury, No. 167, Confidential, Aug. 27, 1896, F.O. 405-72, p. 60.
37. Satow to Salisbury, No. 216, Nov. 14, 1896, F.O. 405-72, pp. 85-86.
38. Satow to Salisbury, No. 29, Very Confidential, Feb. 18, 1897, F.O. 405-73, pp. 47-48.
39. Satow to Salisbury, No. 32, Feb. 18, 1897, F.O. 405-73, p. 48.
40. Satow to Salisbury, No. 37, Feb. 25, 1897, F.O. 405-73, pp. 48-49.
41. Satow to Salisbury, No. 39, Mar. 1, 1897, F.O. 405-73, pp. 50-52.
42. Satow to Salisbury, No. 40, Confidential, Mar. 1, 1897, F.O. 405-73, pp. 52-53.
43. Satow to Salisbury, No. 90, April 30, 1897, F.O. 405-73, pp. 74-75.
44. Satow to Salisbury, No. 256, Secret, Dec. 17, 1897, F.O. 405-80, pp. 39-40.
45. Satow to Salisbury, No. 37 (telegraphic), Dec. 24, 1897, F.O. 405-73, p. 177; reprinted also as No. 185, p. 204.
46. Satow to Salisbury, No. 261, Confidential, Dec. 28, 1897, F.O. 405-76, p. 72.
47. O'Conor to Salisbury, No. 49 (telegraphic), St. Petersburg, Mar. 16, 1898, F.O. 405-76, p. 161.
48. Satow to Salisbury, No. 45, Mar. 31, 1898, F.O. 405-77, p. 143.
49. Satow to Salisbury, No. 83, May 10, 1898, F.O. 405-80, pp. 117-18.
50. Satow to Salisbury, No. 67, Confidential, Apr. 1, 1899, F.O. 405-88, p. 47.
51. Satow to Salisbury, No. 108, Jun. 22, 1899, F.O. 405-88, p. 65.

52. Satow to Salisbury, No. 170, Very Confidential, Oct. 16, 1899, F.O. 405-87, pp. 117-18.
53. Satow to Salisbury, No. 241, Very Confidential, Aug. 5, 1895, F.O. 405-64, p. 169.
54. Satow to Salisbury, No. 245, Aug. 19, 1895, F.O. 405-64, p. 170.
55. Satow to Salisbury, No. 254, Confidential, Aug. 31, 1895, F.O. 405-65, pp. 6-7.
56. Satow to Salisbury, No. 83 (telegraphic), Sept. 3, 1895, F.O. 405-64, p. 10.
57. Satow to Salisbury, No. 258, Confidential, Sept. 12, 1895, F.O. 405-65, pp. 7-8.
58. Satow to Salisbury, No. 85, Secret, Sept. 13, 1895, F.O. 405-64, p. 158.
59. Satow to Salisbury, No. 265, Very Confidential, Sept. 25, 1895, F.O. 405-65, p. 51.
60. Satow to Salisbury, No. 270, Confidential, Sept. 27, 1895, F.O. 405-65, p. 30.
61. Satow to Salisbury, No. 277, Very Confidential, Oct. 7, 1895, F.O. 405-65, pp. 31-33.
62. Satow to Salisbury, No. 5, Jan. 14, 1896, F.O. 405-70, pp. 65-70 and No. 8, Jan. 14, 1896, F.O. 405-70, pp. 70-72.
63. Satow to Salisbury, No. 53, Mar. 14, 1896, F.O. 405-71, p. 15.
64. Satow to Salisbury, No. 196, Oct. 22, 1896, F.O. 405-72, pp. 77-78.
65. Satow to Salisbury, No. 48, Very Confidential, Mar. 12, 1896, F.O. 405-71, p. 43.
66. Satow to Salisbury, No. 261, Confidential, Dec. 28, 1897, F.O. 405-76, p. 72.
67. Satow to Salisbury, No. 16 (telegraphic), Mar. 19, 1898, F.O. 405-80, p. 64.
68. Satow to Salisbury, No. 40, Very Confidential, Mar. 26, 1898, F.O. 405-77, pp. 142-43.
69. Salisbury to Satow, No. 21, Very Confidential, Foreign Office, Mar. 31, 1898, F.O. 405-76, p. 247.
70. Satow to Lord Lansdowne, No. 2, dated Peking (hereafter deleted), Jan. 2, 1901, No. 97, enclosure 2, F.O. 405-103, pp. 86-88.
71. *Ibid.*
72. Satow to Lansdowne, No. 11, Jan. 8, 1901, F.O. 405-104, pp. 12-13.
73. Satow to Lansdowne, No. 33, telegraphic, Feb. 5, 1901, F.O. 405-103, p. 17.
74. *Ibid.*
75. Fraser to Lansdowne, telegraphic, No. 160, dated Hankow, Feb. 25, 1901, F.O. 405-103, p. 127.
76. Scott to Lansdowne, No. 24, dated St. Petersburgh, Feb. 27, 1901, F.O. 405-103, p. 129.
77. Fulford to Satow, No. 6, dated Newchwang, Feb. 8, 1901, F.O. 405-105, pp. 179-80.
78. Satow to Lansdowne, No. 56, telegraphic, Feb. 27, 1901, F.O. 405-103, p. 130.
79. *Ibid.*
80. Satow to Lansdowne, No. 61, telegraphic, Feb. 28, 1901, F.O. 405-103, p. 136.
81. Satow to Lansdowne, No. 58, telegraphic, Feb. 28, 1901, p. 135.

82. Lansdowne to Satow, No. 49, telegraphic, dated Foreign Office, Mar. 1, 1901, F.O. 405-14, p. 3.
83. Lansdowne to Satow, No. 48, Confidential, dated Foreign Office, Mar. 1, 1901, p. 4.
84. Lansdowne to Satow, No. 55, telegraphic, dated Foreign Office, March 4, 1901, F.O. 405-104, pp. 50-51.
85. Satow to Lansdowne, No. 64, telegraphic, Mar. 5, 1901, F.O. 405-104, pp. 51-52.
86. Satow to Lansdowne, No. 66, telegraphic, Mar. 6, 1901, F.O. 405-104, p. 53.
87. *Ibid.*
88. Satow to Lansdowne, No. 67, telegraphic, Mar. 6, 1901, F.O. 405-104, pp. 53-54.
89. *Ibid.*
90. Fraser to Satow, No. 26, Confidential, dated Hankow, Mar. 5, 1901, F.O. 405-105, pp. 187-88.
91. Fraser to Satow, No. 28, Confidential, dated Hankow, Mar. 6, 1901, F.O. 405-104, pp. 188-89.
92. Satow to Lansdowne, No. 69, telegraphic, Mar. 8, 1901, F.O. 405-104, p. 61.
93. Lansdowne to Satow, No. 59, telegraphic, dated Foreign Office, March 8, 1901, F.O. 405-104, p. 63.
94. Fraser to Satow, No. 30, dated Hankow, Mar. 9, 1901, F.O. 405-105, pp. 204-205.
95. Satow to Lansdowne, No. 71, telegraphic, Mar. 11, 1901, F.O. 405-104, p. 74.
96. Lansdowne to Satow, No. 59, dated Foreign Office, Mar. 13, 1901, F.O. 405-104, p. 82.
97. Satow to Lansdowne, No. 78, Secret, telegraphic, March 17, 1901, F.O. 405-104, p. 113.
98. *Ibid.*
99. Satow to Lansdowne, No. 82, telegraphic, Mar. 19, 1901, F.O. 405-104, pp. 124-25.
100. Satow to Lansdowne, No. 84, Secret, telegraphic, Mar. 19, 1901, F.O. 405-104, p. 125.
101. Satow to Lansdowne, No. 110, Confidential, Mar. 21, 1901, F.O. 405-106, pp. 46-47.
102. Lansdowne to Satow, No. 74, Confidential, dated Foreign Office, Mar. 20, 1901, F.O. 405-104, pp. 127-28.
103. Lansdowne to Satow, No. 70, dated Foreign Office, Mar. 20, 1901, F.O. 405-104, p. 129.
104. Fraser to Lansdowne, No. 7, dated Hankow, Mar. 22, 1901, F.O. 405-105, p. 303.
105. Brenan to Satow, No. 21, dated Shanghae, Mar. 23, 1901, F.O. 405-105, pp. 303-304.
106. Lansdowne to Brenan, No. 5, telegraphic, dated Foreign Office, Mar. 23, 1901, F.O. 405-104, pp. 146-47.
107. Satow to Lansdowne, No. 91, telegraphic, Mar. 23, 1901, F.O. 405-104, p. 148.
108. Satow to Lansdowne, No. 99, telegraphic, Mar. 28, 1901, F.O. 405-105, pp. 52-53.

109. Fraser to Satow, No. 41, Confidential, dated Hankow, April 1, 1901, F.O. 405-106, pp. 67-68.
110. Fraser to Satow, No. 42, Confidential, dated Hankow, April 4, 1901, F.O. 405-106, p. 69.
111. Lansdowne to Satow, No. 101, Confidential, telegraphic, dated Foreign Office, April 5, 1901, F.O. 405-105, p. 73.
112. Lansdowne to Satow, No. 103, telegraphic, dated Foreign Office, April 5, 1901, F.O. 405-105, p. 73.
113. Satow to Lansdowne, No. 109, telegraphic, April 7, 1901, F.O. 405-105, p. 84.
114. Lew Kwun Yih to Sir Chihchen Lofêngluk, dated Nanking, April 7, 1901, F.O. 405-105, p. 96.
115. Lansdowne to Satow, No. 96, dated Foreign Office, April 9, 1901, F.O. 405-105, p. 99.
116. Lansdowne to Sir C. Scott, No. 105A, dated Foreign Office, April 17, 1901, F.O. 405-107, p. 201.
117. Seymour to Satow, Confidential, dated "Alacrity," at Wusung, June 1, 1901, F.O. 405-108, p. 103.
118. Fulford to Satow, No. 36, dated Newchwang, June 22, 1901, inclosure in Satow to Lansdowne No. 243, Confidential, dated Peking, July 4, 1901, F.O. 405-109, p. 126.
119. Lansdowne to Satow, No. 231, telegraphic, dated Foreign Office, July 15, 1901, F.O. 405-108, p. 43.
120. Satow to Lansdowne, No. 333, Confidential, Sept. 7, 1901, F.O. 405-111, p. 59.
121. Satow to Lansdowne, No. 380, Oct. 2, 1901, F.O. 405-112, p. 73.
122. Hosie to Satow, No. 59, dated Newchwang, Sept. 25, 1901, *Ibid.*, p. 73.
123. Tientsin, Oct. 7, 1901, *Ibid.*, p. 74.
124. Satow to Lansdowne, No. 439, Secret, Nov. 17, 1901, F.O. 405-117, pp. 15-16.
125. *Ibid.*, p. 17.
126. Scott to Lansdowne, No. 343, Very Confidential, dated St. Petersburg, Dec. 11, 1901, F.O. 405-113, pp. 55-56.
127. Satow to Lansdowne, No. 30, telegraphic, Jan. 25, 1902, F.O. 405-117, p. 61.
128. Lansdowne to Satow, No. 32, telegraphic, dated Foreign Office, Jan. 29, 1902, F.O. 405-117, p. 66.
129. Satow to Lansdowne, No. 37, telegraphic, Feb. 6, 1902, F.O. 405-118, p. 4.
130. Lansdowne to Satow, No. 38, telegraphic, dated Foreign Office, Feb. 8, 1902, F.O. 405-118, p. 7.
131. Satow to Lansdowne, No. 43, telegraphic, Feb. 13, 1902, F.O. 405-118, p. 21.
132. Satow to Lansdowne, No. 44, telegraphic, Feb. 14, 1902, F.O. 405-118, pp. 22-23.
133. Satow to Lansdowne, No. 46, telegraphic, Feb. 16, 1902, F.O. 405-118, pp. 26-27.
134. Satow to Lansdowne, No. 49, telegraphic, Feb. 21, 1902, F.O. 405-118, pp. 100-101.
135. Lansdowne to Satow, No. 48, telegraphic, dated Foreign Office, Feb. 24, F.O. 405-118, pp. 110-11.

136. Satow to Lansdowne, No. 61, Confidential, Mar. 11, 1902, F.O. 405-120, pp. 78-80.
137. Satow to Lansdowne, No. 78, Confidential, Mar. 26, 1902, F.O. 405-121, pp. 25-27.
138. Satow to Lansdowne, No. 72, telegraphic, Mar. 29, 1902, F.O. 405-119, p. 70.
139. Lansdowne to Satow, No. 70, telegraphic, dated Foreign Office, Mar. 21, 1902, F.O. 405-119, p. 72.
140. Satow to Lansdowne, No. 83, telegraphic, April 8, 1902, F.O. 405-120, p. 6.
141. Satow to Lansdowne, No. 106, Very Confidential, April 22, 1902, F.O. 405-122, pp. 49-50.
142. Satow to Lansdowne, No. 108, Very Confidential, April 22, 1902, F.O. 405-122, p. 50.
143. Satow to Lansdowne, No. 331, Nov. 6, 1902, F.O. 405-128, p. 63.
144. Hosie to Satow, No. 74, dated Newchwang, Nov. 7, 1902, inclosed in Satow to Lansdowne, No. 340, dated Peking, Nov. 14, 1902, F.O. 405-133, p. 5.
145. Hardinge to Lansdowne, No. 350, Very Confidential, dated St. Petersburg, Nov. 13, 1902, F.O. 405-127, p. 36.
146. Townley to Lansdowne, No. 364, Secret, dated Peking, Nov. 27, 1902, F.O. 405-127, p. 53.
147. Townley to Lansdowne, No. 14, telegraphic, dated Peking, Jan. 13, 1903, F.O. 405-133, p. 33.; also Townley to Satow, No. 17, Confidential, dated Peking, Jan. 13, 1903, F.O. 405-133, pp. 133-34.
148. Townley to Lansdowne, No. 378, Very Confidential, dated Peking, Dec. 16, 1902, F.O. 405-133, pp. 67-69.
149. Townley to Lansdowne, No. 2, Very Confidential, dated Peking, Jan. 1, 1903, F.O. 405-133, pp. 102-104.
150. Townley to Lansdowne, No. 81, dated Peking, Mar. 27, 1903, F.O. 405-134, p. 34.
151. Lansdowne to Sir M. Herbert, No. 117, telegraphic, dated Foreign Office, April 25, 1903, F.O. 405-134, p. 31.
152. Townley to Lansdowne, No. 161, Very Confidential, dated Peking, April 23, 1903, F.O. 405-134, p. 176.
153. Townley to Lansdowne, No. 106, telegraphic, dated Peking, April 28, 1903, F.O. 405-134, p. 52.
154. Lansdowne to Townley, No. 66, telegraphic, dated Foreign Office, April 28, 1903, F.O. 405-134, p. 55.
155. Sir C. Scott to Lansdowne, No. 26, telegraphic, dated St. Petersburg, April 29, 1903, F.O. 405-134, p. 56.
156. MacDonald to Lansdowne, No. 22, telegraphic, dated Tokyo, May 1, 1903, F.O. 405-134, p. 66.
157. Scott to Lansdowne, No. 117, dated St. Petersburg, April 27, 1903, F.O. 405-134, pp. 69-70.
158. Scott to Lansdowne, No. 119, dated St. Petersburg, April 29, 1903, F.O. 405-134, pp. 70-71.
159. *Ibid.*, p. 72.
160. Scott to Lansdowne, No. 126, Very Confidential, dated St. Petersburg, May 4, 1903, F.O. 405-134, pp. 76-78.

Notes

161. Townley to Lansdowne, No. 110, Secret, dated Peking, May 2, 1903, F.O. 405-134, pp. 66-67.
162. Townley to Lansdowne, No. 173, Very Confidential, dated Peking, May 4, 1903, F.O. 405-134, pp. 202-204.
163. *Ibid.*, pp. 204-205.
164. Townley to Lansdowne, No. 213, Confidential, dated Peking, June 1, 1903, F.O. 405-135, pp. 33-34.
165. Townley to Lansdowne, No. 186, Secret, telegraphic, dated Peking, July 22, 1903, F.O. 405-135, p. 42.
166. J. N. Jordan to Lansdowne, No. 48, Confidential, dated Seoul, April 18, 1903, F.O. 405-134, pp. 158-159.
167. MacDonald to Lansdowne, No. 38, Very Confidential, dated Tokyo, June 19, 1903, F.O. 405-134, p. 193.
168. MacDonald to Lansdowne, No. 47, Most Secret, telegraphic, dated Tokyo, July 2, 1903, F.O. 405-135, p. 2.
169. Lansdowne to MacDonald, No. 88, Secret, dated Foreign Office, July 3, 1903, F.O. 405-135, p. 4.
170. Scott to Lansdowne, No. 172, dated St. Petersburg, June 22, 1903, F.O. 405-134, pp. 213-14.
171. Townley to Lansdowne, No. 216, Secret, dated Peking, June 3, 1903, F.O. 405-135, p. 35.
172. Sir Garrett O'Moore Creagh to Townley, Tientsin, May 29, 1903, F.O. 405-135, p. 37.
173. Scott to Lansdowne, No. 226, Very Confidential, dated St. Petersburg, Aug. 5, 1903, F.O. 405-135, p. 83.
174. Scott to Lansdowne, No. 244, Very Confidential, dated St. Petersburg, Aug. 20, 1903, F.O. 405-135, pp. 104-107.
175. Scott to Lansdowne, No. 243, dated St. Petersburg, Aug. 20, 1903, F.O. 405-135, p. 77.
176. MacDonald to Lansdowne, No. 61, Confidential, telegraphic, dated Tokyo, Aug. 6, 1903, F.O. 405-135, p. 81.
177. Satow to Lansdowne, No. 219, telegraphic, Sept. 9, 1903, F.O. 405-138, pp. 100-101.
178. Satow to Lansdowne, No. 344, dated Peking, Oct. 6, 1903, F.O. 405-139, p. 80.
179. See Satow to Lansdowne, No. 223, telegraphic, Peking, Sept. 21, 1903, F.O. 405-135, p. 223.
180. Satow to Lansdowne, No. 329, Most Confidential, Sept. 24, 1903, F.O. 405-139, p. 61.
181. Satow to Lansdowne, No. 333, Most Confidential, Sept. 25, 1903, F.O. 405-139, pp. 77-78.
182. See also Satow to Lansdowne, No. 247, telegraphic, Oct. 29, 1903, F.O. 405-139, p. 43.
183. Lansdowne to Satow, No. 312, dated Foreign Office, Nov. 4, 1903, F.O. 405-139, p. 58; Satow to Lansdowne, No. 381, Nov. 9, 1903, F.O. 405-146, pp. 44-45.
184. Satow to Lansdowne, No. 406, Nov. 29, 1903, F.O. 405-146, p. 48.
185. Satow to Lansdowne, No. 268. telegraphic, Dec. 14, 1903, F.O. 405-139, p. 110.
186. Satow to Lansdowne, No. 277, telegraphic, Dec. 24, 1903, F.O. 405-139, pp. 121-22.

187. Satow to Lansdowne, No. 440, Secret, Dec. 28, 1903, F.O. 405-146, p. 133.
188. Satow to Lansdowne, No. 453, Confidential, Dec. 31, 1903, F.O. 405-146, pp. 134-35.
189. Satow to Lansdowne, No. 8, telegraphic, Jan. 13, 1904, F.O. 405-146, p. 36.
190. Satow to Lansdowne, No. 13, Jan. 17, 1904, F.O. 405-146, p. 53.
191. Satow to Lansdowne, No. 16, Jan. 17, 1904, F.O. 405-147, pp. 18-19.
192. Satow to Lansdowne, No. 17, Very Confidential, Jan. 18, 1904, F.O. 405-147, pp. 19-20.
193. Confidential addition to Satow to Lansdowne, No. 14, telegraphic, Jan. 19, 1904, F.O. 405-146, pp. 55-56.
194. Lansdowne to Satow, No. 23, dated Foreign Office, Jan. 24, 1904, F.O. 405-146, p. 68.
195. Satow to Lansdowne, No. 20, Jan. 20, 1904, F.O. 405-147, pp. 20-21.
196. Satow to Lansdowne, No. 25, Confidential, Jan. 25, 1904, F.O. 405-17, pp. 26-27.
197. Satow to Lansdowne, No. 22, telegraphic, Jan. 26, 1904, F.O. 405-146, p. 73; Lansdowne to Satow, No. 25, telegraphic, dated Foreign Office, Jan. 26, 1904, F.O. 405-146, p. 74.
198. Satow to Lansdowne, No. 39, telegraphic, Feb. 9, 1904, F.O. 405-146, p. 121.
199. Satow to Lansdowne, No. 62, Feb. 24, 1904, F.O. 405-147, p. 59.
200. Satow to Lansdowne, No. 47, telegraphic, Feb. 13, 1904, F.O. 405-146, p. 140.
201. Satow to Lansdowne, No. 54, telegraphic, Feb. 19, 1904, F.O. 405-146, p. 149.

Index

Alcock, Sir Rutherford, 6
Alexeieff (Alekseev), Admiral Evgenii Ivanovich, 128, 130, 136, 158, 165, 210, 213, 224, 235, 243-66 *passim*
Alexeieff (Alekseev), Kir Alekseevich, 86, 92
Allen, Bernard M., 19, 283
Allen, General, 263
Allen, Horace N., 49-50
An Kyong-su, 93
Anderson, F., 203
Anglo-Japanese Alliance, 30, 33, 121, 123, 172-73, 177-78, 182, 188, 222, 237, 246, 256, 268
Aoki Shuzo, 28, 30, 33, 54, 75, 93-99, 122
Arisugawa, Prince, 85
Asaina Kansui (Asahina Masahiro), 21-24, 33-34, 61, 62, 64, 69, 77, 83, 87-89, 91, 110, 116, 122-23
Asaina Masatoshi, 22
Ashridge Repository, 39
Austria-Hungary, 12, 44, 275
Azevedo Castello-Branco, José, 277-79

Balfour, Arthur James, 69
Belgium, 12, 69, 204, 227, 275, 277
Benckendorff, Count Aleksandr Konstantinovich, 205
Beresford, Lord Charles, 122
Bertie, Francis Leveson, 10-11, 177
Bezobrazoff, A. M., 245, 251-52
Bishop, Mrs., 76
Blagovestchensk, 228, 230, 232-33, 236
Bland, Sir Nevile, 15-16
Bonar, 226
Bowra, C. A. V., 198

Boxer Uprising, 4, 9, 10, 12, 32, 168, 197, 200, 241, 247
Bredon, Sir Robert E., 11, 203, 235
Brenan, Byron, 148, 287
Brinkley, Captain Frank, 61
Brodrick, St. John, 10, 100
Brown, J. M. McLeavy, 85-89
Bruce, Sir Frederick, 235
Bülow, Prince Bernhard von, 171
Buller, Sir A., 72, 86, 88, 204-205
Bullock, Sir Alexander, 33

Campbell, (C. W. ?), 168
Campbell, F. A., 15
Cartier, 91
Chagin, Ivan Ivanovich, 89, 98, 124
Chamberlain, Joseph, 160
Chang Chih-tung, 31, 93, 134-62 *passim*, 202, 227, 239-40, 246, 258-59, 263
Chang Pohsi, 260-61, 263
Chang Shun, 217
Chemulpo, 63, 70, 89, 92, 157, 270, 276-77
Chiang Wên-hsi, 128
Chihli, 130, 144, 148, 157, 189-90, 245, 253-75 *passim*
China, *passim;* partition of, 1, 2, 13, 30-31, 121, 122
Chinese Eastern Railway, 167-68, 192, 202, 216, 223-24, 228, 230, *see also* Manchurian Railway
Ch'ing, Prince (I-k'uang), 30-31, 127-280 *passim*
Chirol, Ignatius Valentine, 79, 205, 265
Cho Pyöng-sik, 88-89
Cho Wi-yon, 52, 61n
Chou-fu, 142, 181
Chou Mien, 128, 130

291

Index

Index

Saburo, 8
Saigo Kichinosuke, 46
Saionji Kinmochi, 26, 43-81 *passim*, 101, 102, 105, 106, 108, 245
Salisbury, Lord Robert Arthur, 9, 11, 13, 27, 34, 44, 47-48, 54, 57, 66-205 *passim*, 283-85
Salvago (-Raggi), Marquis Giuseppe, 277
Sanderson, Sir Thomas, 10, 30, 86, 205-207
Sannomiya, 64, 114
Sansom, Sir George, 14, 18-21, 283
Sapporo Agricultural College, 20
Satow, Sir Ernest Mason, *passim*
Scott, Sir C., 132, 161, 199, 210-11, 223-25, 247, 257, 266, 288-89
Seoul Memorandum, 81, 83, 84
Sewall, Dr., 21
Seymour, Admiral, Sir Edward H., 155, 204
Shanhaikwan, 131, 143, 145, 167, 175, 181-99 *passim*, 238, 248, 257-58, 267, 270
Shantung, 11, 139, 150, 168, 204, 238, 241, 244, 271, 278
Sharratts, General, 162-63
Shen Ong-hi, 88, 90
Shêng Hsuan-huai, 148-49
Shiba Shiro, 127
Shibusawa Eiichi, 241
Shimonoeski, Treaty of, 3, 101, 104-106, 111
Siam, 8, 15, 16, 33, 93, 99
Siberian Railway, 34, 37, 45, 48, 113, 121, 123, 258, 276
Siebold, Philipp Franz von, 19
Sill, John M. B., 49
Sino-Japanese War, 1, 3, 24, 27, 33, 43-101 *passim*, 193, 257, 267
Soga Sukenori, 75
Sone Arasuke, 54
Soyeshima Taneomi, 108
Spain (and Spaniards), 8, 12, 44, 275
Speyer (Shpeier), Aleksei Nikolaevich de, 56, 58, 67-93 *passim*
Staal, de, 75
Stein (Shtein), Evgenii Fedorovich, 96
Stipanow, 209
Strachey, John St. Loe, 205

Sugiyama, 92
Sundius, 137, 162, 170

Taft, William Howard, 282
Tai-wön-kun, 47, 52, 54, 79, 83
Takahira, 95
Takashima Tomonosuke, 83
Talienwan Bay, 21, 74, 90n, 92, 113, 115-16, 120-21, 251, 272
Tang Shao-yi, 35, 237, 254
Tani Moriki, 22
Tani (Tateki ?), 64, 75
Temperley, H. W. V., 16
Thailand, *see* Siam
Thomas's, 54
Thomson, R. L., 83
Tibet, 203, 205
Tientsin, 156, 166-67, 179, 189, 197, 199, 223, 226-27, 238, 248, 253, 255, 274
Tientsin Provisional Government, 165, 167, 189, 192-93, 196
Ting Ju-ch'ang, 46
Toda, 24, 77
Tong Hak insurrection, 45
Tosa, Prince of, 8
Tower, Reginald, 157, 160
Townley, Walter, 207-10, 213, 218-19, 288-89
Tripartite Intervention, 3, 28-29, 32, 101, 104, 105, 107, 108, 117, 193, 240, 243
Trowbridge, 226
Tsai, Taotai, 264
Tsên Ch'un-ming, 166
Tsêng Chi, 128-30, 133, 217, 271
Tsitsihar, 113, 195, 228, 230, 232-33, 236, 263
Tsuneya, 94
Tsushima Strait, 33, 72, 74
Turkestan, 137, 142, 145, 203
Turkey (and Turks), 48, 153
Twenty-one Demands, 13n
Tz'u Hsi, 4, 10, 11, 14, 166, 193, 204, 206, 245, 253, 265-66

Uchida Yasuya, 34-35, 160-282 *passim*
United States (and Americans), 1, 11, 12, 14, 25, 36, 50-52, 55, 58-59, 65-66, 78, 88, 96, 115, 135, 137, 142, 160-282 *passim*

295